CULT, A LOVE STORY

ALSO BY ALEXANDRA AMOR

Historical Mysteries

Charlie Horse

Horse With No Name

The Outside of a Horse

Water Horse

The Horse You Rode In On

A One Horse Open Sleigh

Juliet Island Romantic Mysteries

Love and Death at the Inn

Children's Animal Adventure Novels

Sugar & Clive and the Circus Bear

Sugar & Clive and the Bank Robbery

Sugar & Clive and the Movie Star

Larry at the Wedding (A Sugar & Clive Novella)

Learn more and receive a free historical mystery novella at
AlexandraAmor.com

CULT, A LOVE STORY

TEN YEARS INSIDE A CANADIAN CULT AND
THE SUBSEQUENT LONG ROAD OF RECOVERY

ALEXANDRA AMOR

The events in this book are taken from memories, letters, emails and journals, and are true as far as the author knows them to be. For clarity some events have been condensed. All the names, including those of some locations, have been changed, except the author's.

Developmental edit by Silvana Giesse

Copy edit by Theresa Best and Jennifer MacIntyre

Cover design by Streetlight Graphics

Cover photograph copyright iStockPhoto.com

Library and Archives Canada Cataloguing in Publication

Amor, Alexandra, 1967-

Cult, a love story : ten years inside a Canadian cult and the subsequent long road to recovery / Alexandra Amor.

Includes bibliographical references.

ISBN 978-0-9734456-3-3

1. Amor, Alexandra, 1967-. 2. Ex-cultists--Canada--Biography.

3. Cults--Canada. 4. Cults--Psychological aspects. I. Title.

BP603.A56 2009 209 C2009-904376-9

For T.S.N.

The best way to make a person small is to make God big.
—Ian Brown, *The Globe and Mail*

PROLOGUE

"God says that I need to move into the new millennium unencumbered."

My boyfriend looked at me from across the kitchen table as he uttered these words. His expression was a mix of grief, shock and steely resolve to do what he felt was being requested of him by the Almighty. It took me a few seconds to realize that what he meant was that he was breaking up with me and that I was the encumbrance he needed to be free of.

When we had begun to date, two and a half years earlier, it had felt like coming home. We were intellectually well matched and had similar tastes and interests in books and films, wine and food. It didn't hurt that we were on the same spiritual path and had both chosen to follow Limori, a self-styled New Age spiritual guru of immense charm and charisma who espoused the seemingly unquestionable values of Love, Light and Truth.

There was enormous chemistry between Michael and me, the kind I'd never experienced before or since, and I delighted in how happy we made each other. It felt like a great pleasure and privilege to experience such a force of nature as this love between us. I'll risk possible accusations of hyperbole and say that the connection between us had such depth and resonance that every time our eyes met I felt a sizzle of recognition and peace. It was like having my soul walk around outside my body.

And now, it seemed, it was over. Without warning, without explanation and certainly without mercy.

He continued. "The karma that needed to be cleaned up between us is now complete, so there's no longer any need for us to be in a relationship."

We were in the kitchen of Wolf's Den, a fishing resort that our guru owned and operated in central British Columbia, and Michael, my suddenly ex-boyfriend, had just emerged from a four-hour telephone conversation with Limori.

"I'll move my things out of our cabin now," he said, "and tonight I am to stay in Limori's suite." Underneath the look of grief and shock on his face, he looked smug and undeniably pleased with himself. Our leader was in Arizona at the moment with her travelling entourage, so as quickly as I was being demoted to ex-girlfriend, Michael was being vaulted to the status of someone spiritually important enough to occupy her palatial and sacred private suite in her absence. It was clearly his payoff for making a difficult and painful decision to choose God over me.

With this information, I was able to decipher a tiny bit about what was happening. Michael's ongoing status as Limori's trusted confidante, right-hand man and most obedient disciple was confirmed and affirmed by his invitation to spend the night in the hallowed halls of her private suite. It was also unfortunately dawning on me that I, on the other hand, was the spiritual miscreant in this scenario. There has to be a bad guy in every story and it seemed I was being cast in that role this time. I had seen this happen again and again over the years to so many of our peers in Limori's group, but I had, until now, not personally been on the receiving end of a devastating, blind-siding blow of this magnitude. Its impact on my position in the group's hierarchy was immediately becoming apparent; I felt myself plummeting toward the very lowest rungs of a perverse, real-life game of Snakes and Ladders. One minute I had been on vacation with my boyfriend, the next I was single, shunned and demonized.

To add insult to injury, Michael had chosen to (or had been instructed to) deliver his news not in private, but at the kitchen table in front of three of our fellow disciples, who lived and worked at Wolf's Den year-round. To my right sat Lisa, resident cook, housekeeper and den mother. Also at the table were Matthew, who had originally owned the resort and at one point been married to our guru, and John, another long-time group member. If the four at the table, and the guru herself (who had been on the phone), could have sent me packing at that very minute to catch a flight back home, they would have.

"TODAY'S FLIGHT has already left, so you'll have to wait until tomorrow to go back to Vancouver," Lisa said.

The next morning, after a sleepless night awash in shock, grief and self-loathing, I crunched my way along the snowy path from the cabin where I'd been staying to the main lodge. Lisa was cooking and said a brief hello, with no enquiry into how I was feeling or if I needed anything. Matthew joined me at the table.

"How was your night?" he asked, chuckling. "I'll bet you didn't get any sleep."

I flinched, as though stung, from Matthew's cruel delight in my misery. He knew intimately what I was going through; he had been on the receiving end of a devastating spiritual pronouncement from Limori more than once. To him, and to all of us, the agony I was experiencing was simply the difficult row it was necessary to hoe if one wanted to truly serve the God that Limori had us believing in. If the lofty end result was our and the world's salvation, then any and all ugly means it took to get there were justified.

3

Michael joined us then, looking at once drained and self-satisfied.

"How are you?" he asked coldly.

There was a hint of blame in his voice, which confirmed my worst fears. Limori had obviously laid the necessity for our break-up squarely at my feet. I had done something wrong at what she would describe as an "energetic level." It would be something invisible to the human eye but vastly important to the balance and order of the universe. As "God's" messenger it was Limori's duty to bring these transgressions to the attention of her followers. I was being put in the paradoxical position of being entirely responsible for what was happening to me and yet completely powerless to change or refute it, given that whatever was wrong was something only Limori could "see."

I couldn't answer Michael's question and for the first time in seventeen hours I felt my eyes begin to tear up. My shock until that point had been so debilitating that through all the hours of agony and emotional turmoil the night before I hadn't shed a single tear, which had only frightened me further. Why couldn't I cry when the worst thing I had ever experienced had just happened? I turned my back to him and stared out the kitchen window, unwilling to let him see me weep, and tried to collect myself. I failed; the waterworks started, then because of his question. They wouldn't stop for years.

We ate breakfast as a group of five, or rather, a group of four and one outcast. The four around me began to play up the artificial mirth and collective bonding that comes with having a pariah in their midst. I was familiar with it because I'd done the same thing to others in our group who had been cast out in the past. They bantered and chatted while I stewed in my own pain at the table. I said nothing and attempted to choke down a piece of toast, but could barely swallow for fear, grief and confusion, and the stifled, unacknowledged outrage that filled my throat.

Michael got serious toward the end of the meal. I watched his "servant of God" mask develop on his face and knew I was in for it again.

"Alexandra, do you have any questions?" he asked in a scathing voice.

Questions!!? I have a million questions! Like, what the hell is going on? How is it that you agreed to dump me after a four-hour telephone conversation with someone else? What happened to us deciding to live together a few days ago? What in the hell did Limori say to you yesterday on that call that could make you jettison me in such a cruel and callous way? And how did I become the enemy so fast? When will you look at me again without that deep, dark contempt in your eyes? And how can I fix this? And why should I want to fix this? Is everyone here nuts? Can't you see that this is CRAZY? It's insanity to treat people like this and call it "God's will." Are you serious? THIS is what God wants? Misery and fear and terror and humiliation and desperate powerlessness? Really? THIS is what God wants?

But I was well trained from ten years of over-ruling these kinds of treasonous and dangerous thoughts and feelings. I voiced none of it. I didn't even really allow myself to think or feel any of it. I had become so skilled at tamping down most of my thoughts and almost all of my feelings for so long that it was like someone was whispering these questions to me from several miles away. In a snowstorm. At night. In a language I didn't speak.

"No," I said, quietly, "I don't have any questions."

PART I

FROG

1

NOBODY JOINS A CULT

Nobody joins a cult. Nobody joins something they think is going to hurt them. You join a religious organization. You join a political movement. And you join with people that you really like.
—Deborah Layton, *Seductive Poison*

The group certainly didn't look like a cult. No orange robes or tambourines. Everyone had hair, not scalp stubble. There wasn't a sign above the door saying, "Check your freedom here." The thirty or so people in the room were standing in small groups of two or three and chatting quietly. As I looked around it seemed like any other group you'd see anywhere in North America, a mix of ages and ethnicities (although predominately Caucasian). The majority of faces were female but there was a smattering of male faces, too. Many were dressed in the standard casual garb of the day: jeans and a T-shirt or blouse. There was the occasional skirt or dress and some people had obviously just come from an office job because they were attired in suits, or dress pants and jackets. We were in a meeting room in the basement of a generic office tower at the bottom of Burrard Street in downtown Vancouver, Canada, not at an ashram in India or a fenced compound in Texas. There was nothing that set off alarm bells in my head. As I said, it didn't look like a cult.

I had moved to this city a few weeks previously and my mother had driven us to the meeting that night. It was July 1989 and I had finished university in Calgary a few credits shy of a degree. As soon as I could, I had packed my dog and few belongings into my Toyota hatchback and hightailed it over the Rocky Mountains to this lush, green, temperate city nestled between the Coast Mountains and the ocean. I was eager to put behind me the end of a relationship, an education I was too young to appreciate and a climate I had come to deeply resent because I often felt it was trying to kill me. Vancouver offered absurdly mild temperatures (compared to Calgary), soft air and beaches, not to mention my family. My mother, stepfather and brother had preceded me to Lotus Land by a few years and my visits to them while I was in school had introduced me to life on the West Coast. I felt like I had come home the first time I visited the area and couldn't wait to make it my actual home. My parents welcomed my dog and me into their lives and home and graciously allowed us to stay with them while I found a job and an apartment and set about building myself a new life.

There in the meeting room, on a Wednesday night, I stepped inside the doorway for the first time and looked around the room at the others who had come for the meditation circle. Before anyone spoke to me, I found myself thinking, "I've found it." It was an impression of such depth and resonance that it stayed with me for years. I hadn't even been aware that I was searching for anything until that moment, but when that thought and that feeling came to me it was like the gonging of a bell inside my chest. I felt almost weak with relief. I would recount this experience many times over the next few years, to myself and others, as an example of how I knew the group was the right place for me and the "one true path" for those like me who were seeking.

. . .

MY MOTHER HAD JOINED the meditation group a few months earlier. During the Sunday afternoon telephone conversations we'd had while I was still in Calgary, she introduced me to the idea that she was learning to meditate, from a woman originally named Jo-Ann, who had recently changed her name to Limori at the behest of her "spirit guides." I privately thought my beloved mama had finally lost her marbles. (I might have even voiced that opinion, given that I was in my early twenties and therefore knew everything.) But a couple of weeks after I'd arrived on her doorstep, bored by the dispiriting business of job hunting and without friends my own age to do social things with, I asked to go with her to the meditation class she'd been enjoying so much.

When my mother told me that she was learning to meditate I was shocked, not because it seemed wrong in any way, but because I had managed to belong to my family for a little more than two decades without the topic of spiritual matters ever being raised. And I mean ever. When I was growing up, our family didn't go to church, but not because my parents were anti-religion. It just never seemed to come up. Now, though, my mother was using words like *meditate* and *energy*, and this was as surprising to me as if she announced that she'd become a tattoo artist or was learning to play the didgeridoo. Sure, I knew that people did meditate, but until that moment my world had never collided with the spiritual one (orthodox or otherwise). She was searching for answers, I later realized, and given the atmosphere in Vancouver in those days she, and later I, was in the perfect place to conduct that search.

Vancouver is a unique city at any time, given its beauty, location and mild climate; despite its big-city cosmopolitan elements, its sensibilities lean firmly toward the left and New Age. Greenpeace, with its unique and previously unheard-of brand of environmental activism, was born in a church meeting room at the corner of 49th and Oak in 1972. Before Live Aid or the Boomtown Rats, Bob Geldof was a music journalist for Vancouver's free weekly newspaper, *The Georgia Straight*. The year 1970 saw the birth of Banyen Books & Sound, which would become one of North America's most comprehensive bookstores, focusing on spirituality, healing arts and Earth wisdom. It still exists today.

In short, there was a vibe of searching that seemed to linger in the very air. The feeling was that things could not continue the way they had been. It was the New Age and many in Vancouver wholeheartedly embraced the changes. My unsettled personal circumstances and emotional make-up left me vulnerable to influence by a charismatic leader at this time, especially given a cultural environment that encouraged freedom of exploration and thinking. Vancouver was (and perhaps still is) tilted more than slightly toward embracing the values of personal freedom and alternative spiritual exploration. Just ask the people who own the hydroponic stores around town.

And naturally, as with any societal trend or vibe, there are those who will work toward change in positive ways (à la Greenpeace) and those who will notice the zeitgeist and use it only for their own personal end.

BY THE END of the first night at the meditation circle, I was hooked on Limori and to the spiritual answers she was offering. Heck, I was hooked before she opened her mouth, such was the depth of my longing to find meaning and purpose in my life and my need to feel I belonged somewhere, anywhere. She had me at hello.

Charisma is a quality almost no one can specifically define, and yet we all know it when we see it. Limori sat at the head of the room, as still as an oak tree and twice as impressive. It might have been possible to pass her on the street without noticing anything remarkable about her, but sitting there at the far end of the room she had such presence that I wanted to soak her into my every pore and had to stop myself from staring at her. Like a movie star, Limori exuded that indefinable something that made me want to be near her so that whatever it was that made her so magnetic would hopefully rub off. She seemed to be somewhere in her fifties; she was physically large, both tall and mighty in girth, and had platinum blonde hair. (Years later it would strike me that she bore an uncanny resemblance to Ursula the Sea Hag from the Disney movie *The Little Mermaid*.) She seemed completely at peace with herself and her place both in the room and in life. Her hair was stylish, and her clothes—a skirt and blouse made of some silky fabric—made no concession to her weight. She was neither hiding her shape nor making apologies for it. To my eye, everything about her announced that she was comfortable in her skin and felt she had value. Being painfully self-conscious myself and lacking in anything resembling self-esteem, I immediately wanted to learn where I could get me some of the confidence that she embodied. If she had bottled this quality I was experiencing I would have bought several cases on the spot.

However, much to my dismay I learned during the first few Wednesday evenings I attended that I was deeply intimidated by her. The same qualities of confidence, presence and authority that I admired in her also struck me dumb. I was grateful to find Limori's protégé, Sheila, much more approachable. Sheila was Limori's opposite in many ways; she was slender, with jet-black hair, a soft-spoken manner and a kind facial expression that suggested poise rather than authority. She was clearly second banana to Limori, but she was not subservient or obsequious. In the court that Limori held, Limori was king and Sheila was queen.

Sheila was, in fact, the reason my mother had joined the meditation circle. In early 1989, my mother and Sheila, strangers to one another, had both been in a class about teaching English as a second language and during a break Sheila approached my mother.

"I never do this," Sheila said, "but I felt compelled to come over here and offer you a free psychic reading."

My mother, although stunned, accepted the offer and later had the reading. At Sheila's suggestion, she also began attending Limori's meditation circle. (I have reflected on whether or not Sheila's approach to my mother was active "recruitment," something common to thought-reform groups. If it was, I believe it was purely unconscious on Sheila's part; in the years that unfolded, recruitment was never one of Limori's demands of those who followed her.)

(A note to the reader: the terms *thought reform* and *mind control* are often used interchangeably in the study of cults. Throughout this book I will use the term *thought reform*. Thought reform is defined by Margaret Singer as "the systematic application of psychological and social influence techniques in an organized programmatic way within a constructed and managed environment. The goal is to produce specific attitudinal and behavioural changes. The changes occur incrementally without its [sic] being patently visible to those undergoing the process that their attitudes and behaviour are being changed a step at a time according to the plan of those directing the program."[1])

After a few weeks of attending what we came to call "the circle," having glimpsed what I thought could be my future, I booked my own appointment with Sheila for a psychic reading. On a sunny weekday afternoon, I got in my little blue hatchback, still tagged with Alberta licence plates, and drove what seemed to be an enormous distance out the Lougheed Highway to Sheila's apartment in Burnaby.

I was early so I sat in my car with jangling nerves wondering what would unfold in the presence of someone who was "psychic." I had never had a psychic reading before. I don't think I even knew what tarot cards were. And I was naive to the point of blindness. If someone said they were psychic, well, then, they must be. In other words, I was not a natural skeptic, much to my detriment. And I was young enough that I perpetually took people at face value and never doubted that anyone uttered anything but the truth, as they understood it.

Upon entering Sheila's apartment at my appointment time, I was much impressed by the serenity and calmness in her home. The two-bedroom suite was very tastefully furnished, without visible clutter of any sort. Although it was early fall it was still warm enough outside that Sheila had her balcony door open so a breeze could blow in. She had a cat, Tulip, and a new kitten named Petunia, both appropriately as black as pitch. What other colour of cat could a psychic have? Sheila was warm and kind, yet professional about getting me settled into the spare bedroom where she would do the reading. I was impressed that she had an entire room in her home dedicated to psychic readings. I certainly hadn't run into this in small-town southern Alberta.

Sheila sat down in an upholstered chair and had me sit opposite her in another. She explained that she channelled a spirit named Sunray and it was he to whom she would turn for information now. While the reading was conducted, Sheila kept her eyes closed and spoke in her own voice. I remember very little of what she told me that day. What I do remember is the feeling of being absolutely astonished that someone was making a living doing something so esoteric and unusual. It was as though an entirely new palate of colours had been unveiled to me, ones I had never seen before and had no inkling ever existed.

In its own way, this reading did quite a bit by itself to cement me to Limori's meditation circle. I had an unexpressed yearning for a life lived outside the box of normal work routine and cubicles. Growing up, every adult I knew had a job that seemed to be defined in this way. They got up in the morning and put work clothes on and commuted to an office where they did something they would later complain about. No adult I had ever known had spoken of following the road less travelled by doing something they were passionate about. To now find someone working out of her home, doing something so unique it was almost obscene was both astonishing to me and powerfully attractive. This defied even the outermost parameters of what I had ever considered to be work, and was entirely foreign territory to me. I thought it was audacious in the most delicious way and it left the strongest impression with me.

Additionally, I marvelled at the serenity I felt in Sheila's apartment. It caught my attention because it was such a dramatic contrast to the anxiety and uncertainty on my insides. I had to get closer to this way of life and find out everything I could about it. I wanted the stillness and peace that I experienced during my hour-long reading more than I'd wanted anything in my life thus far. I glimpsed the top of my own personal Everest that day and was determined to climb up to it, at any cost.

AFTER THE READING, I continued to attend the meditation circle regularly, but with more eagerness than before. I felt I was onto something really special, something that I badly needed and had been missing for a long time, if I had ever possessed it.

A few weeks later, on a Wednesday night, driven by my desperate need to possess the peace I had glimpsed at Sheila's apartment, and despite my awe and intimidation, I screwed up my courage and approached Limori, at the front of the room. I literally knelt down in front of where she was sitting.

"I feel I need to spend more time with you," I said, dry mouthed and shaking inside.

She looked off, over one of my shoulders into the middle distance, as she always did when she was "tuning in."

I waited. When she had her answer from "Spirit," her eyes came back to mine. (Note: words in this text with quotation marks around them are used in the context of Limori's cult. For explanation of these terms, please see Chapter 3 and the glossary at the end of the book.)

"Call me at the house," she said.

"Okay. Thank you." I got up and returned to my seat, dejected that she had not more warmly and immediately opened her life and heart to me—although of course her response to an almost-stranger was perfectly reasonable. Was she supposed to leap off the chair she was sitting on and pull me into her arms and declare that she had been waiting her whole life for the moment I would approach her? Yes, as a matter of fact, I think that was what I was expecting. My somewhat inferior sense of self craved the fulfillment of a fantasy of extreme acknowledgement. The absence of my fantasy moment notwithstanding, I was still hopeful that when I called her I would be invited to spend some time with her. And if that happened, perhaps the yawning gulf in my soul would find some solace.

THERE IS an analogy that is widely used in the study of cults—you may have heard it used by environmentalists when they discuss global warming. It is commonly called the Frog in Boiling Water scenario. It is such a widely known and commonly used analogy in this field of study that in fact, for a while, the Well-spring Retreat and Resource Center in Albany, Ohio, a cult recovery centre, used a frog as their corporate logo.

The analogy is based on scientific fact and goes like this: if you put a frog in a pot of room-temperature water on a stove and slowly turn up the heat under the pot, the frog will not register the slow and subtle change in temperature and, eventually, will boil to death without ever having realized it was in danger. However, if you first boil the water in the pot and then drop the frog into the boiling water, the frog will immediately sense the danger and jump out.

I haven't even met you but I can say for sure that you're just as smart as that frog in the second scenario. If, on your first visit to a spiritual, political or business group, you were instructed to leave your spouse and give your young children away to be raised by their grandparents and marry someone from the group whom you barely knew and leave your home and quit your job to go and live in a remote wilderness lodge and work for no wages seven days a week, year-round, all because a fat, blonde woman with an Austrian accent at the front of the room said that God was speaking to her in a voice only she could hear and it was He who said you should do these things, you, and every other person on the planet, would run screaming from the room and never, ever look back.

But that's just the trouble. If it were that easy to spot thought-reform techniques being used on a group, gurus would go out of business faster than you can say "Is it just me or is it a little warm in here?" At first, everything seems normal and comfortable, there at room temperature. The people are friendly, there's an element of purposefulness and meaning that has perhaps been lacking in your life and you're pleased to find a group of like-minded people with whom to explore spiritual (or political or business) questions. Besides, even medical doctors agree that learning to meditate is good for your physical and mental health. The woman teaching the class is charismatic and a little out there, but she is also a breath of fresh air and she makes you feel pleased with yourself because she comments on how she can see right away that you are special.

The bad news is that self-appointed gurus like Limori become skilled at knowing exactly what temperature each and every person in the group needs to be cooking at to provide her with the greatest element of power, control and manipulation. Looking back, I can see now that our guru knew exactly when to turn up or lower the heat that was directed at every one of us.

Suffice it to say that no one, frog or human, would knowingly subject themselves to the danger, lies, betrayal, manipulation, and life-shattering choices that become everyday occurrences once one is enmeshed in the hierarchy of an authoritarian leader. We join groups that turn out to be cults because we believe in the people in the group. We believe in the words that the leader is saying, and then slowly, slowly, degree by degree, we become used to the warmer temperatures. A skilled guru turns the temperature up one more degree for each individual only when that person has become perfectly comfortable at their current setting.

INITIALLY, flattery and compliments that propped up my self-esteem were Limori's way of acclimatizing me to her leadership. After my request to spend more time with her, I contacted her as instructed and was granted an audience with her, much to my delight. One afternoon I drove out to her home and spent the afternoon in her back garden.

Limori has the irresistible gravitational pull of the Death Star; there were almost always at least four or five hangers-on in her orbit. She had been in the business of grooming herself as a guru for a few years before I met her and had, as a consequence, already recruited a number of true believers who had left their lives and homes to follow her.

At the house that day, there was Alice, Limori's right-hand woman, who, for the entire decade that I was involved with Limori, was never more than six feet from her, except when she was sent off on an errand for God. Present also were Brent and Rose Marie (a married couple), John, and Matthew, whom Limori would soon marry. A few years later, when I myself moved in to live with Limori, I would learn that this was the normal state of affairs around her. She was never alone, and when I met her she had obviously already learned the number-one essential skill every guru needs: to get people to abandon the life they had before they met her and live continuously in her presence, serving her and doing what she called "God's work."

I would also learn on that first day that being with Limori was a bit like being in a spiritual amusement park. The rules that I thought governed life up until that point were challenged in a way that made me feel giddy with the possibility that anything could happen. She spoke her mind about anything and everything; being polite was obviously much less important than being truthful. No topic was ever off limits – sex, weight, the judgments of others: nothing was taboo.

Four or five of us sat around an umbrella table on Limori's back patio. Too intimidated to speak, I listened to them discuss matters of the soul and "energy." Every topic had enormous spiritual significance, from the food we ate to the clothes we wore to the attitude we had toward politicians.

Most of all I was mesmerized by Limori's utter lack of apology or indecision about anything she was saying. She had a conviction about herself, the messages she was relaying from Spirit and how the universe worked, which was, to a lost soul like me, as comforting as a warm bed on a cold night. This mammoth conviction caused her to exude a sense of purpose the likes of which I had never seen. She was on a mission from God and, boy, the importance and significance of that mission and her fearlessness about it were powerful balm to my weary soul, which was certain of nothing.

I imagine that many of us have moments of feeling lost when we are twenty-two years old. It is not an easy time in life. I've had friends say to me that they wouldn't repeat their twenties for anything, and these are people who had everything going for them. It is an era in life when we've left the shelter of our family of origin but we're not yet fully formed, even though we feel we should be. After all, we've been educated, we have the legal rights to marry, vote, drive, own livestock. We've begun earning our own money for perhaps the first time and begun using words like "career" and "mortgage" and "sub-prime lending" even if we're not entirely sure what they mean. There's a sense of "Ta da! Here I am, world! What now?" The world usually responds, however, with a great deal of indifference, which, for me, was disconcerting, disappointing and more than a little frightening.

Before I met Limori, I remember thinking, "Am I supposed to know what I want to do with my life? Am I supposed to know what really matters to me?" She was providing easy answers to these very difficult questions and I was more than grateful for it.

I didn't yet know what mattered to me. As many of us do, I had arrived at adulthood damaged and wounded from a childhood that was shall we say, slightly less than effective when it came to helping me develop things like confidence or a sense of self. I placed far more value on pleasing everyone around me than on figuring out what my own wants and needs were. I was like a Catholic nun crossed with Rebecca of Sunnybrook Farm: serious, almost humourless, fearful, asexual and riddled with unnecessary guilt. But, boy, was I pleasant! I was the kid my friends' parents wanted to have because I was so quiet and obedient. It was sometimes hard to tell when I was in a room; my need to please often caused me to disappear into the wallpaper. I had been raised in a military family, where order and obedience were valued more than independent thought. My mother and father divorced when I was eleven and, being the first-born child, I seemed to react to that event by developing the habit of taking on too much responsibility for everything around me.

All this, coupled with total ignorance about how healthy and whole people operate in the world ("Whaddya mean I'm not supposed to feel anxious every waking moment?"), meant that I was a psychological disaster waiting to happen. I believe that if I hadn't been pulled into Limori's orbit I would have entered into an abusive marriage, or a string of them. (Many of the techniques that cult leaders use to entrap and abuse their followers are identical to the strategies used by abusive spouses.[2]) I desperately needed approval, assurance that I mattered and for someone, anyone, to tell me that they loved me. I was a perfect, although not unique, storm of insecurity and lack of self-awareness, with a deep and sincere desire to make the world a better place.

On that sunny afternoon on her patio, Limori offered words not only of love and assurance that I was special, but of meaning and purpose of the highest order. For someone like me, who believed that at my core I was worthless and powerless, to hear that I was of vast importance in "God's plan," well, I was like a wriggly puppy having her tummy perpetually rubbed. I basked in the idea that my life, and therefore I, could have meaning. She made a quiet fuss over me that day, pointing out to the others around her that I was "clear" (i.e., psychic or extremely intuitive). She took my measure by looking not at my physical body but at my "aura" and instructed Alice to do so as well. They proclaimed that I had a beautiful aura and was an "old soul" with wisdom and understanding well beyond my years. I succumbed to their flattery and the attention they paid me, which was oh, so welcome.

The information that Limori shared always had to do with values and practices that seemed wholly good: following one's heart and listening to one's own "guides," doing good things to change the planet in constructive and positive ways, projecting positive energy to other people, living without judgment of others, etc. The message Limori brought was not one of doom and gloom or the urgency to save the universe from darkness. (That would come later.) For the moment, she talked to her spirit guides constantly and had us tuning in to practice our psychic abilities as well. It felt like being a part of a great cosmic magic troupe, where anything could and did happen.

AND SO, based on my first experiences with Limori and feeling as though I had found something essential that I had been searching for my entire young life, I found myself belonging to a group of kind, thoughtful, big-hearted people who were interested in all the values and virtues that seemed significant and worthy.

There were no sacrifices, human or otherwise, during our Wednesday night meditation meetings. No fire and brimstone (yet), no demands from Limori's seat that we do anything odd or repellent, no violations of anyone's personal boundaries. The group was, at that point, all about peace, love and understanding. We met once a week, from 8 pm to 10 pm. There was a small drop-in fee that enabled Limori to rent the space we used. We often spent the first part of the evening in discussion; from around the ring of chairs, members of the group would ask questions of a spiritual nature and Limori would answer them after tuning in to her spirit guides. Later we would partake in a guided meditation that Limori or Sheila and their spirit guides led.

The meditation circle was my introduction into the importance of community in a human life. For perhaps the first time, I felt surrounded by people who got me. The world of higher education had not made me feel at home, and for my last few teenage years before going to university, living with my father and stepmother hadn't felt much like a home either. To meet a group of people who were interested in the deeper questions of life and spent time reading and exploring and questioning seemed almost too good to be true. I cannot emphasize enough how the feeling of belonging somewhere filled a void in me and at the same time made me hunger for more. Because of the tremulous place I was in, in my own life, the satisfaction of that feeling made me hold on for dear life. With the exception of my mother, stepfather and brother, it was all I had. I looked forward to Wednesday nights with feverish anticipation and wished that the circle was held on more than one weeknight.

. . .

I ESPECIALLY ENJOYED that my mother and I were experiencing this journey together. For the previous six years while I finished high school, and then during four years of university, I had lived with my father in southern Alberta. My mother lived in Toronto and then Vancouver. This new and interesting topic of spirituality was a great place for us to meet intellectually and use as a venue to get to know one another again, after many years in a long-distance relationship. We had discussions about spiritual questions that we would not have had otherwise and we shared the same social circle, which was not only unique but comforting for me, as I had not yet made friends in my new city.

Soon after moving to Vancouver I acquired my first grown-up job, at the Vancouver Public Library. I was so enchanted and bewitched by what I was learning on Wednesday nights that I felt compelled to share it with the new friends I was making through work. I was the eager new recruit to spirituality and felt that no matter what problems ailed someone, Limori, Sheila and their spirit guides could easily solve them. This was the miracle cure and the answer to questions that had plagued not only me but (and in all sincerity, I believed this) all of humanity, since the dawn of time. I felt that via Sheila and Limori I had my own personal and direct telephone line to the heavens. Henceforth, no problem would go unsolved, no pain unsalved. I was high on the feelings of certainty and purpose I had found and I wanted everyone to give this new drug called spirituality a try.

At the same time, I began to feel a little bit separate from people. It was as though a secret that few could understand or share had been bestowed upon me. Unbeknownst to me at the time, this was the beginning of the "us versus them" feeling that every cult ingrains in its disciples. Like seeds growing in the soil, from the surface it looks as though nothing is happening, but just below, tiny roots are taking hold. Each Wednesday night my thirst for greater connection with the spiritual would be quenched, yet I would leave wanting more and more.

Limori was cautious about using the word *God* initially, though the underlying message was very clear that she, and therefore we, were serving the good forces of the universe. For the first little while she used the words *spirit* or *spirit guide* when she talked about the otherworldly guidance that she received in the form of auditory messages. These spirit guides were firm but gentle and advised us on matters such as the colour of clothes to wear to enhance our energy or the type of crystal necklace to wear to strengthen our ability to communicate with our own spirit guides.

Soon there was one specific spirit guide, named Azeen, whom Limori channelled exclusively. Azeen was said to be "an aspect of God's purest light." His (Azeen was referred to as a he) guidance started out by being similar to that of the former spirit guides but progressed to advice about relationships, careers and family members who were perhaps "flirting with the darkness." Later, probably circa 1992 or 1993, it would be announced that Limori was now strictly channelling God Himself. We had been inched along to this point for so long that this extraordinary proclamation caused barely a ripple among the faithful.

See what I mean about the frog in boiling water? If someone walked up to you on the street and said she was channelling God Himself and that every word out of her mouth was coming directly from the Almighty, you would no more believe her and become one of her disciples than you would strip down to your birthday suit and stand on your head, right there on the sidewalk, singing "I'm a Little Teapot." And neither would I.

But slowly, just like that frog in the pot, degree by degree, belief by belief, I bought it. All of it. And I was proud and honoured to do so.

MANY HUMAN BEINGS experience times in life like the one I experienced in the late 1980s and early 1990s, where we leave an old way of being, not quite sure yet what our new life will look like. Divorce, a family death, job loss or gain, a geographic move – any of these events, and many, many others, can leave us feeling as if we are between worlds, with no place, psychologically or physically, to call our own. This kind of upheaval happens over and over again in life, and each event brings with it its own type of discomfort and disorientation.

My experience is that part of what makes transitions like this so painful and awkward is that when we leave behind one set of criteria by which we define ourselves, we haven't yet formed a new set. We feel we are nowhere and no one. It requires a specific set of emotional skills to be able to sit with the discomfort and dis-ease that arises from not knowing how to define ourselves at these times. When we don't have that skill set, we tend to rush toward and grasp onto anything that will return to us a feeling of being on solid ground, where we can once again define ourselves. Perhaps we charge into a new job or relationship, one we know is ill suited to us, simply because it feels like solid ground, after days or weeks of being emotionally at sea. Experts say that when we experience a period of great transition or upheaval we become vulnerable to cults and cult leaders. However, obviously not every person who experiences transition or enormous change in their life joins a cult. Why are some people vulnerable and others not?

I can only use my own life as an example of this vulnerability. I was twenty-two years old, with no job, an incomplete degree in psychology, no home of my own and no friends, in a new city, with very little sense of who I was or who I should be. As with any circumstance in life, timing was everything. For me, joining a group that would turn out to be a cult required the perfect mix of ingredients, like a complicated soufflé. There was the sense of not knowing who I was, mixed in with a period of great physical upheaval, tossed together with a need for a community, a deep yearning for understanding of how life worked and a sincere desire to leave the world better than I found it. Now add a charismatic and stealthily manipulative authority figure, whose eccentricities were intriguing but not yet dangerous, someone not at the full strength of her power but close to the beginning of her journey as a guru, so her actions and words were not yet threatening or bizarre enough to repel. Slowly and carefully blend all these elements together, et voilà! A devoted disciple is born.

2

INTO THE MYSTICAL

One man's magic is another man's engineering.
—Robert A. Heinlein

The inauspicious start of my relationship with Michael was the polar opposite of the dramatic way it would end ten years later. We met on my first night at the meditation circle. He and my mother had come to know each other in the group and so, as she and I chose our seats and the circle began to form, she introduced me to him. My mother was on my right side and Michael was on her right. As she introduced us Michael leaned around her to say hello and shake my hand. Later, he would say that as he leaned around and our eyes met, he heard a click in his head. I had no such inkling or intuition about what we would come to mean to one another. In fact, I don't clearly remember this meeting at all, but he retold the story several times, years later, when we began to date.

I do remember that he came over for dinner a few weeks after we met. My mother and Michael, in addition to knowing each other from the meditation circle, worked together at an environmental newspaper that Sheila and her husband, Warren, had just started up. My mother was the editor of the newspaper and one of the writers. Michael wrote articles for the publication, as well as providing business-related advice to Sheila and Warren. As a result, in the first few months that I was living under my mother and stepfather's roof, Michael was invited over for dinner a few times and I came to know him a little better than I yet knew anyone else in the group.

After my initial shyness subsided, something drew me to him. He had a worldliness and intelligence about him that was paired with vulnerability, which I found an intriguing and magnetic mix of characteristics. There was such intelligence and perception in his eyes that when he looked at me I felt as though he wanted to understand me. Together with his natural ease and charm, this made him attractive to me and I felt less of the intimidation I usually felt around men.

I suppose I looked to him as a mentor at first. Or as someone in a category somewhere between mentor and friend. I was trying to make friends and he seemed to enjoy my company well enough. There developed a quiet ease in our new friendship and something that I would later come to recognize as good chemistry. Not of the romantic sort, at least not yet, but of the kind that one rarely finds in friendships over the course of a lifetime. We just clicked.

In addition to providing business consulting for Sheila and Warren's fledgling newspaper, Michael was self-employed. He and two business partners, who also belonged to the meditation circle, were raising money and promoting a petroleum and mineral mining resources company that traded on the Vancouver Stock Exchange. This meant that he worked at home and consequently could welcome me into his apartment when I chose to drop by during the week on my days off from the library, something that soon became a weekly habit.

On these visits to his tiny apartment near Granville and Broadway, I was very grateful to have a friend I trusted and who, I was surprised to find, seemed to enjoy my visits as much as I did. At this time in my life I was a bit like a six-month-old Great Dane puppy who hasn't grown into its feet yet, crashing around in my life with a big, baffled look on my face, completely oblivious to my impact on others and not yet used to whatever propriety might exist in the adult world. It didn't occur to me that Michael was a man and I was a woman; he was simply a friend and quickly becoming a calming and guiding presence in my life.

We chatted about the spiritual lessons we were learning from Limori and discussed challenges and questions we had about how the world might work, all viewed through the lens of Limori's spiritual teachings. I also remember going to him for advice about career choices. I had been considering going back to university to get a master's degree in library science, but the longer I worked in the public library the more I realized that this was not my calling. I groped around, as one does in one's twenties, searching for other career options that might suit me. I was onto graphic design one day and being a Montessori school-teacher the next. Michael, who was sixteen years older than I, very patiently listened while I grappled with the life choices that come with being an adult.

He had an emotional maturity about him that was appealing to me and a level-headed jocularity about life that was in refreshingly sharp contrast to my customary anxiety about every life decision, from choosing a career to what to have for lunch. He was infectiously enthusiastic about many things. If he was fired up about something that mattered to him, he wanted to share his discovery with others. And he loved to love people. What quality could be more appealing in a human being? He could find admirable and precious qualities in almost anyone. He appreciated those things that were unique about those he cared about and had a way of zeroing in on people's personal characteristics without seeming judgmental or critical. He genuinely enjoyed people, and his perception of what made those around him tick was almost spooky. He could find the most annoying people amusing simply because he took the time to wonder what motivated them and observe their behaviour without taking it personally, something I admired immensely.

Over the next few years our relationship would grow into the best friendship I'd ever had. Michael saw me in a way I hadn't felt seen, ever. In his presence, I ceased to be invisible to the world. He noticed, and more importantly appreciated, qualities about me that no one had ever mentioned before. He not only accepted me, but also gave me the sense that I was acceptable just for being myself. He was the first person I had ever known who tried to understand me, not for how I related to him, but for who I was in the world.

It's very scary being a child in a grown-up world, but there I was, a wounded child in the body of a woman. It was this quality of gentle curiosity about and perception of his fellow human beings – me included – that drew me to him as we began to get to know one another. Later, as my feelings of friendship began to deepen, this quality only made him easier to love. Michael, with his bright eyes, gentle, intelligent humour and big-brotherliness was a very welcome influence in my life. He saw me, and I will never be able to adequately express how much that meant to me at the time and means to me still.

Michael was the first to admit that he had always been attracted to women he felt needed rescuing. I certainly fit into that category, although there was no romantic attachment between us at the time. He was dating a woman named Jessica, whom he'd met at his Toastmasters club, and the fact that he was already in a relationship made me feel even safer. We could just be friends. Relegating Michael to the category of friend/mentor suited me just fine.

WHILE MY GROWING friendship with Michael gave me my first

taste of being seen and valued, the mystical practices and events in Limori's meditation circle served to make me feel like I was special. After our afternoon in her back garden, Limori continued, on some Wednesday nights, to make a fuss over me and make me feel like I had special spiritual talents. I received many messages in the early years of my involvement with her group that I was wise beyond my years and a clear channel for spirit. She would encourage me to tune in to my spirit guides and projected confidence that there was no question I could do this. Unconsciously, I began saying to myself that this was something I could build character and personality on.

As clinical psychologist and meditation teacher Tara Brach says in her book *Radical Acceptance*, "Those who feel plagued by not being good enough are often drawn to idealistic worldviews that offer the possibility of purifying and transcending a flawed nature."[1] In my case, believing that I was learning to tune in to spirit guides and see visions of the truth had me feeling like I was special for the first time in my life and perhaps not as flawed as I had felt until then. After a childhood of unremarkable school grades and no special achievements, of feeling constantly battered and berated by the beliefs I had about myself, which told me I was without value and, worse, that my very presence took up space and time that could be better used by someone else, it was extraordinary to feel . . . well, extraordinary. This was something to latch onto, to give my life purpose and clarity, and to prop up my ailing sense of self.

One Wednesday evening I was sitting in the group not feeling at my best. I had had a minor disagreement with a co-worker at the library that day, which had a negative effect on my mood. I was sitting in my chair trying to pay attention to what was going on in the group but mostly just feeling miserable. My body language must have conveyed this quite clearly; I was slumped, noodle-spined, with head and eyes cast down, when I felt Limori's gaze land on me.

"Alexandra, what is going on with you today?" she asked.

"Oh, I just feel kind of crummy," I replied. "I had an argument with someone at work and I'm sure I was in my ego about it." I was trying to own up to my responsibility for the way I felt and brush Limori off at the same time. I didn't feel like being poked and prodded this evening about my "ego positions."

There was a pause, and the room was silent while everyone waited to see what Limori would do (or what she would be guided to do, as we understood it).

"Come here," she said at last.

Reluctantly I stood up and walked to where she sat, resplendent in an ivory silk dress with a wide, velveteen belt, a turquoise silk scarf and open-toed high heels. Her blonde hair was poofy around her face at that time, and she wore minimal makeup, although her fingernails were acrylic and she had a French manicure.

"Come here," she said again as I got close to her, and held her arms up as if to embrace me. "Here." She patted her lap. "Sit on my knee."

I felt ridiculous but I complied, turning my back to her to face the rest of the circle and perching my rear end on one of her knees. She put her arms around my waist, cupping my hands in hers, and had me lean back so that I was resting against her chest.

"Now," she said, "what is your favourite animal?"

The question disarmed me because it was so completely not what I expected. "The barn owl," I replied, not certain it was my favourite animal, but it was what popped into my head.

"What do you like about barn owls?"

I wasn't sure, but her question made me search for an answer. "They're quiet. They have nice eyes. I like their colour and shape."

"Now," she held me a little tighter and addressed her next question to the group, "can you see the barn owl in Alexandra?"

After a short pause in which I felt terribly self-conscious, Karen answered, "Yes, she has beautiful eyes like a barn owl."

"That's right," Limori said, "and what else?"

I still felt like a fool, one grown woman sitting on another's knee with the group looking at me, but bubbling up underneath my embarrassment was pleasure. This positive attention from Limori was not unwelcome, and to be singled out by our guru and treated in such a tender way made me feel loved, not only by her, but also by God.

"She's wise," Gary answered.

"That's right!" Limori's vocal timbre became deep with approval and I could feel her behind me nodding at Gary, one of her main protégés. She shifted her weight and adjusted me on her knee so that I turned sideways and we could look at one another. "Azeen says that you are to remember that, like the barn owl, you are quiet with your wisdom. It shines out through your eyes. He relies on you to bring that knowing, that wisdom, here to the group but also to the other parts of your life. Your co-workers may be jealous of who you are, which is why they argue with you. But you can simply face them, without drawing them into a quarrel, and know that Azeen is with you. Okay?"

"Yes."

"Good girl. Now get off my knee; my leg is falling asleep."

We all laughed as I stood up and returned to my seat. She had the pitch-perfect timing of a comedienne and always knew how to close with a joke.

The sense of community that Limori offered and the friendships I found in the group began to fill a void in me. There were many incidents like the one I've just described, where I was singled out and made to feel that the sense of worth I'd been searching for did exist somewhere inside me. And this didn't just happen to me; Limori made the same sort of fuss at different times over my mother, over Michael and Jessica and over each person who came into the group. The longer the person stayed, the greater the number of incidents of special treatment they could rely on receiving.

For me personally, in addition to being exposed to what was essentially a seduction, I also had my own little transcendent moment. It was private and personal, but somehow I managed to attribute it to Limori's greatness, rather than to my own spiritual journey, and it served to bond me to her even more strongly.

AFTER SIX MONTHS of living in an alcove in my mother's upstairs hallway in Kitsilano, I had finally made the mental adjustment to the upward difference in the price of rental suites compared to Calgary and was ready to commit to leaving the parental nest. I found a basement suite in a charming, tree-lined neighbourhood called West Point Grey, which was perfectly suited to my dog, Patches, and me. It had a backyard she could claim as her own and was within walking distance of my job at the library. It had all the standard features of a basement suite – low ceilings, tiny windows at ground level, constant noise overhead from the main part of the house and an odd, elongated shape – as well as a few additional idiosyncrasies. The kitchen was an eight-foot-long stretch of countertop that contained a hot plate, sink, microwave and fridge, but no stove or oven, and there were very few cupboards. One entered the suite through the laundry room, which flooded when it rained (and it's almost always raining in Vancouver), due to a poorly placed downspout from the second floor. The bedroom was so small that it was reminiscent of a coffin, as Michael remarked the first time he saw it. I had a futon bed at the time and had to assemble it in the room because there was no way I could have gotten it in otherwise. The room was about one foot wider than the bed itself and about half a foot longer and had a low ceiling. It was like sleeping in a very small cave.

Despite its idiosyncrasies, it was home and I would live there for almost three years.

One night, as I lay in bed, I experienced what I would describe as my first (of only three) truly mystical, inexplicable, mind-bending spiritual experience. It occurred apropos of nothing. I had had what I would describe as a fairly normal, boring day: I'd walked the dog before breakfast, after work and before bed, as always. I'd worked at the library, checking books in for people and checking them out for other people. It wasn't a Wednesday so I hadn't been to the meditation circle. I may not have spoken to anyone from the group, although I don't remember clearly if I had or not.

What is crystal clear is what happened after I crawled under the sheets. I lay on my back, my eyes open, perhaps mulling over what the next day might hold, with Patches there on the end of the bed, snuggled in for the night. Suddenly there was a noise, as loud as someone abruptly closing a book in a quiet room, a cross between a pop and a whoosh. It was loud enough that it startled me out of my reverie and immediately my eyes opened wider, because the ceiling above me became a shimmering mass of light. From corner to corner to corner, every square inch turned into a clear, white light that was thick, almost gelatinous, and filled, filled, with additional lights that sparkled and shined like the Milky Way on overdrive. As I watched this happen, with awe and wonder, the light flowed downward, absolutely evenly, until it filled the entire bedroom. It was like a cup was filling up, only from the top down.

Well, colour me surprised. It was so extraordinary and so real, and I was so aware that I was conscious and not yet sleeping, that all I could do was lie there and gawp, breathless. I wasn't afraid, just curious and interested. In fact, I had a pervading sense that, although this radically bizarre thing was happening, I was completely safe. I didn't feel awash with bliss or anything, but I did feel perfectly at peace, safe and calm.

As soon as the light had completely filled the room, so that I was lying in the middle of a cube of thick, clear, but infinitely sparkly light, I had what I can only describe as a vision. Suddenly, I felt and saw myself standing before a large, unidentifiable figure. I had that recognizable dream feeling of being me-but-not-me. The figure in front of me, which was not a person and had no identifiable characteristics, was, all the same, a presence. Neither of us said anything, but again I felt perfectly safe. Then this figure, presence, whatever-it-was handed me a sword. Or rather I found myself reaching out my left hand and a sword was placed in it. An honest-to-god sword with a carved handle and a glinting silver blade almost as long as I was tall. As soon as I held the sword in my hand, the scene changed. The figure/presence was gone and I was standing all alone, sword in hand, in what seemed to be a tiny village, a collection of one-storey buildings with thatched roofs. I noticed that "I" was still female and dressed in a sort of tunic and skirt, and that my hair was darker than my normal colour and cut in a chin-length bob.

And then it was over. My eyes were still open and everything evaporated. The light, the vision, the feeling of holding a sword in my hand. All gone. I was lying again on my bed, in my dark little cave, with my dog at my feet and what I can only imagine was a fairly stupid look on my face.

"Huh," I thought. "That was beyond weird." I lay there, stock still, for a few minutes to see if anything else would happen, but nothing did. I replayed the scene over in my head a few times, my eyes searching what I could see of the ceiling and walls for remnants of what the light must have left behind. It had been so thick I couldn't believe it could disappear completely without leaving some trace. But there was nothing there. I lay awake for quite a while after that, adrenalized by the surprise of what had just happened, confused, and not a little bit baffled.

The next day happened to be my day off, so after breakfast and a long walk with Patches I hopped on a bus and made the journey across town to ostensibly run some errands. If I'd had more courage I would have admitted to myself that my true destination was Michael's apartment.

When I had made my way there, he was as happy to see me as ever. As we chatted about whatever else was going on that day, I worked up the courage to tell him what had happened to me. In the morning light, while Patches and I had strolled the quiet streets of our neighbourhood, I had re-examined the experience of the night before. It seemed no less real then, but I did have some misgivings about seeming crazy if I shared it with anyone (as I do now, almost twenty years later, while I write this). I delayed telling him and continued putting it off until we were almost getting ready to put our coats on and go out and have something to eat for lunch.

"You know, there is one other thing," I said, as he started to make standing-up motions from his place on the couch. I was nervous; my voice felt trapped inside my tight throat. What if he thought I was completely nuts?

"What's that?" he asked and settled back down into his seat. As always, the look on his face was one of concerned and perceptive interest. If something mattered to me, it mattered to him.

So I told him the whole story, sword and all.

When I was done, he was quiet for a few seconds and I thought, Oh boy, here it comes. He's going to ask me to never drop by on my day off again and suggest that I consider medication.

After a short pause, what he said was, "You have to tell Limori this." He believed me, much to my relief and, like me, he thought that what had happened was some sort of spiritual event. And if anyone could explain it, our leader could.

I was still very intimidated by Limori and protested that we shouldn't bother her in the middle of the day, but Michael insisted and went to his phone and dialled her number. When he got through to her, he explained that he had me with him and that something significant had happened to me and he wanted me to explain it to her myself. He handed me the phone.

So I told the story again, feeling a little more confident with this retelling. Limori listened and "um hmm'd" a bit. When I finished she said, "Well, of course. Azeen has shown me images like this about you for a long time. You are a soldier for God and now you know that too."

I was relieved that she too believed me and flushed with pride that she and Azeen thought well of me. I felt a small moment of bonding occur between us, and I was pleased and proud about that as well. Her response was more muted than Michael's and contained less overt enthusiasm, but she was warm and I appreciated that. When the call was finished and I hung up, I was left with a small sense of denouement, wishing that she had made a bigger deal about my experience, but I quickly decided that this was my ego seeking approval and brushed away any feelings of disappointment.

LOOKING BACK NOW, as I recount this episode for the first time in two decades, it occurs to me that the most prominent feeling I had during Limori's response to me was that what I was telling her was not news to her. As I've been writing, I've been reflecting that from the point of view of a guru who was grooming a disciple it had to be this way. As an omniscient leader, she could not react with surprise to what I shared. She had to leave me with the impression that, of course, she had already seen what the human eye could not see.

Years later, as part of my recovery from Limori's influence, I would come to read an excellent book about authoritarian control and cults called *The Guru Papers* by Joel Kramer and Diana Alstad. Kramer and Alstad explain that for a guru, "[t]he need to appear right when presenting oneself as a spiritual knower is greater than in any other arena because knowing is what makes one essentially different from seekers."[2] The feeling of denouement that I had when I hung up Michael's phone was a result of being met with this mask of knowing everything, which Limori perpetually wore. She couldn't be excited or delighted or react in wonder with me. She had to keep her guru persona in place and assure me that anything I knew, felt or experienced, she had long ago "been there, done that, bought the T-shirt."

At the time, though, her lack of enthusiasm disappointed me. I noticed it, as I said, but chose to ignore it. And it is only now, in hindsight, that I can see that our conversation had a secondary effect on me. The experience of seeing the dense, sparkly light slowly filling my room from the top down and having a vision of a village that was so real I could smell the clear, crisp air of it, was, hands down, the most interesting and perhaps profound thing that had ever happened to me. To this day I am not certain exactly what it all meant, but what I am certain about is that it did happen and it was far outside the reach of my everyday experience of life up until that moment. It was beyond extraordinary.

But what happened after I spoke to Limori was that I attributed this event to her. She convinced me with her few sparse words and her all-knowingness that this sort of thing happened to her every day, and she left me with the impression that if I stuck close to her, it would be commonplace for me as well. It was my proximity to her, I gathered, that had caused such an event. The event itself and her calculated measure of it proved to me that she was the spiritual guide she said she was.

This specific event was a huge part of Limori's entrance into my life and my heart. I wanted the mastery she seemed to possess, and my yearning only increased after the Night of the Glowing Ceiling. I wanted to know the truth about the way things worked and she seemed to have direct access to the sources of this. So began a decade of trying to be enough like her that glowing ceilings would become commonplace.

THE TECHNOLOGY OF COERCION

When people show you who they are, believe them.
—Maya Angelou

Acircle is the most egalitarian of shapes; every point on its circumference is an equal distance from the centre. At every meeting of Limori's mediation group, she required that we sit in a circle. The shape of a circle, she said, emphasized the spiritual equality of those sitting in it. Her verbal message was that she was the same as the rest of us and that we all had equal rights and were equally valuable in "God's" eyes. On the Wednesday nights that the group met, which were drop-in evenings that anyone could join, Limori channelled to us that the circle was like a necklace, a chain of individuals who formed a whole. Later, when an additional, invitation-only Thursday night group was created, she told us that this special group formed a solid band of light in the form of a circle.

Yet with all this talk about circles and their egalitarian nature, Limori always managed to make her place in the circle resemble the head of a table, so the circle was not actually a circle at all. She did this by sitting in a chair that was different than everyone else's, if we were at her home for a weekend workshop, for example. Or if we were outside, sitting in plastic lawn chairs, Limori would be the one person sitting in a wicker chair with a cushion. In the space that was rented for years for the Wednesday and Thursday night meditation groups, her place in the circle was immediately beneath the spiritually significant paintings hanging on one wall, and the circle radiated out from there.

Her commanding presence and charisma also served to make her the centre of attention. And she never seemed to miss an opportunity to ensure that we were receiving subtle, non-verbal messages, via clothing, jewellery, seating arrangements and so on, that she was somehow better than the rest of us and therefore had the authority to lead us, while verbally proclaiming that we were all in the service of God together. In what was perhaps my first reaction to the contradiction between Limori's verbal and non-verbal messages, I remember thinking that this sitting-in-a-circle business had become a bit Orwellian; some members of the group were definitely more equal than others. But I would always banish that treasonous thought as soon as it arose, chiding myself for questioning something as simple as seating arrangements. I had also already begun to absorb the message that everything Limori did and said was directed by God, and therefore there must be a solid spiritual reason for this dissonance between her words and her actions.

I WAS GETTING USED to Limori, but not necessarily getting to know her. She continued to be as charming and charismatic as she had been on the first night I met her. I had learned that her every conversation centred around God and Spirit and the spiritual work she said she was compelled to do. She was always perfectly presented, with never a hair out of place or an outfit that did not scream regality, even when she was lounging at home. I learned that she had a grown son and also an ex-husband somewhere in her past. She was Austrian by birth but had immigrated to Canada at some point, exactly when I did not know. She never engaged in small talk and dissuaded those of us in her presence from doing so as well, because small talk was irrelevant to one's spiritual development. So the snippets of information that I picked up about her life before she created the meditation circle were few and far between.

I would like to be able to describe more about Limori's character and personality, but the truth is that beyond the act she was putting on about being in God's service 24/7 I didn't learn much else about her. My experience of joining the group was like being thrust onto a stage midway through the first act of a play. There wasn't time or an appropriate moment to ask for the action to stop, so that I could catch up and have the other characters' motivations explained to me. It was all I could do to simply try to absorb the meaning and significance of everything Limori was saying and feel as though I belonged there myself, under the floodlights. There was an urgency to everything she said and did – the universe was already in deep trouble with threats from the forces of evil – so the underlying and sometimes overt message that I received was that we didn't have time to mess around "getting to know one another" or learning at a pace that was comfortable for each person. The universe was in crisis now, now, now, and I needed to catch up to the plot as quickly as possible and set aside any questions I might have.

Getting personally close to her was impossible. For one thing, she was constantly surrounded by a gaggle of hangers-on, each in their own way competing for her attention and favour; unless I booked a psychic reading with her, I was unable to get any one-on-one time with her. And, for another, she ensured that the dynamic in each of her relationships, including mine, was a guru–disciple paradigm, not a friendship. She had to be the person in authority at every moment; she could never appear to be confused or frightened by life, or bogged down by the gritty, petty details that we all encounter. She couldn't have us experiencing her as just another sweaty human being travelling through life. She had to be different and set apart from the rest of us, while simultaneously giving the impression that we were all saving the world together. When I felt uncomfortable about our circle of chairs having a "top," it was this dynamic that I was experiencing. It turns out that it was essential for Limori to set up the group dynamic this way.

ONE STORY about Limori clearly shows how she had to be the authority at all times. It was known as the Pear Tree Story, and became an extremely valuable part of the group lexicon.

On a spring or early summer day, Limori and several of her inner-circle disciples were sitting outside in the backyard at her house. For some reason, fruit trees were being discussed and pear trees were specifically mentioned. Limori got up to walk into the house and fired a comment over her shoulder: "Pear trees don't grow in Vancouver."

Consternation ensued. Those who were present were thrown into a fit of confusion because several of them had seen the fruit tree in question growing in Vancouver lawns and gardens. Yet here was their guru, whom they believed only ever spoke The Truth, telling them something that directly contradicted their own experience. What to do? Whom to believe? (For the spiritual student, it was a deeply perplexing and disturbing problem: the one who channels God saying one thing and one's personal experience saying another.)

Limori returned to the patio a few minutes later to discover this perplexity and confusion on the faces of her followers. When they explained what was causing all the discomfort, Limori laughed and agreed with them. "Indeed," she said, "pear trees do grow in Vancouver. Can't you see the lesson I am trying to teach

46

you?" Everyone relaxed; Limori had not made a mistake. They could rest easy that she did, indeed, know everything.

A GURU MUST BE INFALLIBLE. She does not make mistakes and say that pear trees do not grow in Vancouver. She does not have bad hair days or feel troubled by an outstanding debt. She does not bring herself down to our level by complaining about her ex-husband or discussing the weather. A guru is on a mission from none other than God Himself, and there is no room in that job description for errors, miscalculations or all-too-human vulnerabilities like emotion and ego.

In *The Guru Papers* Kramer and Alstad explain that authoritarian rule, by its definition, assumes that a leader knows better for her followers than the followers know for themselves.[1] They further explain the phenomenon of this type of relationship like this:

> It would be difficult to surrender to one whose motives were not thought to be pure, which has come to mean untainted by self-centeredness. How can one surrender to a person who might put his self-interest first? Also it is difficult to surrender to someone who can make mistakes, especially mistakes that could have significant impact on one's life. Consequently, the guru can never be wrong, make mistakes, be self-centred, or lose emotional control. He doesn't get angry, he "uses" anger to teach.[2]

In my experience, this assumption of a guru's infallibility is the cornerstone of all the other manipulative strategies for control that the guru uses. If we had not been taught to believe that Limori was infallible, we would have been free to question her behaviour and teaching methods, not to mention her messages from God, and therefore she would have had a much-lessened influence on our lives.

Limori must have known this, for when I joined the group she had already been working at establishing herself as infallible and would continue to work on members both new and veteran to grind this belief in. Everything she did hinged on her followers believing that God was speaking through her. And as the Pear Tree Story illustrates, she used every conversation, every word, every gesture and every opportunity to emphasize that she was without ego and everything she did was "for our own good."

According to cult expert Steven Hassan, a destructive cult is "a pyramid-shaped authoritarian regime with a person or group of people that have dictatorial control. It uses mind-control techniques to keep people dependent and obedient."[3] The International Cultic Studies Association (ICSA), a non-profit research and education organization and global network of people concerned about psychological manipulation and abuse in cultic groups, defines a cult this way:

> A cult is a group or movement exhibiting great or excessive devotion or dedication to some person, idea or thing, and employing unethical manipulative or coercive techniques of persuasion and control (e.g., isolation from former friends and family, debilitation, use of special methods to heighten suggestibility and subservience, powerful group pressures, information management, suspension of individuality or critical judgment, promotion of total dependency on the group and fear of leaving it), designed to advance the goals of the group's leaders, to the actual or possible detriment of members, their families, or the community.[4]

THE PEAR TREE STORY, in addition to being an example of the

ways in which Limori convinced her followers of her omniscient nature, is also an excellent example of the term coined by Robert J. Lifton: *thought-terminating cliché*. Lifton is a psychiatrist and author, well known for his studies on the psychological effects of war, and for his seminal work on the subject of coercive persuasion, *Thought Reform and the Psychology of Totalism*.

In his book, Lifton introduces eight criteria that can be used to measure any group or environment to see if totalism exists in the group.* Where it does exist, Lifton says, "a religion, a political movement, or even a scientific organization becomes little more than a cult."[5] (*For a list of all eight criteria, please see the appendix.)

The sixth of Lifton's criteria for totalism is loaded language: "The language of the totalist environment is characterized by the thought-terminating cliché . . . Words are given new meaning – the outside world does not use the words or phrases in the same way – it becomes a 'group' word or phrase."[6]

The terms that Limori's group used had a context and history in the group that was unique, and often their general definitions had little bearing on how we used them. Many of the terms had a colourful and meaningful history to us, which could be summed up in the word or phrase. As a group, we had a shared history and stories of events that had significant spiritual meaning for us. When we named those events with a word or phrase they became filled with all the contextual spiritual lessons that Limori had been trying to teach us in that moment. For example, anytime anyone raised a question about Limori's methods or teaching, or questioned whether or not something she had done had exhibited egoic properties, one of us might pipe up and say, "But remember the Pear Tree Story." The mere mention of the phrase itself did exactly what Lifton describes: it stopped our thoughts of dissent and questioning. We would remember the story and all its messages about Limori working for our good and that her every action was undertaken to teach us, and any thoughts of discomfort with her methods would be set aside.

"Oh, right," I would think. "Limori only has our best interests at heart and would never say or do anything that was harmful. If I don't understand her methods at this moment, I probably will when I've achieved more spiritual growth." The underlying message I was delivering to myself during these internal dialogues was, "Any failure to understand is always mine, not hers. And any action that looks hypocritical or untrue simply means that I have failed to grasp what Limori is trying to teach."

In its most benign form the shared language of a community gives that community cohesiveness, a sense of familiarity and intimacy and a way to shorthand explanations or narrative. We experience this phenomenon to one degree or another in almost every community we belong to, whether it be centred around work, family or hobbies. Take up any new hobby, such as motorcycling, video games or collecting Smurfs, and one of the first things you'll notice is that you need to learn the language of the community that participates in that hobby. There are words that are new to you that describe the materials and equipment you'll be using, the techniques and skills you'll need and the history of the hobby. It's a mini-culture all its own and one of the key elements that makes it unique is the language the members use.

The same goes for a cult, but as with most everything else in the cult experience, the language is taken to an extreme and used not simply to inform but to control. As Lifton says, the language also reinforces the sense of separation of the group from the outside world. I can vividly recall the puzzled looks on the faces of newcomers to our group as those of us who had been indoctrinated for years spoke in a shorthand that was so ingrained and closed it became almost impossible for anyone new to gain entry into our world. Yet if and when someone did persevere and begin to understand the language we spoke, that new understanding became a huge part of their beginning to feel like a member of the community.

As I've been writing this memoir, I have been swapping stories and reminiscences about the group with a woman named Gayle, who is also an ex-member of Limori's cult. Gayle left the group in the mid-1990s, after living with Limori and some of her other followers at Wolf's Den Fishing Lodge for a few years. She and I became reacquainted in the early part of this century when I tracked her down using that ubiquitous tool, the Google search engine.

Gayle and I often find ourselves stumbling across a particular word and will burst out laughing with the shared knowledge and discomfort that the meaning of the word used to hold. Words as simple as *energy*, *ego* or *truth* or a phrase like *Being in your heart* were so laden with years and years of meaning and spiritual context that Gayle and I have remarked to each other on several occasions that we couldn't use them, even in a non-spiritual context, for years after leaving the group. To this day, when anyone uses the term *the truth* in my vicinity, a small part of me recoils in painful reminiscence.

The Truth was one of Limori's most powerful weapons. Only she had ultimate access to it, and she wielded it with immense power. She and Alice repeatedly explained in the first couple of years I knew them that The Truth (I put both words in capital letters because the phrase held so much significance) was the ultimate tool that could be used to thwart the forces of evil or darkness in the universe. The motto of Limori's group became "Love, Light and Truth." We were told that the Dark (the negative or evil forces in the universe) wanted love and light but they were afraid of The Truth; therefore, a servant of God would always be looking inside herself for The Truth.

Sounds harmless enough. The catch was that Limori was the only person with knowledge of The Truth. The phrase quickly became, for me, another thought-terminating cliché. Anytime I disagreed with something Limori said, which wasn't very often, or with the way she treated someone, I would tell myself, or others would tell me, "But what she says is The Truth." The unspoken part of that message was, "You cannot argue with it or dismiss it or not use the advice she is giving you." And further, "If you do disagree with The Truth, then obviously you are serving the Dark and not the Light."

ANYTHING SAID with enough conviction will appear to be true. I was reminded of this one night recently while renting a movie. I was at the counter of my local independent video store, paying for my video, when another customer approached the counter and asked the women serving me, "Who directed *The Magnificent Seven*?"

The store clerk paused for just a second and then said, "Sergio Leone." The tone in her voice and the expression on her face made me believe her. This, combined with the fact that she was behind the counter and therefore a film expert, gave me no reason to doubt her. I had no idea who directed *The Magnificent Seven* but at that moment I would have sworn it was Sergio Leone.

It isn't. As I fished money out of my wallet to pay for my rental, the sales clerk said to the other customer, "Let me double-check." Turns out the correct answer was John Sturges.

But this little exchange reminded me of an expression Michael coined while we were in Limori's circle: Not always wrong but never in doubt. He most often applied it to Gary, one of Limori's top protégés, but I would later realize it applied to Michael himself and most accurately to Limori. It was not only what Limori said that sucked me into her grasp, it was how she said it. No matter what, every word she spoke was offered with complete conviction. She could say the most outrageous things and sound as if she were simply stating a scientific fact. "Lisa is the incarnation of the Angel Gabriel" seemed as grounded in reality as saying, "Ice forms at temperatures below zero degrees Celsius." And, just like the video sales clerk, she had set herself up in an area of expertise where she had absolute authority, only hers was spirituality.

A few years ago, I took an online marketing class. One of the first lessons was this: In order to create more sales, set yourself up as an expert in your field. Human psychology causes us to trust those we believe are experts. Limori obviously understood this principle long before I did.

MY PASSAGE from that of an outsider who was new to the group to a full-fledged member could be charted by my grasp of the group language. After a year of Wednesday nights, I knew the Pear Tree Story off by heart and had added many new words to my vocabulary such as *ego, spirit, chakra,* and *negative energy* and learned their group-specific definitions via discussions each week. With a little trepidation but more excitement, I began participating as well in the weekend workshops that Limori held locally. The first one I attended was in her home in Port Moody.

There were perhaps twenty of us there, seated around her living room in a circle of chairs, with the other living room furniture moved to other parts of the house. There was never a formal agenda or structure to these workshops; Limori was not teaching a methodology that could be replicated or a paradigm that could be memorized. She was acting at the behest of God, we believed, and therefore we were willing to let her lead us wherever she said God wanted us to go. We spent some of the time during the workshops meditating, and would report afterwards on what we'd "seen" or felt or experienced during the mediation. Limori would then, from her seat at the top of the circle, comment on our experience and explain what her spirit guides said it signified. The meditations themselves were often guided; that is, someone in the group would lead us through a visualization (in the early days it was usually Limori but later others of us were granted permission to do this) and then we might spend some time in silence. The meditations could last up to an hour, but were more often thirty or forty minutes long.

We were there to learn at the feet of someone we believed was a spiritual master and had God's ear. To that end, during these workshops, God was available through Limori via her spirit guide, Azeen, to provide us with guidance about changes we needed to make in our lives and personal selves in order to better serve Him and strengthen our ability to be spiritually "clear." Unspoken was the eternal hope that we would eventually be able to receive His guidance ourselves.

At some point during the first day of the workshop, either before or after a meditation, Limori would look around the room until eventually her gaze would fall on one person. She would make a few introductory enquiries about that person's life, both inner and outer, until she discovered an "ego position" that the person was dealing with. Then the rest of us would sit back, relieved that the spotlight had momentarily fallen on someone else and, like an audience at a tennis match, our heads would swivel back and forth between Limori and her chosen subject as they talked. Or, rather, as the person confessed and Limori gave them God's guidance about what the root cause of their particular problem was and what they should do about it.

DURING THE SATURDAY afternoon of my first workshop, Limori's eyes land on Gary.

"How are you, Gary?" she enquires.

"Fine, thank you."

This slightly clipped response produces scattered nervous laughter around the group as we wait for Limori to drill deeper to discover what Gary's ego position is. He is being coy with her, but we know, as he does, that such skirting around whatever Limori is seeing will not last long.

"How are things with your mother?"

"Good," he replies. "She and Dad just returned from a vacation in Italy."

"Really... hmmm." Limori glances meaningfully at Alice on her left. As their eyes meet they nod and smile knowingly to one another. Now Alice is in on whatever it is that Limori is seeing.

"How was your parents' vacation?"

"Good. Fine." Gary shifts nervously in his seat. "I think."

At this point Limori might as well have yelled, "AH HA!" She has found a chink in Gary's armour. Instead she asks, "When did you last speak to them?"

"Ah, well, a couple of weeks ago, I guess."

"You guess?"

"Well, let's see, maybe three weeks ago. Well, maybe closer to a month..." He trails off.

"Ah yes." Limori smiles and settles a little deeper into her chair, her hands clasped together and resting, as ever, on her ample midsection, her ankles crossed on the floor. "When exactly did they return from vacation?"

"Oh, about three weeks ago." Gary is smoothing his mustache now and trying to appear perfectly at ease with this line of questioning.

"So, you haven't spoken to them since they got back. Is that right?"

"Yeah, I guess that's correct."

"Hmmm." Limori rolls her eyes toward Alice again and smiles with closed lips as though she has a delicious secret that she'd just love to share. "Now, why would a son not call his parents to ask about their vacation? I wonder why that would be?" She asks this question innocuously, but the irony is not lost on any of us. Why Gary hasn't called his mum is obviously of paramount importance.

And then we're off. For at least an hour Limori "works" with Gary to unearth the "issues" he has with his mother and what ego positions he is holding onto that are preventing him from having a clean relationship with her. During this work of Limori's we all listen in and try to learn as much from the discussion as we can. She will poke and prod and find the root cause of any behaviour, or find and address "judgments" that the subject of her work might have. Like a magician, she can make issues appear where no one else can see them.

Over the years and during the numerous workshops that are held, men and women alike shed many tears, as Limori touches old, unhealed emotional wounds and brings them to the surface to be exposed, all in the name of spirituality. We are taught that we cannot be clear servants of God unless we excavate and clean up any and all emotional baggage and ego positions we have.

The benefit of this method for someone like Limori, who was trying to build a community of followers, is that if you're human you've got baggage and an ego. Limori never had to inquire very far into anyone's business before she stumbled onto an unhealed wound or ego position she could manipulate for her purposes. Remember, we wanted to be clear in order to serve God, and she imprinted us with the idea that the way to do this was to bring forward and deal with all our "issues."

After I'd left the group and begun researching cults, I learned that this type of discussion and feedback from the guru is what Robert J. Lifton calls confession; it is his fourth criteria for thought reform.

> Sessions in which one confesses to one's sin are accompanied by patterns of criticism and self-criticism, generally transpiring within small groups with an active and dynamic thrust toward personal change. Confession is an act of self-surrender.[7]

The "sins" that we were confessing to were the possession of ego positions. My experience was that the type of group confession that Limori ensured we participated in had three specific outcomes, in addition to Lifton's self-surrender, which bound me to Limori and the others in the group.

First, it created in the group a perverse sense of intimacy. We came to know each other's emotional wounds thoroughly because of these public disclosures. Knowing someone else's deepest, darkest, most painful wounds usually comes about only after years of being in a relationship with a spouse, partner or therapist. Yet we were forced into that type of intimacy because of these public workshops with our guru. On occasion, those who had just joined the group or just met Limori found themselves forced into this type of confession in only their second or third meeting with her, and in front of the rest of us.

The second outcome (and the flip side of the intimacy coin) was that each of us was provided with ammunition with which to measure our own spiritual growth against that of others. For example, I might think to myself, "Lisa still holds onto her attachment to physical possessions and I don't do that any longer, so I must be further along on my spiritual path than she is."

The third outcome was that the cathartic after-effect of delving deeply into one's emotional wounds bound me to Limori as though she was my saviour. If you've ever been in therapy, you may recognize the feeling of being completely emotionally drained at the end of a therapeutic session. I experience this as a feeling of rawness, as though several layers of my skin have been peeled away. But I simultaneously experience relief and a feeling of safety, because I have been treated with compassion and gentleness. Something that I have been carrying around with me, while painful to bring to light, has been examined face on and I have survived the process, leaving me feeling both vulnerable and cleansed.

In the non-therapeutic setting that was Limori's living room, the feeling of raw vulnerability after being workshopped meant that I falsely attributed any feelings of relief to her gifts as a psychic and a servant of God. Limori had no right to stray into this type of emotional and psychological territory with any of us. She was not professionally trained as a psychologist or psychiatrist, nor were we in a therapeutic setting. Yet she brought those elements into the group under the guise of spiritual work. Consequently, I felt that I owed any spiritual growth that I had experienced to her. She repeatedly violated my emotional boundaries and I thanked her for it.

LIMORI ALSO USED these weekend workshops (and later the week-long ones) to reinforce Lifton's third criterion, the demand for purity.

> The world becomes sharply divided into the pure and the impure, the absolutely good (the group/ideology) and the absolutely evil (everything outside the group.) One must continuously conform to the group 'norm.' Tendencies toward guilt and shame are used as emotional levers for the group's controlling and manipulative influences.[8]

The demands for purity and for confession tie in perfectly with each other. By shining the spotlight on any one of us at any time and probing us into confession, Limori was constantly reinforcing in each of us that we were never pure enough. We were continually put in the position of being forced to confess our impurities and then shamed for having them in the first place. If, during the course of an enquiry from Limori, we denied or defended the presence of an ego position or other spiritual failing, this would only be declared an even greater failing than if we'd admitted our fault up front. Not being willing to face The Truth was the ultimate slap in the face to God, to Limori and to our own spiritual growth. So at any moment one could be called out for either having an impurity or failing to see the impurity. It was a never-win situation.

And naturally, this strategy worked in Limori's favour because no one can ever rid themselves of all their ego positions and impurities. We were held in a constant state, as Lifton says, of guilt and shame. Additionally, the promise of attaining any measure of spiritual growth was never fulfilled because we always, always had more ego positions to work through. The carrot of spiritual clarity and attaining Limori's level of enlightenment was perpetually dangled in front of us but it was always out of reach.

ONE OF LIMORI'S theoretical premises was that we were each developing our spiritual "muscle." This was one reason given for the need for the weekly meetings and weekend or weeklong spiritual retreats that we attended over the next few years. She told us that we were all spiritual beings and in order to best serve God we needed to strengthen the spiritual skills that we had. We needed to learn how to be in tune with God via psychic communication – clairaudience, clairvoyance and the like.

We were told that each of us had these natural spiritual abilities and developing them was a simply a matter of practice and diligence. Unlike sports or music or dance, possessing talent and/or natural ability were not important. We were all capable, she said, of communicating with our higher selves, our guides and, it was implied, God. For every issue (an argument with a co-worker, a recalcitrant child, a decision between a blue dress and a red one) we were invited to "tune in" to see what Spirit had to say.

However, as with every authoritarian relationship, because Limori was the teacher, she had the ultimate say about whether the answers an individual received while tuning in were accurate or clear. Clarity was the ultimate goal for every one of us. Limori herself was the "clearest" of all, and we aspired to reach her level of clarity by defeating our ego positions and meditating as much as possible.

But here I had my first experience of a double bind. For while Limori's approach to teaching us seemed to empower us, it actually served to do the opposite. We were taught that our hearts, the centre of ourselves, always knew The Truth. This mantra was repeated over and over . . . and over again. "Trust your heart," we were told. "It always knows The Truth." However, another contradictory mantra was also drilled into us, from the earliest days. "If what your heart knows to be true contradicts what Limori says, then your heart is wrong."

So, always trust your heart; it is always right. But also be willing to dismiss it because it can be wrong.

This was a means of control cleverly disguised as a spiritual principle and it was incredibly effective. We recited it to each other in Limori's absence—"always trust your heart"—for it seemed so empowering. The phrase became an integral part of our loaded language. But inevitably decisions that we made, choices that felt right for someone when they "tuned into their hearts," could be overthrown by a mere glance from the ultimate authority on The Truth, the clearest one of all: Limori.

Under the guise of learning to trust ourselves and develop our relationship with God, we were actually learning the opposite: to trust no one except Limori. She gradually became the ultimate authority we all looked to for confirmation of our every feeling, thought or spiritual message.

Double binds cause their own unique sensation in my body. I feel as though my brain has slipped a cog. All thought leaves my head and I feel slightly paralyzed, as though time has just stopped. Double binds contradict logic. My body knows this and clearly tells me so, while my brain remains wrapped in knots, trying to figure things out.

Of course, when I was learning to accept double binds as the rule of law in Limori's group, I knew none of this, but my body did. It never stopped telling me that what I was learning didn't make sense. However, the sinister, dangerous beauty of authoritarian rule is that at the same time that Limori was manipulating me, she was teaching me to ignore any signals from my body or mind that would contradict her position of power. The analogy I use is that gurus teach us to build a dependence on compass points that are outside ourselves. We become completely dependent on these external references because we are simultaneously being taught that our internal compass is faulty.

NOT KNOWING any of this at the time, I became fully integrated into the spiritual community I'd found. The feeling of being specially chosen by God was reinforced by spending weeknights, some weekends and later a week at a time in a spiritual setting with others who were on the same path. My social circle had grown, but was almost entirely comprised of those in the group, and I spent most of my spare time with them as well, especially Debbie and Amber, who were both single like I was, and close to my age.

I'll reference Robert J. Lifton again, and his first criteria for thought reform, milieu control: the control of human communication within an environment. One of the elements of milieu control that Lifton cites is a mind-control guru setting up "a sense of antagonism with the outside world; it's us against them."[9] This was certainly the case with Limori's group; we were continually immersed in messages about the sacredness of what we were doing, the importance of our work for God. The difference between of all of us who were there, willing to listen to and follow Limori, and those who were not in the group, and therefore had less value in God's eyes, was often brought to our attention.

One of the reasons I found myself wanting to develop friendships with others who followed Limori's teaching was that I had early on absorbed the group message that life consisted of two types of people: "us" and "them," "them" being literally everyone on the planet who did not believe in or follow Limori. She planted the seeds of us against them in many ways, some subtle, some not so much.

For example, we were a community of searchers. It was our desire for a deeper understanding of life that brought us to Limori in the first place. Therefore, most naturally, many of us spent a great portion of our time in the exploration of the world and the spiritual ideas put forth by those both ancient and recent. The need or desire to understand our place in the universe most often led to reading – everything from Paramahansa Yogananda to Carlos Castaneda, Shirley MacLaine and Black Elk, to the teachings of Buddha and the channelled work of Emanuel, and back again. At times, in a Wednesday night meeting, someone would bring up an idea they'd been reading about and contemplating and ask Limori for Azeen's explanation of the topic. The answer would invariably come back, usually laced with gentle humour, agreeing with some of what the referenced author said, but also, ever-so-subtly, undermining the author's authority and the veracity of their message, and implying once again that it was only Limori herself who knew The Truth.

Later, when we were more enthralled and more closely tied to her, she might say, "Azeen says that Yogananda's message has been twisted somewhat and that what he really meant was . . ." Or she would even tune into the teacher (Jesus, Buddha, etc.) himself and bring his message directly to us. The underlying implication was that if you want the real truth, you cannot trust even the books that a spiritual teacher has written; you must hear The Truth from the source itself, and Limori was the one person who could connect with these wise masters and give us the message they intended. With "us" you got The Truth; with "them" you could never be sure.

Additionally, to create a stronger feeling in the group of "us versus them," those among us who had partners or spouses who did not attend the group would very quickly find that person thrown into a light of suspicion. The messages would begin subtly and at once build up the group member's perceived standing in God's eyes, while at the same time implying (or stating) that the non-attending partner was deficient in some way.

For example, a group member might share a dream with Limori that had seemed spiritually significant. Limori would respond by affirming what the member thought and then, with a wink and a smile, say something like, "But your husband wouldn't understand such an advanced concept, would he?" Her tone would be kind and jovial, but the message would be crystal clear. The group member was advancing rapidly toward spiritual enlightenment, but unfortunately her spouse was not quite as special and not able to keep up. The group member would eventually be told they were "being held back spiritually" by their spouse. And when someone's spouse came into question by Limori, and she began to really lean on the group member to consider leaving the marriage, she always had a trump card to play: "Do you choose God or do you choose your spouse?"

What a conundrum for the serious spiritual student! It was the very choice Michael would be required to make several years down the road, both in his marriage and later in his relationship with me. Marriages began to dissolve at an astonishing rate for those group members whose spouses did not attend. It was a powerful strategy and one that worked very well for Limori, for once someone had left their spouse they were even more strongly bound to her, their guru.

Another way that Limori created an environment of "us versus them" was to demonize those who left the group. Leaving was the worst-case scenario, from a spiritual perspective, according to Limori. Whenever anyone did leave the group, the event actually ended up working in Limori's favour, because she could take the opportunity to emphasize to those of us who remained that it was her group and her group alone that was working for God. When referring to a departed member Limori would shrug her shoulders and sigh.

"That's his choice," she would say, "but he is making things awfully difficult for himself. He'll be back when he's had enough pain."

Or, "She just couldn't face The Truth. Her ego is fully in charge now. She will regret the decision to leave, maybe not immediately but eventually."

Each time someone left the group, Limori would respond by continuing to weave this spell of "us versus them." I slowly grew to believe that the only way to serve God was to stay in the group. I absorbed the message that to leave the group was to turn my back on God; anyone who walked away from Limori and her group was walking into the dark and dangerous existence of those who served only their ego and, therefore, the Devil. This belief was reinforced much more strongly in a few years when a couple of members who had been very close to Limori took their leave. She declared that they would be dead within six months because of their refusal to serve God and their choice to serve the Devil.

Interestingly, when these types of predictions were proven wrong – when we bumped into a ex-member on the streets of Vancouver, say, or heard through the grapevine that someone had moved or married or started a new business and, therefore, was not in fact dead – Limori had us so well trained that no one ever confronted her about her inaccuracy. She achieved this by making anyone who departed into He Who Shall Not Be Named. To bring up the name of a former member of the group would be to bring "bad energy" into the group. On the rare occasions that someone made the mistake of doing this, Limori and Alice would clutch their stomachs and roll their eyes and describe how "black" the energy in the room had become and how sick this was making them, simply hearing the person's name. Therefore, we learned very quickly never to refer to anyone who had left the group and certainly never to question the fact that Limori's prediction of debilitation and death for this individual had not come true.

THE "US VERSUS THEM" strategy was also used within the group, as part of its hierarchical structure. At the bottom of the hierarchy was everyone who attended the Wednesday night meditation meetings. Everyone who came to Wednesday night was "special" in God's eyes and was treated as such, but they weren't as special as they could be. The next rung up the ladder contained those who had been asked by Limori to join the invitation-only Thursday night circle. This group was smaller than the Wednesday night group, and included only those who were deemed by Spirit to be worthy of this honour. The Thursday night meeting was similar in structure to Wednesday night, with a mix of meditation, discussion and confession. Those in the Thursday group, however, were looked upon by those in the Wednesday group as having additional spiritual merit.

I envied my friends Michael, Lisa and Karen, who had been invited to breathe the rarified air of Thursday night. Belonging to this group meant special access to Limori, it seemed to me, because the group was smaller and there seemed to be greater intimacy between her and its members. Needless to say, it became my life's ambition to be invited to the Thursday night group; I wanted to "belong" at a higher level and I suppose I expected that joining this elite crowd would be the final solution to the self-esteem issues that continued to plague me despite my dedication to meditating.

WHEN I FINALLY WAS INVITED, I did feel a greater sense of belonging and remember feeling superior to those in the Wednesday night group who had not received the call.

. . .

THE FINAL RUNGS above the Thursday group in the hierarchy were those who lived at Wolf's Den, and above them was just Limori herself.

WITHIN THESE BROAD categories there were also mini-hierarchical steps; those who travelled with Limori when she spent months in Hawaii or Arizona were slightly elevated from those who lived full time at Wolf's Den. Those in the Thursday night group who were invited to private events at Limori's home were slightly elevated from those who were not, etc.

Kramer and Alstad, in *The Guru Papers*, describe the hierarchical structure of a cult as providing security, and that was certainly my experience. The further I moved up the ladder, the more secure I felt about my purpose for God and the better I felt about my value as a human being because I belonged to a group that I believed were God's chosen people. "Since spiritual hierarchies contain ready-made steps for advancement they offer quick access to feeling better through improving. . . Moving up the rungs brings power and respect," Kramer and Alstad say. "The organization's hierarchical structure neatly fits the disciples' psychological need to make progress, and to be able to evaluate themselves (measure their progress) with regard to others. Whatever one's position, one can feel better than those who have not progressed so far."[10]

And, as I describe in the prologue, there was a perverse game of real-life Snakes and Ladders perpetually being played within this hierarchical structure. As people moved in and out of favour with our guru, their position in the hierarchy would change. Someone could go from living at Wolf's Den to being excommunicated, living with Limori's son and daughter-in-law as their nanny and housekeeper. When that person returned to favour, they would return to Wolf's Den and their job as nanny might be filled by someone new, who was "bringing in bad energy" and needed to clean up their act. Those of us living in Vancouver knew that we'd slipped a few notches in the group hierarchy if Limori stopped taking our phone calls or ignored us on Thursday night. But whatever one's status in the group, exalted flavour of the month or miscreant, our belief was that life outside the group, among those who did not serve God, was profoundly worse than anything we could encounter inside it.

It was a very black-and-white world I began to live in, and a black-and-white morality that I adopted. Inside group: good. Outside group: bad. What Limori says: Truth. What anyone else says: to be confirmed or denied by Limori. And honestly, it was a relief to fold myself into a doctrine and morality that had no uncertainty. I didn't even think of it as morality; everything was simply The Truth or Not The Truth.

For those of us living in Vancouver, the cult was non-residential. That is, we all lived in our own homes and had jobs that occupied our days. Debbie, Amber and I became good friends, going to movies and dinners on the weekend. Spiritual topics were never far from our conversation, and any challenge that any one of us encountered at work or with family was always examined, using our much-loved spiritual rhetoric. My friendship with Michael continued to grow as well. He was never far from my thoughts, and we spent many an afternoon in his shoebox-sized apartment getting to know one another. His girlfriend, Jessica, was naturally suspicious of our relationship, but she had nothing to fear from me. Despite the fact that I was falling in love with Michael, I was completely unaware of my own feelings for him and had no interest in examining them. My upbringing, combined with a naturally shy and introverted personality, meant that by the time I met Michael I was more than slightly emotionally stunted, so indeed, I was no threat to Jessica. I was simply grateful to have Michael's friendship and mentorship. He was a darn good listener, too.

As my friendships with Michael, Debbie, Amber and others in the group continued to strengthen, so did my attachment to Limori and her teachings. With my new friends, I attended the Wednesday night meditation classes faithfully and continued to crave more of everything our guru had to say. In those first couple of years with her I felt a burning eagerness to be asked to serve God. "Ask me to move to Wolf's Den," I would think to myself, "and I'll gladly do it." If she had asked me to do almost anything I would have gladly leapt at the chance to obey and serve. I wanted to be told what to do and what to believe. It was effortless for me to switch my allegiance and obedience from the authoritarian rule of a parent to the authoritarian rule of my guru.

I would soon have an opportunity to spend more concentrated time with Limori at the first weeklong workshop, to be held at Wolf's Den Fishing Lodge. Three of Limori's disciples had been living in the primitive and run-down resort almost since I had joined the group, and had been slowly but surely renovating and improving it so that it could be operated as a business. It was the perfect place for a spiritual retreat, with cabins for up to twenty-five of us to sleep in and a lodge and kitchen that could support us while we worked up an appetite meditating and clearing out ego positions. I didn't know it at the time but events at this workshop would ripple outward for years afterward and have a direct impact on my life, my relationship with Michael and eventually on my departure from the cult.

4

CANADIAN ASHRAM

The way to love anything is to realize that it might be lost.
—G. K. Chesterton

Wolf's Den Fishing Lodge, the seat of Limori's spiritual kingdom, is located on a lake in the middle of a remote Canadian wilderness region called the Chilcotin Plateau. The lodge itself sits on the crest of a small hill that leads down to the lake on a piece of property roughly three hectares in size. The freshwater fishing in this lake and others surrounding the lodge is world-class, and in winter the area is renowned for its cross-country skiing and ice fishing. In June, the blackflies will eat your head if you're not paying attention.

The word *remote* only begins to describe this part of the world. The main highway that runs through the Chilcotin to the British Columbia coast has an 80-kilometre (50-mile) stretch that, as of this writing, is still unpaved. The BC Ministry of Transport calls it a highway but technically it's still a gravel road. Telephone service didn't arrive at Wolf's Den until the 1990s; before that, a radiophone provided contact with the outside world. The closest town, named after the lake that Wolf's Den sits on, is a 20-minute drive from the lodge. Please keep in mind that I'm using the word *town* loosely. If you're looking for peace and quiet, you've found the Promised Land.

I drove to the workshop with three other women from the group. It took all day: east on Highway 1 out of Vancouver, then north up the Fraser Canyon, trail of the Cariboo gold rush in the 1860s and '70s. When we hit Williams Lake we turned northwest and followed Highway 20 as it angles toward the coast again. Wolf's Den sits midway between Williams Lake and Bella Coola on the coast. Throughout the drive all four of us chattered away as only women can. We took turns driving, ate junk food, stopped frequently for bio breaks and, of course, discussed spirituality. The sun shone as mile after mile of quiet, single-lane highway spooled away in our wake. I'd never seen this part of BC before and was fascinated as we squeezed between the walls of the Fraser Canyon and then were spat out onto rolling grassland at the canyon's top end a few hours later.

I was nervous about attending my first spiritual workshop. And excited. I'd never participated in anything like this before. There was the familiar sense of spiritual purposefulness that sang quietly in the background of my mind. Like the Blues Brothers, my fellow travellers and I were on a mission from God, and it felt so good to be certain of something.

Beyond Williams Lake, there were several hundred miles of the highway, still unpaved at that time, and the journey slowed down as we allowed for potholes and the corduroy effect that large transport trucks leave in their wake. Finally, road-weary and cramped, we pulled off the highway and bounced down a long gravel driveway that eventually terminated at the lodge. This was Limori's unofficial ashram, the seat of her growing empire, although I didn't think of it as such as the time. She and her ever-present sidekick Alice greeted us warmly with hugs and inquiries about our journey. We were shown around the lodge, then later the property. It was the first time any of us had been here.

Limori was the warm, genial hostess, clearly enjoying her role as matriarch of the brood that was gathering under her wings. She was also obviously proud of the work that those who lived at Wolf's Den had done under her tutelage and direction, to rescue the lodge and its outlying cabins from the neglect and wear they had suffered in recent years. She proudly showed us through all the buildings, pointing out all that had been done and mentioning the numerous changes that were to come. The lodge and all the cabins were rustic split-log design, perfectly befitting the surrounding wilderness landscape. The lodge had a fair-sized kitchen, which opened to the main living room via a pass-through window and a set of swinging doors. This room, with red carpet salvaged form Limori's home in Port Moody, would serve as the main workshop space and the place we would eat our meals, buffet style. Fitted with huge picture windows, it offered a spectacular view of the lake and its far shores.

The lodge was furnished gracefully but without flash. Limori had a way of creating physical beauty wherever she went, even in these somewhat primitive circumstances. Limori and Matthew's bedroom was on the far side of the living room. Alice and her then-husband John slept in a cabin nearby that, before the arrival of electricity, had been an icehouse.

We were each assigned a cabin to share with two or three others. There were about twenty of us; the five men stayed in one cabin and the women in the others. The cabins were without running water or electricity, and each had a woodstove for heat and a nearby outhouse. During that first workshop, all twenty of us shared the one bathroom in the lodge. We were each given a five-minute window every other day to shower so that we would not overwhelm the septic system. In later years, as the business of the lodge expanded, a shower house would be built to service the cabins.

Throughout the late afternoon and early evening, cars bearing fellow group members arrived. The passengers would disembark and receive the same welcome and tour that we'd had. Some of Limori's followers lived in BC's interior, and those of us from Vancouver saw them only at workshops such as this. It was a bit like a reunion as everyone slowly gathered in the living room, even though some of us had seen each other just a few days earlier. As the crowd grew, a feeling of anticipation began to permeate the atmosphere, and I became conscious of my curiosity about what would occur this week.

Once everyone had arrived, we were all seated in the living room and without instruction we grew quiet, ready to listen to whatever Limori and her "spirit guides" had to offer us. She was there in regal splendour as usual, dressed in a custom-made silk skirt and matching top, while the rest of us were mostly in jeans. As the chatter in the room slowly petered out, she clasped her hands around her belly, closed her eyes and made the small nodding motions and quiet, private murmurs of assent to the spirit voices she was listening to that we had come to learn meant she was "tuning in." She would often laugh at something Spirit had said and then open her eyes, still chuckling, and let us in on the joke she and Azeen were sharing.

A few guidelines were outlined for the week, such as the instruction that no one was to leave the property. Limori emphasized that she had drawn in good spirits to protect us while we were here but if we strayed past the property boundaries we could break the protective seal at the property line and endanger ourselves and everyone else. This was another reminder that we had to constantly be on guard and wary; doing God's work incited the wrath of the "dark forces," and coming to Wolf's Den en masse like this meant that the Devil would be really pissed at us. Cabin assignments were to be strictly followed – as with everything else, the cabin assignments were decided upon with Spirit's guidance and the "energies" were balanced by pairing certain people together. Meals would be taken communally in the main lodge with breakfast at 8:00 a.m. Alice was in charge of the kitchen and would be preparing the meals for us, but we would help with cleanup. Whatever happened or was shared by anyone at the workshop was strictly secret and was not to be shared with anyone once we'd returned to our regular lives.

After these rules had been outlined, we were free to spend the first evening as we wished, catching up with our compatriots and winding down from the long drive. Limori floated among us and held court. She continually provided bossy instruction to those who lived at Wolf's Den about tasks to be done immediately or in the coming days or weeks. "Open a window; we need some fresh air. Close the door or the cats will get out. Brent, is there firewood stacked at each cabin? Alice, what is that smell? Turn off the stove —you're burning the soup. Rosemary, get me a platter to put this on. No! Not that one. The blue one. Ugh, I'll do it myself. John, is there enough toilet paper in each outhouse? Go check. No, I said, go check. 'I think so' isn't a good enough answer," etc. This bossiness was one of the things that always bothered me the most about Limori, and being here in close quarters with her for several days in a row made my discomfort with the relentlessness of it, and her control over those around her, begin to grow. Everyone around her was always treated as if they were four years old and couldn't make the smallest decisions for themselves. But, as with every other warning sign and feeling of discomfort, I dismissed how I was feeling. "She's not bossy," I thought. "She's just particular."

The first night, the cabin I was assigned to was warm with both heat from the wood stove and the intimacy and community of the four women who were my bunk-mates. We took turns stoking the fire and brushed our teeth using water from a jerry can balanced on an old wooden chair in the corner. Some of the women in my cabin were the ones I'd driven up with; others were not, but we all knew each other and shared the common bond of a deepening desire to do good spiritual work. Ironically, I was assigned to share a double bed with Michael's girlfriend Jessica; Amber and Debbie were each on a tier of a bunk bed on the other side of the room. As we all nestled down under the blankets and our chatter quieted down, I could hear the loons calling to one another on the lake that was one hundred feet from the cabin door.

In the middle of the night, when I got up to use the outhouse, the flashlight beam bounced ahead of me, illuminating a tiny patch of ground in front of my feet. The darkness of the night was so thick it felt like a velvet blanket around my shoulders. Other than my flashlight there was not a single manmade source of light to be seen. On my way back to the cabin, I stopped briefly, turned off the light, and rolled my neck back to look heavenward. The abundance of stars seemed almost unreal, they were so crowded onto the patch of sky I could see through the tops of the trees. When viewed from Vancouver, the night sky looked nothing like this.

The morning came soon enough and, as instructed, the group was at breakfast by 8:00 a.m. Limori ate with us in the living room, and not for the first time I observed, perhaps unconsciously, the strange dynamic that accompanied her. She seemed to be trying to blend into the crowd and have small, casual conversations with those seated near her, but she also appeared to be highly attuned to whatever was going on anywhere else in the room. Midsentence, she'd interrupt herself and call across the room to the kitchen to correct Alice about the way she was doing something. Or she'd seem to be engrossed in one conversation but then interject herself into another conversation going on elsewhere in the room and correct someone about a point they'd made. It was like witnessing omnipresence, first hand. Her energy, for lack of a better word, was in every corner, in every conversation and in every head in the room.

And this peculiar dynamic wasn't one sided. Although we

were all sitting and chatting in small groups of two or three and eating breakfast off our laps, we all had our antennae pointed toward Limori. I would strain to stay present with those I was talking to, all the while making sure I didn't miss anything Limori said, for every word from her was, I felt, a blessing, a message from God and a gem not to be wasted. I could see that others were doing the same; I'd stop in midsentence and realize that the person I was talking to was looking at me but that his or her attention was with Limori, wherever she was in the room. There was a pull on her at all times. Wherever she went we were like hungry orphans grabbing at her skirts: "Please, Miss, feed my soul."

When breakfast was complete we each took a seat on the couches and chairs that encircled the room. We all knew the routine well and settled down quickly, assuming the position of the good meditation student: hands clasped in our laps, feet flat on the floor, spines straight, breathing deeply and slowly. I had a vague idea of what to expect, but I also knew there would be experiences I had not anticipated. I had never been on a week-long spiritual retreat, or any other kind of retreat for that matter, but given my experience with the group on Wednesday nights and at the weekend workshops, I assumed this would be much the same, only on a larger scale.

Limori began by tuning in and channelling to us about the spiritual work that would be done that week, a theme continued from the night before, only now in a less warm and welcoming tone. We were getting down to business and it was impressed upon us that this week held enormous significance in God's plan and in order for that plan to come to fruition we would have to be willing to step up and do whatever was required of us. As usual there was a tenor of gravity to what Limori was saying, and I was filled with the now-familiar twin feelings of urgency and self-doubt. There wasn't enough time to get everything done that God wanted done and, even if there were, I was probably not up to the task. This always left me feeling that I must work as hard as possible and go to whatever lengths were required to meet this bar that had been set so high, which, of course, was how the message was supposed to make me and everyone else feel. We were it. The twenty or twenty-two people here in the room with Limori were God's only true servants on Earth, and if we couldn't face the darkness within ourselves in order to bring more light to the world, then all was lost.

So, with that twisted bit of logic firmly in place, we were assigned our task for the day. We were each given a pad of paper and a pen and instructed to go off on our own and write down all the secrets we held in our hearts and minds and anything we were ashamed of having done, large or small.

"The only way to serve God," Limori instructed, "is to clear yourself of these things that you are holding onto. Write down what you are ashamed of and what you hide from others. Get these things out of your body and onto the paper and you will be free of them. In this way you will become a clearer vessel for God to work through. Secrets and shame that hide in the darkness are magnets for the Devil. He will use every bit of darkness that hides inside you to thwart God and to ensure that God's plan can never be fulfilled. We must remove these hooks from inside you so that they cannot be used in such a way. Bring everything into the light and it will no longer have a hold on you."

We were given three hours. There was to be no talking among us, but we could go anywhere on the property. I wrote earnestly, searching every nook, cranny and memory inside me and dragging up whatever I could think of that was shameful or secret. As did everyone else, it seemed: all around the grounds, on lawn chairs by the water and on porches and at kitchen tables, we wrote until our wrists ached.

After lunch, as we settled back into our seats around the living room, I felt that I could see pride and relief on everyone's faces. Some chagrin too, but mostly pride. Limori asked us how the experience was, and a few of us chimed up with explanations of what the exercise had been like. She listened and nodded sagely, as always, and then dropped the bomb.

"Now, you will all read out loud to the group what you have written."

"What?!" Amber exclaimed. "I didn't know we would be sharing this information." Her face was deeply flushed and she moved restlessly in her seat, eyes wide and shocked.

"I know," Limori said. "I didn't say earlier that you would be sharing what you've written but Azeen says that in order to completely clear out the shadows from within you, each of you must do exactly that."

More of us shifted in our seats and squirmed with discomfort.

"Who wants to go first?" Limori looked around the room, her eyes passing over each one of us until one brave soul volunteered to do what each of us was dreading.

And so the afternoon passed. And then we continued for the duration of the following day. It took up to an hour (sometimes more) for each person to read aloud what they'd written and then have Limori/Azeen respond to what had been shared. We confessed to everything from shoplifting chocolate bars as a seven-year-old to adultery and more. Lisa told us of a child she'd given up for adoption when she was a teenager and an abortion she'd had in her early twenties, events that even her husband didn't know about. Norman, whose wife Nelly was also a member of the group but not there among us at the workshop, volunteered that he'd insisted on having anal intercourse with his wife. I am a fairly private person so the experience of listening to everyone's deepest, darkest secrets hour after hour was agonizing.

When it was my turn to read what I'd written, my secrets and shameful events paled in comparison to those of some of the others in the group; I wasn't perfect by any means, just young. I hadn't had as much time or inclination to accumulate secrets, though I still flushed to my roots while I read what I had written.

I was very happy when the chore was over. Limori/Azeen didn't have much to say to me afterwards, much to my relief.

In hindsight, it wouldn't have mattered what any of us had shared. This was simply an exercise in confession. We were baring our souls in an exercise that bound us to Limori and increased that false sense of intimacy between us. (I really did not want to know about Norman and his intimate relationship with his wife – that's an image I will never be able to scour from my brain.)

At the end of day two, when every last person had read the contents of their notepad (except Limori of course; she didn't participate in these exercises – that would have lowered her to our level), relief and a small sense of accomplishment spread through the room. Limori told us it was a good beginning and that now we could build on this work in the following days at the workshop. During the evening of the second day we were free to do as we liked. Most of us relaxed in the lodge: reading, playing cards, drawing or chatting with one another.

One member of the group, Victor, was a shy, gentle, some-what socially awkward man in his late fifties. He was an engineer, whose family origins were Estonian. Tall and reed thin, he reminded me a bit of Ichabod Crane. Very much an introvert, Victor kept to himself and during free time at workshops he would often go off by himself, to his cabin or for a walk in the woods. An avid outdoorsman who loved canoeing and kayaking, he was the sort of person who was obviously much more comfortable in communion with nature than with people. As a group, we often teased him about his idiosyncratic habits and I am not proud of the borderline abuse he received from me and his other peers in the group simply because he was a bit different. One of the strongest underlying messages that took hold in the group was that to be different was dangerous. We were all required to fit into a mould that had limited parameters, from the clothes we wore ("women should be feminine and wear skirts and dresses, and men should take pride in their appearance and not dress in a sloppy way") to any inclination to have close relationships outside the group, to speech patterns that were outside the group norm. So Victor's inclination to spend time by himself, possibly the result of an introvert's natural need to recharge by being alone, often made him the target of teasing or, in more serious cases, of being workshopped by Limori.

On the third day of the workshop, as we settled into our chairs in the living room, Limori began the day by channelling a meditation. We each assumed the position and meditated while Spirit spoke through her about the mystical and magical events that were changing the universe as a result of our hard work during the previous couple of days. Limori's guided meditations always had vivid visual images (a bit like the Disney film *Fantasia*) of light and dark and the battles supposedly going on in the universe, of which we were told we were an integral part.

When the mediation was over that day, Limori scanned the room with her raptor's eyes and they eventually settled on Victor.

"Victor, I noticed you weren't with the group last night during the evening," she said.

"Nope," Victor replied. He was always a man of few words.

"What did you do?" Limori asked.

He explained that he'd gone for a walk after supper and then to his cabin to read.

"You didn't feel like coming back to the lodge to be with the others?" Limori's tone was not yet accusatory or blaming, but she was not messing around either.

"Nope."

"Hmmm. And why do you think that is?"

For the next hour, Victor was workshopped. In no uncertain terms, it was impressed upon him that keeping himself separate from the group was an ego position and that when he spent his free time alone he was separating his "energy" from that of the group and that to do so was to keep himself separate from God. It always came back to that. Whatever issue was being pointed out to any one of us, the bottom line was always that we were somehow, and in some way, defying God or rejecting God or not doing enough for God. And it was always as heartbreaking as being told you'd disappointed a parent.

I have no idea what this specific workshop experience was like for Victor, but I know that whenever I was workshopped I felt shame (for not doing enough or not doing the right thing for God) and a distinct sense of worthlessness because I'd failed. But I was also always left with a deepening feeling of resolve. I would try harder. I would do better. I would make Limori, and by proxy God, proud of me. I would not let them down again. I would do so well that she and God would never have to take me to task again. I would be the perfect pupil, the perfect servant, the perfect being of light in an increasingly dark world.

I believe that this particular feeling of resolve was one of the key elements that kept me in the group, and in Limori's clutches, for so long. No one wants to be a failure and, most especially, no one wants to disappoint those beings whose approval we crave the most. When we are children, it is our parents whom we need to please. This is a natural, instinctive desire; if we are bonded to the adults in our family they will provide for us and protect us. Approval equals survival in the early life of a human animal. When we as adults are enticed and seduced into a cult, it is the guru to whom we look for approval. The twin tactics that Limori used, of building me up ("you are each so vitally important in God's plan") and tearing me down ("you have failed again by letting your ego get in the way of your service to God") kept me unbalanced and entrenched in self-doubt, yet simultaneously and perpetually hopeful that I would receive the total acceptance and affirmation of my worth that I so desperately wanted.

The more deeply I became involved in the group and the more firmly the ideas and beliefs that Limori taught became ingrained, the greater became my need for her approval and praise. It seemed a bit like how I imagine a drug addict to be: I was always chasing my next fix of praise or approval, yet with each fix I became more and more dependent on the drug until it became impossible to live without. Just as an addict will eventually cheat or lie or steal to obtain their fix, I would gradually begin to go to further and further lengths to obtain mine, lengths that eventually included doing things that were morally and ethically reprehensible to me.

But for now, I was not clearly seeing any of this and simply skated from one spiritual event to another with the group to which I had become bonded. At Wolf's Den I was trying to enjoy the experience of my first weeklong workshop, although I always felt the strain of the emotional upset when people were worked over by Limori. And I was in a constant battle with my body, which was sending me clear signals that this was not a safe environment and something was wrong. But I ignored the nervous stomach and uneasiness I perpetually felt or, more commonly, tried to find a spiritual reason that would explain why I felt this way. Was I in my ego? Or was I unwilling to fully surrender to God's will? These were usually the conclusions I came to when my stomach was in knots from dawn to dusk, and I would resolve, once again, to work harder and be a better servant.

After workshopping Victor about his need for solitude, Limori channelled to us that this day was to be a day of silence. We were not allowed to speak to anyone until she instructed us to do so. We were allowed to go anywhere on the lodge property, however, and reflect in silence. It was suggested that we spend as much time as possible outdoors. So instructed, we trooped silently out of the lodge, wearing warm jackets and sometimes hats against the autumn chill in the air.

The three cabins where most of us were staying were set in a crescent around a little clearing that bordered the lake. The cabins crouched there with their backs to the forest and their tiny front porches facing the lake. Almost everywhere else on the property the trees marched directly down to the edge of the water, and were sometimes so close that their roots had been submerged by the shifting, eroding shoreline. But near the cabins there were a small clearing, a rocky beach, a pit for bonfires and a rock, half as large as a car, squatting on the shore, discarded carelessly by a passing glacier millennia ago. On this day of silence, I fell into a pattern of sitting somewhere on the property, in the trees or on a log, soaking up the silence, meditating and contemplating, as we had been instructed to do. Then, when I felt inspired to, I would change locations, easing the creaks and chill out of my limbs and walking slowly and meditatively until I found the next place I wanted to sit. Sometimes I would simply walk in irregular loops around the property, trying to warm up. Most of the others in the group seemed to be doing the same thing. I would bump into them occasionally as we each moved about the property like paper boats on a pond.

Mid-afternoon, as I moved from the shelter of the trees at the property's crest, down the narrow gravel driveway that led to the cabins, I could see Michael perched atop the sentry rock in the clearing, staring out at the lake. It was a gorgeous fall day. The air was so clear and clean that breathing had become a conscious pleasure. Occasionally a fish would leap out of the lake, which always filled me with joy and wonder. "Why do they do that?" I thought. "Are they playing?" The gentle splash that hailed their return to the lake would be carried hundreds of metres on the silence. I would often not see the fish leap, but simply hear the splash it made, carried from a distant point on the lake.

As he sat on the rock, Michael's waist was at about my shoulder height. I approached him and smiled, self-conscious about being silent, but determined to follow the rules anyway. And then, quite out of character for me, while still standing I leaned my right hip against the rock and my head and right shoulder against Michael's waist, the crinkly sound of his jacket filling my right ear. He put his left arm around my shoulder and together we gazed out at the lake, joined together like two complementary puzzle pieces. My breathing slowed, my shoulders relaxed and I felt safe. And accepted. The two best feelings in the world.

The tops of the trees swayed with a slight breeze that we could not feel at ground level. The lake water gently and rhythmically tickled at the pebbles on the shore. Michael and I stayed where we were, quiet and connected, for maybe six or seven minutes. We had never had this much physical contact for such a length of time. During the course of a normal day, in our friendship in the city, I would never have snuggled up to him in such a way. For one thing, he was dating Jessica and I would have felt duplicitous if I had touched him other than for a quick hug. For another, I was morbidly self-conscious and afraid of men in general. But in the communal circumstances of the workshop, and with the requisite silence of the day protecting me from some of my self-consciousness, my barriers were lowered briefly. Our embrace soothed me. My body and spirit relaxed in a way I hadn't experienced before. I wished I could stay there all day but, too soon, I felt it was time to move on. I stood up straight and removed my arm from where it had lain on the rock, behind Michael's behind, smiled at him again and turned back the way I'd come. I took a few steps toward the forest that surrounded the cabins, and there, coming out of the woods along the path, was Jessica. We smiled at each other silently and I knew that she would see Michael herself in a moment. After we'd passed one another, before I entered the envelope of the woods, I looked back and saw that she had joined him at the rock, leaning into him just as I had.

Upon returning to the lodge at lunchtime, I could sense that something was amiss as soon as I entered the front hallway, where our boots and coats were stored. When I got into the living room, a few of my compatriots were already gathered with Limori and Luke, Limori's "spiritual husband." Limori and Luke were seated in chairs at the far end of the room and Luke was holding his right arm on his lap at an odd angle. Even from fifteen feet away I could see that there was a wooden splinter sticking out of the palm of his hand.

At the time of this workshop, Limori was legally married to Matthew, who owned the property of Wolf's Den. But she was also spiritually married to Luke. They had known each other before I joined the group, though I didn't see much of Luke because he lived in the interior of BC. I would only encounter him at events such as this, where he would travel to join the group. Limori had proclaimed sometime in the last year that Luke was the reincarnation of Jesus Christ. His importance in God's plan was paramount and, as such, he was of particular importance to Limori herself. When she had told the group that Spirit had instructed her, while continuing to be married to Matthew, to marry Luke in a spiritual ceremony, there had been a few raised eyebrows but no outright objection, at least none that I was privy to. Anyone who heard the news was already heavily enough involved with the group that they swallowed what Limori proclaimed, and I remember feeling grateful even to be allowed to witness this part of God's plan. Not repelled by the impropriety of the situation, or curious about the dysfunction of it, but grateful. Yeesh. The spiritual marriage was not something Limori, Matthew or Luke spoke of in public (i.e., with co-workers or friends outside the group). I pointedly asked Limori one day whether she and Luke slept together. No, she had replied, they did not, and indeed Luke was required by God to be celibate for the rest of his life.

"What happened?" I quietly asked those close to the doorway as I entered the room.

Karen, who was nearest to me, answered, "Luke fell outside and landed on that splinter. It's so big that they're afraid to take it out. They might have to drive to Williams Lake to find a doctor."

The splinter was enormous and most of it was buried in

Luke's palm. "Splinter" is not even an accurate description. It was a chunk of wood, which obviously had one very sharp end that was imbedded into Luke's palm. He must have been in considerable pain, but he stayed composed and even joked with Limori while they decided what to do.

It emerged, as members of the group drifted into the lodge for lunch, that Brent, one of the men who lived full time at Wolf's Den, and Luke had already been to see the nurse on the nearby Indian reserve. She had advised that due to the nerves and tendons close to the splinter she was not qualified to extract it. She suggested that Luke make the 320-km (200-mile) trip to Williams Lake to have it removed. Limori, Alice and Gary conferred about what to do. They quickly determined that Brent would drive Limori and Luke to the hospital in Williams Lake and Gary and Alice would share the duties of supervising the workshop that afternoon – but not before this accident had been noted as a significant spiritual event. Almost everyone was gathered in the room now, and Limori began to channel.

"As we have all been told," she began, channelling God Himself, "Luke is the reincarnation of My son, Jesus of Nazareth. This splinter is symbolic of the crucifixion that he experienced many years ago. It is a reminder that My work goes on and that you, My children, must be ever vigilant about continuing to bring My light and love to the Earth. The battle is not nearly over and we have much to do." She carried on for several more minutes. We listened, as we always did at these times, in absolute silence and with total conviction that we were being told The Truth.

Once the channelling was complete, Luke, Limori and Brent gathered themselves and their things and left for Williams Lake. It would be at least a four-hour drive each way. Before departing, Limori gave Alice and Gary a few instructions about how to proceed with the afternoon. We were to eat lunch and then continue the day in silence.

I was a little tired of silence at this point. Tired and bored and fed up with being chilled while sitting outside on the ground or on a log or a rock. It was a beautiful fall day but this was not the tropics. After a few hours of being outside without moving much, the cold had crept into my bones. But I followed the instructions as everyone else did and made do with short, rebellious trips into our cabin to warm up. Even there, though, the chill could be felt because the fire in the woodstove wasn't lit. I crawled under the blankets on my bed, fully clothed, for a few minutes and felt horrifically guilty the entire time for disobeying orders. I dared not go as far as lighting the woodstove; the smoke from the chimney would instantly give me away.

Limori, Luke and Brent arrived back at Wolf's Den late that night and we didn't see them again until the following morning. Luke's hand was bandaged but he was smiling when he greeted us as we gathered for breakfast. The hospital in Williams Lake had successfully removed the wood from his hand and he had apparently narrowly missed serious nerve damage. This was championed by Limori as a sign that "God was at work with us," and we spent almost the entire morning listening to the tale of the drive down to the hospital and the spiritual significance of everything that had happened en route. An old pickup truck had pulled out onto the highway to cross at one point, directly in front of Brent, and he'd had to avoid crashing into it by driving into a ditch.

"That was the Devil, of course," Limori said. "He was trying to prevent us from reaching the hospital. But I drew in the Light and God protected us. We are constantly under attack and must be vigilant at all times."

That day we meditated and Limori workshopped various people for whatever ego positions they were holding onto, but it was our evening free time that held the next surprise. Once again, most of us were gathered in the living room of the lodge after supper. Michael and I happened to be sitting on the floor with our backs against a couch. Limori was seated to our right, on a chair. She and Michael conferred for a moment and I noticed them glancing at Jessica, who was across the room. I couldn't hear much of what they were saying because they were speaking quietly, and I was trying to appear as though I wasn't listening because the conversation appeared to be private, although, as with anything that went on in Limori's orbit, I desperately wanted to know every detail. Finally, I heard her say to Michael, "You know what you have to do," and she glanced at Jessica again.

Michael seemed to gather himself up inside, and then stood up and went over to where Jessica was sitting and pulled her up to stand with him. The two of them stood in front of the fireplace at the end of the room and Michael asked Jessica to marry him. Everyone in the room had grown quiet as they turned to watch; we all sensed that something significant was going on, and when Jessica accepted we all clapped and cheered.

I felt shocked and saddened, of course. In the last few months I had become more in touch with my feelings for Michael so it was painful, naturally, to watch him propose to Jessica. But I tried as best I could to stifle what I felt and pretend at least to be happy for the betrothed couple. Limori immediately began talking about the spiritual significance of this union and about how much it mattered to God and all his angels. She began planning for a spiritual wedding to be held the next night, our final night at the workshop.

The following day was mainly spent preparing for the wedding. In the early evening, we all gathered in the lodge, wearing the best clothes we had brought with us. I had not brought very much in the way of fancy dress clothes with me – not many of us had. Jessica borrowed her bridal outfit - a blouse and skirt - from Alice. A huge table was laid along the length of the living room and Gayle had painted and calligraphed beautiful name cards for each one of us at our place setting. As we gathered in the room for the ceremony and dinner, Limori announced that we were to witness a double wedding this evening, as Gary and Karen had decided to get married as well. Each couple stood on either side of Limori, at one end of the table. The couples held hands and Limori held the hands of the grooms, who were closest to her. The rest of us stood at our places around the table and listened while Limori channelled and officiated this spiritual wedding between the two couples. After the ceremony, we enjoyed a feast that Alice had prepared and spent the evening in celebration of this event. Naturally, Limori painted this double wedding as having enormous spiritual significance and importance to the forces of good in the universe that we were working for. During the celebration and the evening that followed I felt a mix of jealousy and pride. Jealousy because Michael was marrying someone other than me. But pride because I was one of "us" and could count myself as one of God's warriors, working for the Light.

The fallout from this evening would last for years. Both couples would eventually legally marry and then divorce. This was a harbinger of the multitudinous couplings and uncouplings that many of the faithful would experience in Limori's group. Although I was not the woman marrying Michael on this night, my life would eventually become intertwined with his and Jessica's marriage in ways I could not possibly imagine at the time.

THE WORKSHOP CLOSED the following day with congratulations from Limori about what we'd accomplished and how proud God was of us for the spiritual work we'd done. She was moved to tears as she channelled Azeen, saying that battles in the universe were being won by the Light and angels were weeping with joy and gratitude. She described the throng of angels she was seeing as being bathed in "God light," reaching their arms out to us in thanks for our work and for our commitment to God. Many of us, me included, were moved to tears as well. My tears were caused by the relief that came with feeling that I was a significant and valuable member of such a special community. I felt intensely proud of myself, in a way I had never felt in any other part of my life, as well as determined to never let God down. I felt like a warrior with a sacred mission, and let me tell you, that's a pretty powerful feeling. It gave purpose and meaning to every part of my life, and that's not something to sneeze at.

To my dismay and grave disappointment, however, I had begun to notice in the previous few months that my stomach often had a serious case of butterflies whenever I was around Limori, and being here at the lodge with her for a week had worsened that feeling. I was concerned for two reasons. First, the group culture told me that if I was afraid or nervous, it meant I had something to hide. I didn't believe that I was consciously hiding anything, but I understood that there could be something amiss with my energy that Limori would point out to me. I was loath to disappoint her and continued to long for her approval, so it tormented me that there could be something wrong with me that she and God would have to take me to task about.

My second reason for concern was rooted in another piece of group dogma: fear allowed "negative energy" to proliferate, and this energy could potentially "hit" Limori. She would often wince and gasp with the pain she said she experienced in her body because of the energy of the people around her. The premise was that she was so spiritually important to the Light that the Dark Side was constantly sending negative energy to hit her in the form of sharp pains in all parts of her body, to weaken and defeat her and therefore God.

Whenever she was workshopping someone, Limori's dialogue was peppered with sharp intakes of breath and flinching that were her way of expressing that she was being hit. In these instances, we were told that it was the anger of the person Limori was dealing with that was allowing negative energy to hit her, but fear was touted as another emotion that could allow the dark forces in the universe to hit her. The technique was a powerful one; we were constantly being reminded of what a powerful and positive force in the universe Limori was. If she weren't, so the logic went, "the negative" wouldn't bother hurting her so much.

For these reasons, the more I noticed the nerves in my stomach acting up, the more afraid I became. And the more afraid I became, the more convinced I was that I was about to hit Limori and be taken to task for all my negative emotions and whatever else was wrong with me. It was a vicious circle and one I would struggle with for years, until I left the group. I know now that the feeling of butterflies in my stomach was my body's way of telling me that something was wrong, not with me, but with the situation I was in. But at the time, the fresh gleam of my pride and purposefulness diverted my attention from what my body was saying to me and I simply tried to deal with the physical sensations by using group rhetoric.

LIMORI BUILT us up on that final day, feeding the very egos she was purporting to try to rid us of, by telling us how proud and grateful God and his angels were. But then her follow-up tactic, which would be repeated with monotonous regularity, was to tear us down again.

The group dispersed on the morning following the final day of the workshop. I joined the three women I had driven up with, and we drove back the way we had come, through Williams Lake and on into Vancouver.

The following week at the meditation circle in the city, Limori looked around the circle with grave disappointment on her face. We were told we had failed her, and therefore had failed God. We had "fallen back into old habits" upon returning to the city and our homes. The positive work we had done at Wolf's Den had been mostly erased because of falling back into our egos and into the habits of "our heads instead of our hearts." This pattern of building us up and tearing us down would continue the entire time I was involved with the group. It was not a pattern I could see until I had taken a step back from what was going on, but it was there. At the conclusion of each workshop we would be praised for the hard work we'd done and for how much progress we were facilitating for God in the battle between Light and Dark. But inevitably our confidence and pride would be crushed by a word from God, delivered through Limori, that He was disappointed by our lack of commitment and saddened by our apparent lack of love for Him. If we loved Him we'd work harder. And so we did.

5

LIVING THE LI(F)E

Sometimes all the prisoner has is the guard.
—From the television program *Life*

B
y the summer of 1992 I had been living in Vancouver and
going to the circle for three years. I had been to
numerous workshops, both weekend and weeklong
ones, at Wolf's Den and I had been asked to join the invitation-
only Thursday night meditation group.

Limori's brand of spirituality had become my whole life. I
longed to learn more, do more and sacrifice myself more for
Limori's God, who I believed was my God too. Limori had
brought me along to the point where I was utterly devoted to her.
I considered the members of the group to be my true family and
working for this god she represented to be my truest calling. I was
a feverish devotee, rarely missing a Wednesday night and never
missing the sacred Thursday nights. My life revolved around the
group and the people in it. I socialized with them on weekends
and meditated with them at our meetings. I spoke to at least one
person from the group every day.

When I re-read my journals from this time, it is easy to see that I was a very young, twenty-something girl who had almost no sense of herself. It is clear to me now that I swallowed whole almost everything Limori said. I had no critical thinking skills to apply to her claims that she was enlightened, nor did I ever question the merit or the veracity of what she said. I wanted so badly to believe in something, anything, that I became enchanted and enraptured by what Limori said and did. I wanted what she had: a close and intimate relationship with God and a strong sense of herself. It would take me two decades to figure out that these are not things anyone else can give you; we each have to build them inside ourselves, for ourselves. But at twenty-five years old I thought that if I just kept trying harder, doing more and pleasing Limori more, I would achieve them. I would find the inner peace I was looking for.

My mother left the group in 1992. She and I had been attending Wednesday nights together for three years or so, but then two things happened. Sheila, Limori's co-facilitator, broke away from the group and formed a circle of her own, and Limori made the mistake of criticizing my mother's partner, John. As I mentioned earlier, this was a common strategy on Limori's part, but it backfired with several people, including my mother. She wisely and rightly resented the tactics Limori was employing to undermine her relationship with her partner, and by the middle of the year she had left Limori and followed Sheila off to another, short-lived meditation group.

This was a tumultuous time for me; Sheila and my mother's split from the group left me feeling that my loyalties were torn. Sheila and Limori had been an especially magical team to be around, both channelling Spirit and both working for God. The fact that they were disagreeing was confusing for me, and I wondered, "How could they disagree when they both have access to higher realms? Wouldn't the spirits be giving the same messages to both of them?" It is a testament to both my naiveté and the state of my mind-controlled brain that I could not take a step back and think logically about this situation. It was two women with egos of their own, clashing about who was in charge. But the only answer to this problem that I was comfortable with in my black-and-white mindset was that one of them was "good" and one was "evil." I landed on the side of the fence that housed Limori and my other friends. But it was especially difficult for me to see my mother leave, because I believed she was turning her back on God.

My devotion to Limori proved strong enough to help me weather this storm, and in the summer of 1992 an opportunity came for me to live with her. She was moving out of the high-rise apartment building that she'd been living in for a few years, to a house she'd rented in a suburb of Vancouver. I was made an offer I felt was too good to refuse; I could live in the house in my own room, and keep my job outside the home. I would thus be part of God's world and work but would not have to entirely let go of my regular life. This was an unusual offer, because those who lived with Limori, with the exception of her spouse Matthew, worked exclusively for her, although without pay. The three women who were then her personal aides had left their jobs and their homes and, in two cases, husbands, and lived a life entirely of service. They spent their days doing Limori's bidding: meditating, travelling with her when required, working their fingers to the bone and generally making her life easier and more pleasurable. All this was in God's name, of course, and they viewed it as an honour to be atop the highest rungs of the group hierarchy. Those who lived and worked at Wolf's Den worked without pay as well, and considered it an equally honourable venture.

As did I. For someone from our group to be invited to live with Limori but allowed to maintain their own life outside the home was unheard of. I was deeply honoured to be elevated in the circle's hierarchy. I was being welcomed behind the Wizard of Oz's curtain and as such felt a deep sense of personal and spiritual achievement, as well as superiority toward my peers who were not offered this opportunity.

I gave the decision very little thought and simply jumped at the opportunity to be closer to God. I was aglow during the weeks leading up to my move, with a life that felt like it had even deeper purpose and meaning. I felt like I really, really belonged now. God loved me and I had proved devoted enough that He was willing to let me live under the same roof as his right-hand woman. This was not just a move from one apartment to another; I felt vaulted up several rungs of the group hierarchy, over the heads of those I served with on Thursday nights, including Michael. In my journal I wrote, "It is a privilege and an honour to live with Limori" and "Only a few people in the world live like this." What I believed when I made the latter comment was that, of all the billions of people in the world, only the handful of us who knew and followed Limori were "doing God's work," and so to live in her home was an opportunity of such exclusivity that I felt humbled by it. I believed that I was living with God's one true voice on Earth.

Michael and another member of the group, Gary, helped me move much of what I owned into storage and then a few possessions into Limori's new house. I was nervous on the day I moved in, but quickly fell into a groove of living comfortably with the odd assortment of followers who were with her at the time.

There was always a honeymoon period when someone moved in with Limori or left their job to work with her full time or moved to Wolf's Den. This was true for me as well. The first couple of months were fun and exciting, living with "God's messenger," and I especially loved being privy to what went on behind the curtain. Spirit channelling sessions that lasted late into the night. Learning about the spiritual significance of everything that Limori did, the clothes and jewellery she bought or had made, the parties she hosted, the teacup puppy she insisted she had to have.

At this time Limori was working as a psychic reader, giving one-on-one readings to people in the impressive all-white living room of the house. I would come home from the business training I was taking and hear her chatting and channelling with someone in the living room, and would quietly make my way to my bedroom so as not to disturb them.

Our guru was almost continuously surrounded by a gaggle of hangers-on. There was her right-hand woman, Alice, who had been in service to Limori ever since I had joined the group. A recent addition to the ranks of full-time assistants was Susan, a woman from the interior of BC, who had been following Limori and coming to her workshops for years and had recently left her husband so that she could fully immerse herself in Limori's teachings. Limori's husband Matthew and I rounded out the residential group. Each day brought the addition of a variety of visitors. These would be members of the group, asking for God's advice about whatever issues they were facing in their life at that time that couldn't wait until Wednesday or Thursday night, or friends of Limori's who didn't belong to the group but who were nevertheless in her sway. Some of these friends spent quite a lot of time at the house soaking up Limori's charisma and the magic dust that seemed to float around in her wake, and also asking for God's advice.

Living in the house reinforced in me the realization that wherever Limori was, workshops were soon to follow. The justification for the way Limori treated us during these workshops came from what Lifton calls sacred science, his fifth criteria for thought reform: "The totalist milieu maintains an aura of sacredness around its basic doctrine or ideology, holding it as an ultimate moral vision for the ordering of human existence. Questioning or criticizing those basic assumptions is prohibited. A reverence is demanded for the ideology/doctrine."[1] Limori was on the highest moral ground, we believed, and therefore we had no right to challenge her methods or her messages.

One such workshop, which occurred very shortly after I moved into the house on St. George's Street, was spectacularly memorable. It involved Susan, Limori's newest personal aide, and began on an otherwise innocuous weekday evening. There were five of us present that night: Limori, Alice, Susan, me and Gary, Limori's first lieutenant, who did not live with us but had come over this night for a visit. We began by casually chatting about personal current events and Limori mentioned several important spiritual events that were going on in the universe.

"Battles are being won by God's army," she said, nodding sagely. "Do you feel that, Gary?"

"Yes," Gary replied, "I've had several very deep meditations in the last week and Azeen keeps showing me a field with victorious soldiers on it."

"Exactly!" Limori said, smiling at her protégé for his clarity. "I've seen that too. And also waves of Light spreading out at the edges of the universe." She paused and closed her eyes to tune in; the rest of us were quiet, responding like Pavlov's dogs to the signal that we should sit in reverence while Limori had a private conversation with God. "I see one dark cloud in the sky, though." Her eyes remained closed while she shared what she was seeing. "Do you see that too, Gary?"

Gary closed his eyes too and I felt a thrill of excitement at being able to watch these two people whom I believed were spiritual masters work.

"Yes," Gary said, "I see it. It's dark, almost steel grey, with black flecks all through it."

"What is it?" Limori asked from her seat. And then, after a short pause, "Or rather, who is it?"

Now I was afraid. My stomach started to churn with a thousand butterflies and I took deep, cleansing breaths, as quietly as possible, to try to calm myself and stay focused and clear. I closed my eyes, as the others had done, and simply tried to be blank inside. No thoughts, no fear, no assumptions about what was going on. I tried to receive information from Spirit but mostly I just saw blankness on the backs of my eyelids. Not that I would have admitted that to anyone in the room.

"It's someone close to you." Gary said.

Shit, I thought. *It's me. Shit, shit, shit. I've screwed up already and I've only been living here a couple of weeks.* What could I have done? I quickly scanned back over the past few days; have I had any judgments? Have I spoken or even thought something that is not The Truth? Have I been in my ego? I couldn't think of anything specific but I could always have missed something. God sees everything after all, so if I'd done something wrong I wouldn't be able to escape it. My butterflies worked themselves up into a frenzy but outwardly I remained calm. I continued to breathe with my eyes closed, not ready to give myself up until called upon.

"Yes," Limori said, "that's what I've been seeing, too. My energy is being interfered with. Azeen won't show me who it is, though. Will he show you, Gary?" (By asking Gary to do this, Limori was making him complicit in what was about to occur. It was a technique she used with all of us, but especially with those very high up in her hierarchy, like Gary, Alice and later Michael and even me, to a certain extent. At the time, it seemed as though Limori was mentoring us. Being with her when she asked people like Gary to do these things felt like she was encouraging them to reach for the spiritual heights that she had supposedly gained. But looking back I see that it was another clever way to ensure that we were closely tied to her. If we were participating in this spiritual work of Limori's, and not simply observing her, then we were naturally inclined to feel more involved with her and with God and to defend the practices/abuse to ourselves. By having us take an active part in workshops, like the one about to occur, we became partly responsible for them.)

Gary was quiet while he continued to tune in. The silence in the room was, as they say, deafening. I felt almost faint with fear, but worked as hard as I could to quash my feelings. Fear had no place in God's house, I believed, and once again I asked myself how I could properly serve God if I was afraid of what He had to say.

Finally, Gary spoke up. "It's Susan," he said.

Ohthankgod, I said to myself, with a relieved but quiet exhale. I was safe for the moment.

We all opened our eyes and looked at Susan.

"What's going on with you lately, Susan?" Limori asked.

Susan looked like someone trying not to look guilty or afraid. "Nothing," she said. "Nothing, I'm perfectly fine. I've had a good week. I had a judgment of Alice yesterday but I caught myself and I've felt fine since then . . ." She stumbled to a halt under Limori's raptor eyes.

"Hmmm, really?" Limori nodded and turned her head from Susan and made meaningful eye contact with Alice. She closed her eyes again briefly and then asked, "How do you feel about Alexandra moving into the house?"

Alice, who had been quiet up to this point, made a grunt of assent. She met Limori's eyes again and they nodded conspiratorially. She was affirming that Limori was on the right track with this line of questioning.

Susan answered, "Good. Fine. It's been nice to have her here. She brings a new, fresh energy into the house." There was a pause and Limori waited until Susan continued. "I had a judgment about her when she moved in. She gets her own room and she gets to come and go as she pleases and that bothered me a bit. I was feeling like she's the spoiled baby. But I have released that and I feel good about her being here now."

Partway through this explanation Limori closed her eyes again. She remained still when Susan finished, so we waited for her next move. The atmosphere in the room had changed from the casual, comfortable feeling of earlier, when we were chatting, to the more familiar strained and charged energy that was always present when Limori was working with anyone. We were all on high alert; we each sat as still as possible, with hands clasped in our laps and feet flat on the floor. No one ever lounged or slouched when this type of spiritual work was going on.

I was, as usual, rigid with fear, and my posture reflected that. I was also concentrating with every fibre in my being; I wanted to see the things in my inner vision that Limori saw and I wanted to understand the same messages that she received from God. I wanted to fit in and I wanted Limori's approval, and therefore God's approval, so I concentrated with every cell, every breath and every thought, trying to understand what was going on within the room, within the people in the room, including me, and outside the room. What was God saying? What was He trying to teach us at that moment? What was the higher purpose of this workshop for Susan? How could I use this moment to change, to improve, to become a better spiritual student? All I wanted was to learn to communicate with God. In that moment, I absolutely believed that this was the way I could learn to do that. This was God in action. I believed that Limori was helping Susan by confronting her in this way and using the spiritual tools available to her to offer Susan guidance and wisdom and an opportunity to grow. Even though I was not the subject of this workshop, I wanted to pay attention to everything that was going on so that I could be the best spiritual student possible.

Limori opened her eyes and began to probe Susan further. "What, specifically, were your judgments?"

"Well, that Alexandra was getting better treatment than I was."

"So you were comparing yourself to her?"

"Yes, I guess I was."

"You guess? Or you were?"

"I was," Susan agreed. "Yes, I was comparing myself to her."

"Is the bedroom you have not good enough for you? Is sharing a room with Alice not good enough for Princess Susan?"

Limori's sneering tone when she said *Princess* made it clear to all of us that this was not a compliment.

Susan attempted to defend herself, "No! It's fine. I like sharing the room with Alice and we've become closer by doing so . . ."

Limori interrupted, "Then why the judgment? Why worry about where Alexandra or anyone is sleeping? Why is it any of your business where God has you sleep? If He asked me to sleep in the road I would do so. If He asked me to leave this house and take only the clothes on my back and let go of all these things [she hissed the word, giving it all sorts of evil meaning] I would do that without question. I would go barefoot and sleep in Stanley Park if that was what He asked me to do. No questions. No judgments. This is what God wants, so I do it." She paused and her gaze, which had been drilling into Susan, relaxed a bit and she looked over at Gary. "Is what I'm being told correct?" she asked him.

Gary closed his eyes and tuned in for twenty or thirty seconds. "Yes," he said, without opening them. "Yes, you are to do as Azeen asks."

Limori sighed, "Ach, that's what I thought. It's never easy, is it Papa?" (Papa was her pet name for Azeen or God.) She looked heavenward as she said this, and then rubbed her eyes with the fatigue of the ultimate spiritual warrior.

"Alice, what do you see? Am I to do what I think I am to do?"

Alice, who had been at this game of tuning in longer than any of us, nodded and smiled with closed lips, "Um hmm."

"I thought so." Limori sighed again, and then delivered her message from God to Susan. "If you are serious about serving God, if you really mean to strip yourself [she emphasized these two words but we didn't yet know why] of your ego so that you can fully serve God, then you will not hesitate to do as I ask. Go into your bedroom, the one that is obviously not good enough for you [her tone was cutting and sarcastic], and make a decision. If you choose to serve God you will come back into this room, in front of all of us here, wearing only that birthday suit that God sent you onto this Earth with. If, as you say you do, you actually want to serve God you will stand naked in front of God and declare your commitment to rid yourself of all your ego positions."

I was mortified by this set of instructions, but my reactions to this workshop were a perfect example of how a cult follower's authentic self is in constant battle with her cult self. In *Combatting Cult Mind Control*, author and cult survivor Steven Hassan describes the dual identity of a cult member like this:

"Given freedom of choice, people will predictably always choose what they believe is best for them. However, the ethical criteria for determining what is "best" should be one's own, not someone else's. In a mind-control environment, freedom of choice is the first thing that one loses. The reason for that loss is essentially simple: the cult member is no longer operating as himself. He has a new artificial cult identity structure, which includes new beliefs and a new language. The cult leader's doctrine becomes the master "map" of reality for the new cult member. A member of a mind control cult is at war with himself. .. he has two identities."[2]

My beliefs about right and wrong, good and bad, ethical and unethical had been warped by my gradual immersion in Limori's doctrine. The longer I stayed in the group, the more I suppressed my old identity and belief system – my authentic self. This real identity, though deeply buried, was still paying attention to what was going on. As Hassan says, it "sees and records contradictions, questions and disillusioning experiences." But for all the years that I was involved with Limori, my cult self overruled and shouted down my authentic self and convinced me that Limori's contradictions and unethical, abusive behaviour made sense and were right and good.

My authentic self, which tends toward shyness and modesty, was horrified by this request from God via Limori's mouth. It seemed degrading, humiliating, shaming, abusive and completely unnecessary, especially in front of Gary, Alice and me. Yet my cult self got busy immediately quashing all these dangerous and treasonous thoughts and feelings and began telling me that "whatever God asks us to do requires our obedience. He has our best interests at heart." And "A little bit of nudity is nothing compared to the energetic battles that will be won if Susan can rid herself of this ego position." And further, "I hope that if I'm ever asked to do something like this I can step up and declare my love and devotion to God without hesitating or worrying about petty little things like modesty and personal privacy."

Susan quietly left the room, a mixed expression of resolve and horror on her face. While she was gone Gary, Alice and Limori quietly discussed the spiritual crossroad that Susan had reached.

"This is a big one for her," Limori said quietly but firmly, her tone serious and concerned. "Susan's always been a bit haughty and has too much attachment to being better than others."

Gary nodded, agreeing. "Azeen said to me that if she does not pass this test that there will be years of darkness to come, for her and for the rest of us."

"Yes, I saw that too," Alice said.

"OUCH!" Limori winced and grabbed her head. "Aye ya, Susan is really angry about this. She is hitting me like crazy."

Then, as quietly as she had left, Susan returned to the room, buck-naked. She looked to Limori for instruction, her hands clenched into fists at her side. Her expression was the one of grim determination that we all wore on occasion when we were around Limori. It said, "I will do anything for God, even this." It was a rigid visage; a mix of fear, self-loathing, vulnerability and utter submission.

"Well, you have made your decision, have you? That was quick." (The sarcasm in Limori's tone implied that Susan had not given this crucial decision the time for consideration that it deserved. Yet if Susan had taken a long time to return to the living room Limori would have made a cutting comment about her reluctance to serve God. One could never win in these situations.) "Come over here and stand by me."

Susan moved to stand beside the white wing-backed chair Limori was sitting in. Her nudity among the rest of us who were clothed was absurd. It was like the proverbial car wreck; I didn't want to look but I couldn't help myself. I squirmed a bit with empathetic discomfort but Susan was stock still, eyes slightly downcast. It's hard to look dignified when you're the only naked person in a room.

"So," Limori began, "you're committed to serving God?"

Susan raised her eyes slightly and looked at her. "Yes."

"What about your superiority to others?"

"I don't feel superior to others."

"You don't? Then why the objection to where Alexandra sleeps? Why the comparison of your sleeping arrangement to hers? If you aren't feeling superior to her, then why would you even consider whether or not the sleeping arrangements are appropriate?" Limori's tone of voice was leaning away from inquisitive and toward accusatory.

Susan began to stammer a bit, "I'm sorry. I did judge the fact that Alexandra has her own room but . . . I don't . . . or . . . I'm not now. I know that God only guides us with what is right and true. I apologize for being in my ego about the sleeping arrangements in this house."

Limori watched and listened to Susan with an expression of distaste and disbelief on her face. "I don't think you are sorry," she said. "I think you're still angry about it. Do you see anger in her, Gary?"

Gary nodded his assent. "Yes, she's very angry."

In my opinion, Susan looked anything but angry. She looked afraid, embarrassed, contrite and naked to me. But if God's messengers, Limori and Gary, were saying she was angry then she must be angry, I thought.

"Oh, boy, you're not going to like what Azeen has just asked you to do." Limori looked over at Gary once again. "I'm getting this clearly, am I? Check for me."

"Yes, you're correct," Gary said, and he chuckled. "You're right, she's not going to like it."

"No, she's not." Limori sighed again, leaving us, as always, with the impression that what was happening and what was about to happen was not her choice, merely her lot in life as God's chosen one. She was simply following instructions, as any pure and worthy servant would. "Susan, go to your bedroom and gather up all your jewellery and bring it here."

Susan left the room once again and returned, still naked, with a jewellery box in one hand and a small, velvet-looking bag in the other.

"Is that ALL your jewellery?" Limori asked, daring Susan to have left anything behind.

"Yes, that's everything."

For the next 20 minutes or so, Limori picked through Susan's collection of jewellery. It was the usual collection of necklaces, rings, earrings and bracelets that many adult women have, both costume and semi-precious items, including her wedding and engagement ring to the husband she had left for Limori. Susan stood at attention beside Limori and answered questions about some of the items, such as where they had come from and who had given them to her. Several items were from Limori herself; she often bestowed gifts of jewellery on the women closest to her. Limori always emphasized that it was God who guided these purchases. From personal experience, I knew that when one received a ring or a necklace from Limori, it came with incredible significance and was treasured as such. On the couple of occasions that I received such gifts I felt so honoured it was as though I had been made a dame of Limori's spiritual empire.

"Well," Limori said, when she finished looking through everything, "this is all ego." She lifted a dripping handful of the pieces into the air and let them fall back with a clatter into her lap. "All ego. Azeen says that you are to hand all this junk over to me until you can learn to live without superiority and without comparing yourself to others in God's flock. I will give it back to you when you've earned it; when Azeen says I can."

"Yes, Limori," Susan said quietly.

"You are to live without these flashy trappings and simply learn to be yourself. To be humble and to learn about real value, not the value that comes from this." She held up a handful of jewellery again and made a sneering, derisive face.

"Yes, Limori," Susan said again.

"Alice, pack up all this stuff and get it out of my sight and put it away somewhere." She looked at Susan, "You, go get dressed. I'm tired of looking at your naked body. Blech." She made a retching noise and shivered as though spiders were crawling over her skin.

Alice carefully began picking up the tangled pile of necklaces and earrings and bracelets from Limori's lap. "Oh, for heaven's sake, Alice, just scoop it up and get rid of it. I can't stand it touching me any longer. Ugh, disgusting. I need to wash my hands. And you too," she said to Alice. "Wash your hands when you're finished dealing with that . . . junk." (Washing their hands would cleanse Alice and Limori of any negative energy that may have attached to them from Susan's jewellery.)

Sadly, the only thing out of the ordinary about this workshop was the nudity involved. Otherwise, this type of treatment of people was well known to me at this point and, although I never became entirely comfortable with the level of cruelty that was involved in this type of "spiritual work," I was familiar with it. I was entirely entrenched in the belief that Limori was working for our best interests and that she only did as God asked. I had stopped asking myself if her methods were justified. I was not comfortable with her methods at all, but I thought my discomfort was my failing, not hers. I rarely brought up the fact that I was often uneasy with the way Limori treated us because if I did, whomever I was speaking to (Gary, Michael, Alice etc.) would tell me that it had to be this way if we were all to become clear and be able to do God's work. I constantly felt that I was failing God because I could not adjust to Limori's harsh way of teaching. I lived in a constant state of battling with myself: trying to justify Limori's behaviour and trying to learn to be totally at peace with how she treated us.

AFTER MY FIRST few weeks living in the house had passed, I was disappointed to find that this fear of Limori and my constant state of anxiety and worry about what was to come did not get better; it got worse. I just couldn't stop myself from cringing every time someone was raked over the coals, as Susan had so memorably been. This discomfort translated itself into a perpetual case of butterflies in my stomach, as I worried about the next workshop that would occur, either to me or to someone else in the house. I realized that I had expected that by living with Limori I would learn to stop being afraid of her and her methods and that I would finally feel at ease with her. I had had the same expectation when I joined the Thursday night group and had been disappointed then as well. It tortured me that I couldn't be comfortable with her: I was always waiting for the other shoe to drop. When she went away for weeks at a time to Hawaii or Europe on spiritual missions, I was at once relieved that she was gone and furious with myself for being relieved. "If I want to serve God," I thought, over and over again, "I have to learn to accept whatever Limori says and does and know that she is helping me and the others, not hurting us." I wrote feverishly in my journal, trying to resolve my conflicted emotions. I referred to myself in those entries as being "spoiled." This is a very telling description. One seven-letter word speaks volumes about my state of mind at the time.

By telling myself I was "spoiled," I was referring to the belief that a) I felt I had been given so much (by being invited to live in God's house) and b) by feeling anything other than joy and gratitude I was spitting in God's face. I believed that I was living under the same room as God's right-hand woman and to be afraid of what she might say or do, or to feel uncomfortable with anything that went on in that house, was to be questioning God Himself and his methods. It was to be putting myself, I thought, above God. My fear and my stomach full of butterflies meant to me that I disagreed with Limori's methods. Ergo, I was challenging God. Only those who work for the Dark Side challenge God, I believed, and so because of my fear and my butterflies I lived in a constant state of self-loathing. It was the same old vicious circle: the more afraid I felt of Limori's treatment of her followers, the more I loathed myself and believed myself to be evil. The more evil I felt, the more fear took hold of me, and I became sure I would "hit" Limori or that she would call me onto the carpet and workshop me. Around and around I went.

Despite constantly chastising myself, my anxiety continued to grow and the battle inside me raged on. I hated myself for being afraid and used every means available to me to talk myself out of how I felt. I meditated several times a day, I wrote in my journal and chastised myself for not wanting The Truth, I thought about my fear obsessively when I took the bus from North Vancouver to the school I was attending. I even began bringing it up more with my friends from the group. I was bothered night and day by butterflies in my stomach; even when I was not in the house or around Limori I was anxious. The tension and stress inside me continued to build until I felt I might burst into tears at every moment. But I stuffed my feelings down inside me as best I could every day and told myself that it was "the negative" making me fear Limori—and that, if the negative won, by convincing me she was someone to fear or that her methods weren't purely motivated by love, then I would end up on the Dark Side myself. I believed that I would be serving the Devil if I allowed myself to listen to the thoughts and feelings inside me that were telling me something was amiss.

The fact that I never did achieve peace with Limori and her cruel treatment of others is a testament to the fact that my body knew that something was not right. The butterflies in my stomach never stopped. They wouldn't back down no matter what I told them with my logical head. I thought they were harbingers of doom, indicating my evil nature; really, they were simply trying to get my attention. This was a hard-won lesson and it took ten years of discomfort for me to learn it. But in the end, it was my blessed body, which never lied to me, that helped me eventually make the decision to leave the group.

At the time, though, I was desperately trying to adjust to life inside the hallowed halls of Casa God. There were minor work-shops going on all the time for all of us who lived with Limori, though none were as memorable as the one with Susan. At least, not until I was asked to move out.

I SOMETIMES WENT to Michael for counsel about the predicament that my feelings had me in. He had disagreed with me about my decision to move in with Limori. Michael was wary of the commitment that he felt the move entailed and thought that as someone in my mid-twenties I should be sowing my wild oats. However, I was hypnotized by the status boost I felt the move gave me and the underlying message I felt the move symbolized, that I mattered to God. My monastic tendencies and my driving need to belong to God's family eclipsed any desire I might have to be free and irresponsible. This was the first time in our friend-ship where we'd encountered such a philosophical difference of opinion and it surprised and confused me, given that I felt Michael was closer to Limori than I was.

As well, during the months I was living at the house, Michael and I didn't see each other as often as before. Limori's house was in a suburb of Vancouver and therefore not nearly as close or as convenient to Michael's apartment as my previous apartment had been.

Fighting for supremacy among the reasons for the distance between Michael and me at this time was the fact that he and Jessica were now living together and preparing for their legal wedding in Hawaii. Since Michael and Jessica's spiritual wedding at Wolf's Den, Michael had become conflicted, to say the least, about getting married. He felt (and rightly so) that he was being forced into a marriage that he wouldn't otherwise choose to commit to. During his adult life he had always been something of a free spirit; he had never married (he was forty-two at the time) and had no desire to settle down. He loved to travel and had spent a year when he was twenty-nine circling the globe, an adventure that was the highlight of his life up to that point. He was not naturally inclined toward the so-called normal trappings of life: career, family and real estate. He usually lived very centrally in Vancouver, and enjoyed the restaurants, nightlife and other activities of a large cosmopolitan city. He was self-employed and had been from the earliest days of his adulthood. All these aspects of his character clearly indicated that this was a person who was more interested in freedom than conventionality or security.

Limori used all these natural inclinations against him. If he really wanted to serve God, she said, he would get over his ego position about not wanting to be married. This trump card of Limori's, "get over your ego position," was supremely powerful because it could be used any time she wanted to control or manipulate someone, no matter how large or small the request was that she was making. Ultimately, every request she made of us had to be accepted because it was God who was asking, and if we refused we were giving in to an ego position. She had us perpetually over a barrel. In the case of Michael's marriage, all she had to do was wait him out and not back down, knowing that eventually he would fold and do her bidding because he was fully committed to his spiritual path, to the God she had sold him and to not giving in to ego positions.

Normally, Michael was my bedrock of support and encouragement. He helped me understand the way the world worked in ways I never would have figured out on my own. So I was sad and bereft during this time because he was not as available to me as usual. He was dealing with his own problems, and I was left to figure out for myself why I was filled with such anxiety most of the time. Anytime I was able to discuss this with him, he simply told me what anyone in the group would have: "Be in your heart. Don't be afraid of The Truth," etc. Coincidentally, that was exactly what I was telling him with regard to his impending marriage.

We were both at war with ourselves: each trying to convince ourselves that doing something that felt wrong was actually right and that if our instinct told us we were uncomfortable or disagreed with God's guidance, our instinct was wrong. Limori was raising the temperature with both of us to see how far we would go for her. She would be successful with Michael and a little less successful with me.

AFTER TWO AND a half months of living in Limori's house, during an informal chat with her and Alice one evening I was given a new name. This was surprising to me because I was still deep in the struggle with my feelings of utter failure about living in God's presence and not being able to relax. Limori said that God said I was to be called Chaye Kaley (pronounced cha-ee ka-lay) from now on. I was surprised but also thrilled by this development. I felt it was another momentous step in my evolution into a true spiritual warrior. By carrying a name that God had given me and living under God's roof I felt I would really be making a statement to the world about who I was and what mattered to me. And once again I thought, "Now I will really belong somewhere and feel at home in myself."

I made plans to change my name legally to this new moniker, but this spiritual carrot was dangled and then, just as quickly, pulled away. A few days after I was given the name Limori said that God had asked me to hold off legally changing it until the New Year.

Limori, Alice and Susan spent Christmas that year in Hawaii. The night before they left I gave them each a gift to take with them to open on Christmas Day, but I was nervous and self-conscious as I did it and Limori's hawk-like stare didn't help. As ever, I desperately wanted her approval but I felt that whatever I did seemed to only increase her disapproval of me. I tripped over my words and thoughts whenever I was in her presence and could barely make eye contact with her. The more obsequious I became the colder she seemed to become to me, which only increased my anxiety and fear.

I resolved through the Christmas break to get a grip on myself. I was alone at the house for a few days, and then spent a few days around Christmas Day with my mother and stepfather in Vancouver. To my disappointment, when the New Year dawned and I returned to the routine of living at the house and Limori and her entourage returned from Hawaii, I was as fearful as ever. Maybe more. Finally, one day in late February, the situation broke.

On a sunny Sunday I made arrangements to go for a walk in Stanley Park with two friends from the meditation circle. I made this arrangement ostensibly to spend time with friends, but my true motivation was simply to be out of the house while Limori was in it. I was beside myself with fear and self-loathing and, as often as I could, I needed to escape the pressure of being near her. As my friends and I walked around the seawall I was desperate to share my anxiety and tortured state of mind with them but I couldn't bring myself to do it. I was so riddled with fear that I thought if I shared what I was feeling, I would hit Limori with my negative energy, even from this distance.

When I returned home later in the afternoon, Lisa was in the living room, visiting with Limori. I went to my bedroom and hung up my coat and, as I walked back down the hallway to the kitchen, Limori called me in to see her. I could immediately intuit that I was in for it. The look on her face was thunderous and Lisa was looking smug, a clear sign if ever there was one that I was doomed. Limori asked me to take a seat and then my own little workshop began.

She began by bringing up the fact that I was not comfortable in the home and that I was avoiding her. (This was true.) Then she accused me of complaining about her to the friends I had just returned from seeing.

"I haven't!" I said to her. This was one thing I was absolutely sure of, although I didn't have the courage or the wherewithal to tell her that I had wanted to talk about her but stopped myself because I was too afraid.

"Azeen says that you are not blending in fully with the family that lives here. You are keeping yourself separate," she said (which meant that I was keeping myself separate from God, a disastrous spiritual crime). She pointed out that I was not spending very much of my spare time in the house (true) and that I didn't really want to be there (also true, even if I couldn't admit it to myself at the time).

She stopped frequently during this tirade and asked Lisa to tune in and confirm if what she was getting from Spirit was correct. Lisa was only too happy to do this. The look on her face was one I was familiar with because I used to look like that, too. I used to feel that Limori approved of me and loved me and valued my clarity and my service to her and to God.

Finally, after being chastised and accused of failing God for an hour or so, I was released and told to think about what choices I wanted to make (i.e., serving the Light or serving the Dark Side). She instructed me to help Alice prepare dinner.

"What can I do to get myself out of this mess?" I thought as I walked into the kitchen. "I have been an utter failure about getting rid of my own fear and now it's coming home to roost. I have failed God and I have failed Limori." I felt as useless and small as I have ever felt.

Alice, who had heard this whole episode from the kitchen, didn't refer to it as I joined her, but asked me to help her set the table for dinner and prepare the meal. She breaded a piece of fish and put it in the oven to bake, while I washed some dishes in the sink. My back was to the oven as I looked out the kitchen window with my hands in warm, soapy water, wishing I were anywhere but here. I wanted to cry. Tears were surging to my eyes and a lump grew in my throat with every breath, but breaking down would only have brought another shit-storm of abuse down on my head, so I swallowed hard and concentrated on what I was doing.

Suddenly there was a loud crackling noise. Alice and I turned to look at one another, eyes wide with surprise. Neither of us knew what the noise was or where it had come from.

"What was that?" Limori called from the living room.

"I don't know," Alice called back.

Limori and Lisa appeared in the doorway to the kitchen and the four of us stood around looking left and right, trying to figure out the origin of such a strange noise.

"The fish," Alice said, and she walked over and opened the oven door. Sure enough, the plate under the large piece of fish had splintered into a dozen or more shards. There was a pause while we all took this in and then Limori looked at me, her eyes shooting daggers.

"This is your doing."

I just stared at her, baffled and paralyzed.

"Your anger. Your anger caused this. Didn't it, Alice?"

Alice looked from the fish to me and then to Limori. "Yes, she's very angry."

I must have looked like a deer caught in the headlights. I had witnessed others in the group getting blamed for physical events that mysteriously occurred, but this was the first time I had been held responsible for such an occurrence.

Limori held my gaze. "You are so angry at being told The Truth about your behaviour that you've caused that plate to crack and ruined our dinner." She huffed out a loud, exasperated sigh, "Alice, turn the oven off. You'll have to pull that fish and all that glass out of there. We can't eat the fish, obviously, so you'll have to think of something else for dinner. You," she turned to me again, "you need to get over your anger at me and decide what you want."

I hovered uncomfortably in the kitchen while Alice cleaned up the mess in the oven, and then we prepared something else for dinner. I passed the meal in misery, speaking only when spoken to. After dinner I helped Alice clean up and could hear Limori's and Lisa's voices in the living room. I was certain they were discussing me and, sure enough, when cleanup was over, I was called to join them.

I sat where Limori indicated and she began by saying that I was not committed to God and that I had not been happy since I moved in with her. "Azeen says that I cannot have your energy interfering any longer with the work I am trying to do. You were given an incredible opportunity to change and to increase your level of commitment to God but you have refused to do that." She repeated her assertion that I had been complaining about her behind her back and refused to believe me when I assured her that I had not. My loyalty to her was stronger than she imagined; I was so devoted to her and her cause that I would not have done or said anything that would have harmed her in any way. She, and all that she represented, was all that I wanted. I wanted to feel comfortable with her and I wanted to be fully committed to her. I was very unhappy with what she was accusing me of, partly because some of it was true and I didn't want it to be. I had hoped that by living here in her home my level of fear and discomfort would wane and disappear, but that had not happened.

She did all the talking; I said almost nothing except to make a few feeble attempts to defend myself. Limori asked Lisa and Alice for confirmation about most of what she said; they tuned in and told her they were getting the same information from Spirit.

"You are very angry," Limori said in conclusion. "You have an absence of love in your heart that I cannot have around me any longer. And you play games."

These were all cardinal sins for someone who said they wanted to work for God with Limori, and even at the time I could recognize that they were part of the standard repertoire of reasons that she would use to banish or reprimand someone. Interestingly, I agreed with Limori's assessment that I was angry – I was angry about feeling afraid all the time. I was furious with myself for not being able to control or master my fear. Consequently, there was also an absence of love in my heart; I was too busy being afraid to feel love.

But there were two parts of Limori's monologue that bothered me, though I barely acknowledged them at the time. First, I was puzzled: if she was so psychic, why didn't she know that I was telling the truth when I said I had not been talking behind her back? And second, even in my numbed and mind-controlled state, I vividly remember the reaction in my body when she told me I played games. I knew that wasn't true. I am not a game player and never have been. I couldn't manipulate or strategize my way out of a wet paper bag. So when she described me as someone who played games, I felt my body disagree. I didn't voice any of this, of course, but I clearly remember the feeling of discomfort that came with these two thoughts, and the subsequent feeling of pushing that discomfort away.

I was told it was time for me to move out of the house, and despite my desire to be a better servant for God I was relieved. The constant war inside me, of being afraid and trying not to be afraid, had worn me out. Yet I was humiliated. In our real-life game of Snakes and Ladders I had just slid down a significantly sized snake, moving myself several rungs down the group hierarchy.

Within a couple of days, I found an apartment and moved into it, alone again after a disastrously short period of living with God. I had failed but I was resolved to try harder. What I didn't realize at the time was that the next year or so would be a mini-version of what I would go through when I ultimately left the cult for good in 2000.

6

NEITHER HERE NOR THERE

There was a power outage at a department store yesterday. Twenty people were trapped on the escalators.
—Steven Wright

On September 11, 1992, Hurricane Iniki made landfall on the Hawaiian island of Kauai. She was a category four hurricane and caused millions of dollars in damage and six deaths. Kauai is called the Garden Island in the chain of Hawaiian Islands and is home to the famous Fern Grotto. Much of the lush landscape on the island was destroyed by the hurricane and it would take years to recover.

Before this, Limori had been travelling to Kauai regularly for several years. She described the Hawaiian Islands as having particular spiritual significance, and Kauai was specifically touted to be one of the most spiritual places on Earth. Whenever Limori returned from her trips to the island, she shared stories of the spectacular spiritual energy that was there and the increasingly significant messages that she received from God and from other spirits whenever she was there. She and Alice would stay for weeks or months at a time and return to the group tanned and replete with the spirit of Aloha.

Limori used Hurricane Iniki to her advantage. Because the hurricane landed on Kauai during daylight hours, and because of the prevalence of video recorders in private homes, there was a tremendous amount of recorded footage of the destruction as it occurred. A few months after the hurricane, a documentary film was released, using people's recordings of the storm, and Limori screened the movie for us one night at the meditation circle. The hurricane was described as the work of the Devil. Limori had been doing so much good energy work while in Kauai, she said, and so many positive things were happening in the universe because of it that the Devil felt he had to strike back, and this was what he'd done.

"But we will not be defeated!" she said. "Michael and Jessica's wedding will go ahead as planned in Kauai and the spiritual work that will be accomplished by the wedding itself will help tremendously to begin to restore the damage done by the Devil and his hurricane."

DURING THE LEAD-UP to the wedding, I was struggling mightily with my banishment from Limori's house and with the feelings that living at the house had stirred up in me and the ones that were coming to the surface while I processed what had happened. I had moved into a studio apartment, and while I was secretly relieved to be living on my own again, I was experiencing for the first time what being an outcast among the group was like.

Shunning was a strategy that Limori's followers had adopted and used from the earliest days of my involvement, but this was the first time I had experienced the fuzzy side of this particular lollipop. We never used the word *shunning*; it is a word I have applied to the particular set of behaviours that occurred when someone was thought to have "dark energy" taking them over.

Reflecting on how shunning was applied in the group, I realize that Limori never gave us instructions about how or when or why to shun. It was something we learned by modelling her and something that felt necessary because of the culture of fear that we lived in. We were always on guard and braced against allowing the Dark into our hearts and minds. We were taught that darkness or negative energy was something one could catch from another person, like the flu. Thus was born an unspoken necessity to shun, to place those who were deemed to have negative energy emotionally and socially at a distance so as not to catch their darkness.

Shunning was always initiated because of spiritual work that Limori had done with someone in the group. At a workshop, or on a Wednesday or Thursday night, Limori would rip someone apart for the negative energy they were bringing into the group or for the lousy job they were doing for God. She would often declare that the person in question needed to somehow "change their energy" so that they were no longer negative. In the previous chapter I outlined examples of both Susan and me receiving this type of treatment. The after-effect was that the rest of the members of the group would pull back from the offending party and essentially shun him or her until a time when Limori would declare that the offence had passed and the person was "back in the Light."

These reversals of fortune could be dramatic; someone could go from being shunned and an outcast to being called to fly to Hawaii or Arizona, or wherever Limori was at the time, welcomed with warmth and generosity, brought back into God's good graces and romanced with jewellery and clothes and, most importantly, Limori's favour. For those of us who were not on the highest rungs of the group hierarchy, the return to an acceptable status would be less dramatic, but no less profound. Limori might be talking to Michael or Gary on the phone one day and say, "Karen has done a lot of good work lately and her energy is clear again."

Gary or Michael would pass this kernel of truth onto the offending person, word would trickle out through the group and the outcast would once again be back in everyone's good graces.

The shunning by the group was most dramatic at Wolf's Den, where the person who was being shunned would be forced to live separately from the rest of the "family" and not be allowed into the lodge for meals or connection with anyone. In the Vancouver group, shunning was much less dramatic than this, but no less effective. As a group we would treat an offending person as if they weren't in the room. We would talk to that person only when necessary. They would not be invited to social gatherings because of their negative energy. It felt like being absent while present. When the person's offensive status had been removed by word from Limori, or by more subtle indications such as her inviting the offending person to "tune in to Spirit," then connection and warmth toward the person would be restored and life for that person would return to normal.

The analogy I use when I talk about shunning is one of a recalcitrant foal being cut out of a wild mustang herd by the matriarch. For that foal, being cut out of the herd is, literally, a matter of life and death. Horses, although large, are animals of prey in the wild and the herd they belong to is what provides a wild horse with safety. A horse on its own, especially a young one, is entirely vulnerable to predators. Equine matriarchs cut foals out of the herd when they have misbehaved. As a system of punishment and creating order in the herd, it is effective because the foals learn how to behave in the social system that they have been born into. If they are not willing to abide by the rules they will be outcast and left on their own to survive.

When one was cut out of the spiritual herd that was our group, it felt as though one's life depended on getting back into the group. On the outside, without the group's approval and acceptance, one felt increasingly vulnerable to the dark energy that was everywhere, waiting to prey on those who were not completely in their hearts. And, just as happens with herds of horses, shunning taught us that our survival in the group depended on abiding by the rules within the group.

In the couple of months between my banishment from Limori's home and the wedding in Kauai, I was consumed with feelings of spiritual inadequacy and failure and felt very alone as I experienced being cut out from my herd. I continued to go to Wednesday and Thursday evening meditations, but I felt invisible and ignored. Limori was not there very often; she was spending even more time in Hawaii preparing for the wedding and the workshop that would follow it. It was a huge relief to me to not have to deal with her every week, but I still sought counselling from Michael and Gary and others about what to do about my ever-present fear and how to "fix" it and "get over my ego positions" about Limori.

IN EARLY MAY, 1993, we flew as a group to Kauai, where Limori and Alice met us at the airport. There were ten or eleven of us from the Vancouver group attending the wedding, plus Brent from Wolf's Den and Luke and Gayle from the interior of BC. Limori's welcome to me was warm and inviting, which surprised me. It had been weeks since I'd last seen her and I had expected the cold shoulder at the very least, or even an immediate attack, but she simply offered me a lei (she and Alice had brought leis to the airport to greet each of us with) and an "Aloha." I wondered if I was noticing the beginnings of being allowed back into the group.

Limori always had something or someone that was her current obsession. These flavours of the month were touted as having great spiritual significance, but their presence in her life, and therefore in our lives, was meteor-like. They burned brightly for short periods of time but often quickly burned out, and were replaced by the next flashy trend to take Limori's fancy. And, of course, everything she did was presented as having great spiritual significance. She never did anything just for fun or for relaxation. Everything, and I mean everything, she touched or grew interested in was presented as a direct instruction or request or suggestion from God.

If Limori touted the benefits of ear candling (a process for removing ear wax), then we all jumped on board and had our ears candled. Those who had it done remarked that it not only improved their hearing but cleared up their spiritual energy, too. If Limori developed an interest in beadwork, then most of the women in the group immediately started beading as well. The beadwork obsession was going on while I lived in Limori's home – I spent many evenings at the dining room table, beading earrings with Limori, Alice and other women in the group who had come over for a visit. If Limori became interested in the ancient Hopi people of the southern US on one of her trips to Arizona, then we all became interested in their culture. She would return from a trip with Hopi jewellery to sell (lots of turquoise and silver during this phase) and, again, women from the group would jump on the bandwagon, buying up what she was selling and wearing it proudly at group gatherings. For a few months in 1992 she was channelling Paramahansa Yogananda very often, so many of us, me included, began reading his books and learning about his philosophy. (Of course, Limori would find sly, subtle ways to undermine the books and point out that because she was speaking directly to his spirit she was the one true authority on his teachings.)

When we arrived in Kauai, her obsession was with Hawaii itself. The energy of the islands was a big topic of conversation whenever she returned from a trip there, and we were told repeatedly that while Kauai had a gentle energy it was also a place where one's issues would come up to face one head-on. It was because of this obsessive interest in Hawaii that Michael and Jessica's, and later Gary and Karen's, weddings were held there. If, at that time, Limori had been obsessed with Bosnia or Australia, then I'm sure that's where the weddings would have occurred. Consequently, during the two weeks that the group was in Hawaii, we were regaled with several educational daytrips to places on the island that Limori said had special spiritual merit she was privy to because the ancient Hawaiian kahunas (spiritual leaders) were speaking to her directly when she meditated. We visited several heiaus (ancient Hawaiian temples, usually in ruins) and met a man Limori had befriended who considered himself a modern-day kahuna. We also went to a place where Kauai sea salt was harvested. (Limori proclaimed that this sea salt had a particularly potent capability for cleansing one's energy. Thus, when we were back home, we had all taken to bathing with it regularly when she brought bags of the stuff back from trips to Kauai.) We also visited the quaint and beautiful town of Hanapepe, known for its artistic community.

One of Limori's people-obsessions during that trip was an artist in Hanapepe named Simon. As a group, we went to a gallery that was showing Simon's work and met the man himself. Limori was deep in seduction mode with him; his energy was perfect, she said. His connection to God and the Hawaiian spirits was clear and clean. Simon himself seemed humble and yet confident about this connection. The positive energy that came through his work was unparalleled, according to Limori, and so we all jumped on the "Simon the spiritual artist" bandwagon; the women flirted with him and gazed at him adoringly, and the men slapped him on the back and surrounded him with camaraderie. Very shortly, the group had arranged to all chip in and buy one of his paintings for Michael and Jessica as our wedding present to them.

OUR SPIRITUAL PILGRIMAGE around the Garden Island continued in the days leading up to the wedding, and the day after romancing Simon we set off in a procession of rental cars to the far north end of the island.

(An absurd but meaningful aside: Limori had arranged to rent six or seven cars for the duration of our visit to the island. She had stipulated to the car rental company that all the cars needed to be white. This symbolized our allegiance to and meaningful presence in God's army. When we arrived to pick up the cars, it was discovered that they were all white except for one, which was teal blue. This, Limori proclaimed, was a sign from God; it had been explained for years that Azeen's colour was this exact shade of teal blue. Azeen/God was showing us that he was with us and that we were his people by placing one teal blue car in our fleet. And, of course, it was Limori who would ride in the teal blue car and lead the way on all our travels.)

Before our arrival, Limori had found a beach and some caves that she wanted to show us. With her car leading the parade, chauffeured by Alice, we wound our way up the island to an almost deserted beach. The day wasn't particularly sunny, which is unusual for that part of the world. It was warm, of course, but I remember slightly overcast skies instead of the usual blazing, extroverted sun. We parked the cars and traipsed over some low dunes to the beach and then bore right, with the sea on our left, until we came to a rocky area set perhaps a hundred yards away from the oceanfront. There were scrubby, twisted trees that reminded me of the arbutus trees in BC growing up through the rocky outcroppings and shallow tidal pools at our feet. Limori and Alice led the way. The trees became a little thicker as we picked our way over the rocks. We began chatting among ourselves as we went, but were soon admonished to keep quiet. This was serious spiritual business and we needed to be respectful of the nearby spirits and of the work that Limori herself was doing by bringing us here. It soon became apparent that we were headed toward a small cliff face, perhaps as high as a two-storey building. There were openings in the rock face;

Limori and Alice moved toward a particular one and, crouching slightly, went inside. We followed, as good sheep do, and found ourselves in a cave as big as a one-bedroom apartment. The cave was not completely enclosed; there were a couple of openings to the sky and it was easy to see the damp cave walls that surrounded us and more tidal pools at our feet. Limori had us stand in a circle. We were all silent and reverential and after a few minutes Limori began to channel. I closed my eyes and listened to her voice amid the drips from the cave walls and, further away, the white-noise whoosh of the ocean outside.

This cave, on this holy island, was a spiritually significant place, we were told. And we were spiritually significant people, because we were here and, more specifically, were here with this spiritually important woman. Our work was vastly important to the well-being of the Earth and its people, and even more so to the millions of souls and spirits and angels, who, unseen by us but ever-present in the universe, were praying for our devotion so that Light might reign in God's universe instead of the Darkness that we were fighting. It was a precarious business, as we well knew, and the ceremony that would take place this week (Michael and Jessica's wedding) was so pleasing to the Great Kahunas for all the good it would do in this "battle of Light and Dark." Much Aloha spirit was flowing this week because of our work here and because the gods were so pleased with us.

But beware: ego and temptation are always on the lookout for a weak soul who wishes to place his or her own needs before God's desires. Vigilance was always required, especially now when so much good work was being done. The Dark was enraged at all the progress the Light was making, simply by us being here, and so it would redouble its efforts to trap us into ego positions and mind games. We must be willing to give up everything for the good fight and commit to surrendering any part of ourselves that did not serve God's will and God's plan.

"Those who do not surrender will be left behind." Limori's

voice echoed a little in this damp chamber. "Those who are willing to surrender will be carried forth with God's armies of light. Will you surrender?" Her voice rose. "Will you? Look around at those who serve here with you, at these souls who are willing to offer all of themselves for God."

I opened my eyes and looked around the group and saw each of them doing the same. Limori was standing with her arms at a 45-degree angle from her body, palms facing out, eyes closed, head tilted slightly back in full channelling mode. Alice stood beside her in exactly the same pose, like a Mini-Me version of our guru.

"Those of you who do surrender to God, who are willing to offer all of yourselves to His purpose, will bow down before me. By doing so you will show that your pride and your ego will not stand against your service to the Light and to God." She opened her eyes and looked around the group, meeting each person's gaze. "If you serve me, you will bow down, on your knees, arms outstretched in submission."

There was a slight pause, while we each grasped what Limori was saying, and then shuffling noises began as we each knelt down on the rocky floor of the cave and bowed forward, arms outstretched, somewhat like the child pose in yoga. It took some time and there was some small effort, as some of the older members of the group had difficulty getting to their knees on such a rocky and uneven surface, but eventually we were all prostrate in front of Limori.

Except for one lone figure. I had my forehead on the floor of the cave and my eyes closed, so it was only when Limori began speaking again that I realized there was one holdout.

"Will you not bow down and surrender to My light, My child? It is not to this woman [Limori meant herself] that you are bowing. It is to Me and to the forces of good in the universe."

I snuck a quick peek to my left under my arm and saw one person standing tall among a circle of people on their knees. It was Brenda, a friend of Karen's. She had never been to Limori's drop-in Wednesday night meditation circle and, as far as I could tell, this trip to Kauai was her first encounter with Limori. Until now she must have simply heard the glowing propaganda about Limori from Karen and decided to join us on this trip. I had not spoken to her one on one yet and had no idea what her personal spiritual beliefs were, but from the display in front of me now I realized she was not buying everything Limori was selling, unlike the rest of us with our foreheads and aching knees pressed into the wet rocks.

"Uh oh," I thought. "That chick is toast. No one stands up to Limori. She must be working for the Dark."

Limori continued to speak to Brenda, using her Voice of God, but Brenda was not to be swayed. She wasn't comfortable bowing down to another human being and that was that. What I was witnessing was independent thought and free will in action. What I believed at the time was that Brenda was a fool who was spitting in God's face and thwarting her soul's opportunity to serve God and surrender her earthly ego.

Eventually, the rest of us were permitted to stand again and we all made our way out of the cave, silent with both reverence and, I suspect, fear. We were afraid that this challenge to Limori's authority would adversely affect the "energetic" work we were trying to do.

I can't recall seeing Brenda for much of the rest of our time on the island. She seemed to shrink into the background, and most of us avoided her for fear of catching her dark energy. After this trip, I would never see Brenda again, and her relationship with Karen gradually disintegrated under Limori's tutelage.

MICHAEL AND JESSICA'S wedding took place on May 15, 1993. The ceremony was held on the grounds of the hotel where we were all staying. Lisa and Alice were Jessica's bridesmaids, while Gary and

Richard, Michael's business partners and spiritual compatriots, stood up for him. Limori was in high-def organizing and controlling mode in the hours before the wedding. She was like the second coming of Hurricane Iniki: shouting at Victor for improperly using the green foam called Oasis for the flower arrangements, shrieking at Alice in a high-pitched tone, the likes of which I'd never heard before and one that raised the hairs on the back of my neck in fear and wonder. She complained endlessly that because we were all so pathetically useless she had to organize everything herself, which meant she didn't have time to properly do her hair or makeup for the ceremony.

It was an uncomfortable day for me, in more ways than one. It's hard to say if I was more uncomfortable about the man I had finally realized I loved marrying someone else or about the spiritual crisis I was in. As far as I could tell, in my muddled state of mind and heart, the ceremony and the reception that followed went beautifully. I was expending a lot of energy suppressing my feelings about Michael. I was afraid to feel much of anything that wasn't supportive of his wedding; it was God, after all, who had requested this marriage, so if I opposed it for the selfish reason of being in love with the groom myself, then I was an even worse spiritual student than I thought. My estimation of myself was at a rock-bottom low already, so I was loath to add any more demerits to my already tragic state of worthlessness by disagreeing with God.

But love Michael I surely did. In my secret heart, I had prayed for the past year that during his machinations about the event, he would talk himself out of following Limori's orders to wed. He came close, but Limori did not back down and when the day of the ceremony arrived, he was fully on board. He loved Jessica, and he loved God. He had managed to completely convince himself to see the purported importance of this marriage in God's plan, as Limori explained it to him. Standing beside Jessica, dressed in white as she was, with the Pacific Ocean behind them,

Michael looked as proud and happy as he was handsome. We danced together at the reception and I felt like a fool and a hypocrite, wanting him only for myself. I smiled and smiled until my cheeks hurt, and celebrated, as Limori put it, this "joyous event, which will bring so much Light to the world."

In the days following the wedding, we continued our educational tours of the island and met a few of Limori's other current obsessions, including a masseuse, whose massages were purported to heighten the state of one's connection to God. After two weeks of arranged marriage, sun, spirituality and fighting Satan, I was more than ready to return home.

FOR THE NEXT year or so, my journals express deep feelings of discontent and discomfort about Limori, her teachings and my place in her world. I wrote that I felt "trapped to be a certain something that someone else defines." I even went as far as observing that any complaints I or anyone else in the group ever had about Limori's spiritual techniques, practices and teachings were always made out to be the fault of the complainer. I confessed to myself that I'd noticed that whenever anyone questioned Limori's motives they were always told that they were "in their ego."

The fact that I was willing to even express these thoughts is a testament to the amount of pain I was in. Under no other circumstances would I have had the courage to think, let alone write down, thoughts such as these – I was, after all, questioning God Himself, or so I believed.

My journals from this time are filled with the cyclical mind-control techniques that I would later (once I leave the group) understand as thought-terminating clichés.

Even though my journals are private and no one ever sees them but me, in them I very hesitantly and in a very cloaked and cautious way expressed feelings of doubt about Limori and what she was teaching. I could hardly admit to myself that I was doubting that her group was the right place for me. But as soon as I did get close to a feeling like that, I immediately stopped it, using group language and clichés. For example, here is a direct quote from my journal, from November 1993: "I shouldn't participate in something that doesn't feel right. But it is my ego that doesn't feel right." [I experience a serious case of mental whiplash when I read that now.] I am telling myself that if it feels wrong to participate in the group, it is my ego that is rebelling against what I'm being taught. If I am uncomfortable, it is my fault and no one else's. The implied message is, if I leave the group I'm giving in to my ego and that would be turning my back on God and serving the devil.

Part of my struggle was reflected in the fact that I had come to a place where I realized that I would never recommend Limori's meditation group to anyone. That was something that tore at me for years, and I even mentioned it to Michael at one point.

"I wouldn't recommend this path to anyone," I said to him one day, as we shared lunch at a café near his office. I used the words *this path* to avoid pointing fingers at Limori specifically, something I was not yet nearly courageous enough to do out loud.

"Why not?" he asked, chewing thoughtfully.

"It's too hard," I answered, but even in that moment, as mind-controlled as I was, I knew my answer was a cop-out and didn't come close to expressing what I really felt. What I wanted to say was, "The way Limori talks about love but acts so cruelly seems hypocritical to me. I think her teaching methods of yelling at us and ostracizing people for things she says she sees in visions or hears from the spirits could be considered to be abusive. And the worst part is, she's using God's name to do it. Doesn't that seem like the pinnacle of hypocrisy?" That was the truth of my experience but I couldn't say it, and if someone had asked me at the time if that was what I felt, I would have vehemently denied it. It was too risky to think and feel that I might disagree with how Limori taught. Who was I to question her methods? Michael was quick to use group rhetoric and thought-stopping clichés of his own to respond to my lame-ass answer, but he would have used these even if I'd told him the full truth of how I felt.

"It's just your ego that doesn't like the challenge and the difficulty of working for God," he said. "If it was easy, there wouldn't be any point to it. It's the hard parts that make it a worthwhile fight. That way, we know we're making a difference in the world and in the universe."

Like a good disciple, I shut up and ate my sandwich.

By THE MID-1990s Limori was spending hardly any time at all in Vancouver. She moved out of the house I had lived in with her and moved her base of operations from the city to Wolf's Den. Matthew, her husband, was granted his wish of living at his resort full time. However, without his income from a job at a local cable company, Limori's finances were strained, and for almost a year the meditation group pitched in and paid the mortgage on the resort each month. Limori divided her time between living at Wolf's Den (in the palatial and luxurious two-storey suite that John and Brent added onto the resort specifically for her) and living for weeks or months at a time in rented homes in Hawaii or Arizona. She began to distance herself from the group of disciples she had collected in Vancouver and it felt like we had slid below the last rung on the group's hierarchical ladder.

During these years, I felt a nagging, persistent sense of longing and pining for Limori when she began to spend longer and longer stretches of time away from the Vancouver group. It was a paradoxical feeling because I was at once relieved that she was not around to chastise me or the others but at the same time sad at being rejected by my own spiritual teacher. Those of us in Vancouver were not allowed to call her or contact her in any way, where in years past she had almost always been available to us for telephone conversations about spiritual questions and challenges. For the next couple of years, she would occasionally grace us with her presence once every eight or ten months. Out of the blue she would show up at a Wednesday or Thursday night meditation circle and we would spend the evening hearing about her journeys to Europe or Hawaii or the southwestern US. She would fill us in on the energetic goings-on in the universe and why her work with Spirit mattered so much and how hard it was on her but how devoted she was to serving God; in this context, her being tired and worn out and staying up all night meditating and being constantly hit with energy were okay with her.

On one of these grace-and-favour visits, after the uplifting euphoria of seeing our leader for the first time in a while had passed and we had heard about her recent exciting and entertaining exploits, the room went quiet and, from her position at the head of the circle, Limori looked around at each of us. Her facial expression became stern and serious and she was quiet for a long time. We all waited, well trained in obeying her subtle signals.

Finally, she sighed and said, "Nothing has changed since two years ago." She was gravely disappointed in us and I could feel my twin nemeses of shame and guilt filling my body and my thoughts. "Nothing," she repeated. "You say that you will work hard and that you love God but in the end, nothing changes. Your egos continue to rule over you and you put God second, then fourth, then nowhere on your priority list. 'Oh, but my job is important'" – she adopted a mocking tone, pretending to be one of us – "'and my house is important and all my stuff is important.' And God falls further and further away from your hearts and your thoughts, until He is nowhere to be found and you are all ego." She sighed again and shook her head, looking around the circle and meeting each of our eyes.

I was left, as ever, feeling that I must try harder and do more, but I was also uncomfortable. A few days after this visit from our guru, I wrote in my journal that I was tired of being told all the time that we were failing. I continued to be disturbed by my guru's techniques, and it was those cracks appearing in my cult self that would eventually lead to my departure from the group. I constantly felt torn in two. For several years I had lived in a near-constant state of agitation. Something was wrong and somewhere inside me I knew that, but the only place I could find to place the blame for whatever was wrong was with myself. I would then try to convince myself that if only I could learn to stop feeling afraid and agitated, everything would be all right. But my body, my inner sense of wrong and right, would not stop whispering to me that something was seriously amiss. Around and around I went in this circle of denial and self-blame.

DURING THE COUPLE of years that Limori was gradually distancing herself from the Vancouver group she had formed, she needed to leave someone in charge of us. That task fell to Gary. He had become our substitute guru and we had developed the habit of turning to him for spiritual advice on matters large and small. He and Limori were very close for a couple of years; he was her local representative, in essence. He was the only person in the group to whom she spoke via telephone; he would then relay messages to us about the spiritual work she was doing and the work that we needed to continue doing.

I looked up to Gary, as did the others in the group. I believed that he was the person closest to approaching Limori's type of "clarity" and, as such, considered him by proxy to have God's ear. Just as I did with Limori, I overlooked any faults he might exhibit or any human imperfections that were present in him, having been programmed to believe that these flaws were tools that God was using to teach us. If he was crass or rude or drank too much, I thought he was doing these things in order to teach.

It was astonishing, really, how easily I was able to transfer my guru-worship from Limori to Gary. She helped that along by promoting Gary to us and touting his clarity and wisdom. Gary had done what all of us aspired to do: he had reached the spiritual pinnacle we were all perpetually aspiring to. Gary's ascension in the ranks of the group sent the message that it was possible to achieve enlightenment and that continuing to apply all the lessons we were learning would one day ensure our enlightenment as well. Gary was proof that Limori's teaching worked; he became the embodiment of the spiritual carrot we were all reaching for. However, just as happened with Sheila before him on the first-lieutenant rung of the group hierarchy, Gary eventually fell from Limori's grace.

He and Karen were legally married in Kauai in 1994, but by early 1996 their marriage was imploding. Karen had been concerned with Gary's excessive drinking since they had become spiritually married and, ultimately, that was one of the central issues that led to her leaving the marriage. Gary began coming to the weekly meditation meetings less frequently during this time, but without an explanation (to me, anyway). When he was not there, the rest of us sat in the circle and shared our confessions or meditated together, co-facilitating one another.

I don't know what specifically initiated the rift between Gary and Limori. My observation was that as Gary and Karen's marriage crumbled, he began to drift out of Limori's orbit. On the nights that he did come to the circle to facilitate, he would obliquely refer to the fact that Limori wasn't returning his calls or that he had not talked to her in quite a while. Before the situation completely soured, he flew up to Wolf's Den at Limori's request to stay for a week, but returned after only a few days. His explanation was that his spirit guides had told him that Limori was using too much oil in her cooking and when he had passed this information along to her, she had not liked it and he had been asked to leave the next day. He laughed at the seemingly trivial reason that he had been sent home, but I suspected that his joking was covering up more serious problems in his relationship with our guru. Whatever the reason for the split, I was for the second time witnessing a major change in the group structure, only this time I would be more intimately involved in the outcome.

One night while Limori was staying at a hotel in Richmond, en route from Wolf's Den to Hawaii, Michael, Jessica and I were invited to visit with her. We were to keep the visit secret from the rest of the group, something I found upsetting and confusing at the time. My training about telling The Truth at all times collided with Limori's wish to keep secrets from the rest of the faithful. I was torn between my loyalty to my peers in the group, whom I loved, and my loyalty to Limori. But, as ever, I puzzled over this contradiction only briefly before deciding that God knew best; if Limori said to keep it a secret, I should do just that.

During this late-night visit, from 8:00 or 9:00 p.m. to 3:00 a.m., Limori referred to Gary only once, saying, "Gary's energy is completely wicked [one of her euphemisms for evil]. And he conveniently only ever calls the hotel when I am not here." She raised her eyebrows, implying that Gary didn't really want to get hold of her so he managed to arrange to call her only when she was not available. "I'm not going to call him back," she said. "He's not worth it."

This was a typical comment about someone who had left the group, or was about to. Deserters were dismissed abruptly and with undisguised contempt for their disloyalty and for the spiritually fatal flaw in their character that had led them away from God. Gary, like all the others before him, including Sheila and Luke (who had left a couple of years before), was categorized as the worst kind of failure and spiritual miscreant. As Michael put it every time someone left the group, "He met an ego position he could not face," and therefore had turned his back on God. No one who ever left was viewed charitably or with the compassion and dignity that someone on a spiritual quest deserves. We were always told that we had free will, but whenever anyone exercised that free will they were branded as a weak-willed loser and as someone who had decided to serve the dark forces of themselves and of the universe, instead of the Light.

Gary's departure left a void in the group. He had been Limori's right-hand man locally for several years, so now Michael stepped into that role. Interestingly, though, Michael was not given the facilitator's chair outright, as Gary had been. Limori awarded the position of co-facilitating the public Wednesday and private Thursday circles to Mildred (our sole septuagenarian member), Michael and me. Michael, however, was our only link to Limori. He spoke to her occasionally and would then relay information from her to us about what ener-getic things were happening that were supposed to be affecting us; her influence was such that we carried on with her teaching even though she was not there. All of us, not just the facilitators, had memorized and absorbed enough of the rhetoric, and the methods she taught, that we could spout it back and forth to one another in any situation: "You're in your ego," and "What does your heart say?" and, my personal favourite, "What is The Truth?"

Because of my continuing conflicting feelings about the group, I was surprised that I had been chosen to co-facilitate. But what the title of co-facilitator did was give me a renewed sense of ownership about the group philosophies. I had temporarily fallen from grace when I moved out of Limori's home, but this move back up in the group hierarchy helped slightly to quell my feelings of dissatisfaction. It drew me once again closer to Limori, even though she wasn't present, and I suspect that was part of the reason I was tapped for the job. Any disagreement I had with the ways Limori taught and led were brushed away as I took over the task of winnowing out members' ego positions and chiding them for not being "in their heart." The more I said these things to the others, the more I believed them, and my cult self took a slightly more dominant position inside me once again.

By 1997, the Vancouver group had dwindled to roughly eleven members, including me, from a high in the early 1990s of fifty or more. Without a charismatic leader there was really nothing to draw anyone new to the group. Now that Mildred, Michael and I were co-facilitating the circle, we were the ones who sat at the head of the circle. The meetings on both Wednesday and Thursday nights were two hours long. We'd gather a little early and set up the chairs. It was Debbie's responsibility to bring a small bouquet of flowers to the circle, for atmosphere and good energy. Amber was our treasurer, so she sat close to the front door and collected the drop-in fee from each of us. At eight o'clock we'd take our seats and tune in to what Spirit was guiding us to do that evening.

The circle was and always had been a place where we all discussed our issues. Each Wednesday and Thursday night was like a mini-workshop; if someone was in their head or in their ego (essentially the same thing) they would either volunteer to bring up what was going on with them, or they would be called on by the facilitator(s). With Limori gone, this format was no different, except that now it was Michael and I who would tune in and work with whoever was having a problem on any particular night. Mildred always sat quietly between Michael and me, listening to what was going on, rarely commenting and always seeming peaceful and serene.

MY FAVOURITE STORY about Mildred illustrates perfectly who she was. As Karen's marriage to Gary was dissolving, she was taking classes to become a doctor of traditional Chinese medicine. She invited many of us from the group to her graduation dinner, including Mildred. As ever, Mildred brought herself to the event in her late-model car and, naturally, at the end of the evening prepared to take herself home. It was winter and therefore dark and cold and, as is so often the case in Vancouver in the winter, it was raining as though there was an ark that needed launching. One of Karen's friends, an airline pilot with a mildly chivalrous nature, asked Mildred if she would like him to take her arm and walk her to her car.

She turned and gave him a withering glance. "Good Lord," she said. "What for?" And with that she unfurled her umbrella and marched out into the night.

Mildred was unlike any seventy-something person I had ever met. She was fiercely independent and had never been married, something quite unusual for someone of her generation. She owned a delightful bungalow in West Vancouver, with a fabulous view of Lions Gate Bridge and English Bay that she'd inherited from her parents yonks ago. The backyard was huge and gorgeous and when the seasons permitted she spent her waking hours out there gardening and being a friend to every bird and bee and cat that came along. She was in far better physical shape than anyone else in the group, yet we were all on average thirty-five years younger than she was. (She took us hiking once on the North Shore mountains, and chose a relatively easy hike for our benefit. Still, she had to slow down during the ascent because none of us could keep up with her.) She was like a combination of the Dalai Lama and Tina Turner; her compassion and moral strength were like a beacon but she could take care of herself in any situation without flinching and would kick your ass if you tested her.

Limori used to comment that Mildred's role in God's plan was simply to bring good energy into our midst. Limori said that Mildred had done enough personal work in her life that she was clear and therefore needed no further work done on her, unlike the rest of us. Mildred had been coming to the group for years, and yet Limori had never, not once, confronted her about any of her ego positions or workshopped her in any way. She was the only person for whom this was true. Everyone else who crossed Limori's path, from waitresses in restaurants to her husband(s), were treated like bugs under a microscope. Except Mildred.

I've often wondered why Limori treated Mildred so differently. At the time, I explained it to myself in the energetic terms I had been trained to apply to any situation. But, looking back, I have a different answer. Limori's relationship with Mildred was the same as her relationship with anyone who followed her: she gauged carefully and continuously how much she could turn up the heat underneath each of us. Mildred was a person whose loyalty to Limori was unwavering, but I think Limori could also sense that Mildred was enough of her own person, and had enough life experience beneath her belt, that she would put up with very little manipulation and bullshit from Limori. Leaving Mildred alone and simply praising her clear energy whenever possible was the strategy Limori used to tie Mildred to her. The more character and backbone someone had, the less Limori would push them. This strategy was also apparent in the way that men in the group got a softer ride than women, but I'll discuss that more in Part 3.

Telling these stories about Mildred makes me reflect about my relationship with her and with the other people in the circle. They were good people, with all the best qualities one likes to find in friends: kindness, humour, grace, caring and generosity. We were people from every walk of life: stay-at-home moms, dentists, artists, nurses, actors, doctors and construction workers. I cared so deeply about each and every person there, and loved very much those to whom I was especially close: Debbie, Amber, Karen and Michael. Every one of us genuinely thought we were doing the right thing. We honestly, honestly believed that we were working for God, and doing positive things for the world and the universe. I would describe many of us as soft-hearted; we were the type of people who bring home stray puppies and well up during sappy TV commercials and care about injustices and worry about the downtrodden. Each person had a good heart and, if circumstances had been different, I know none of them would have hurt a flea.

And yet, because of the knots that our brains were tied into, we were unutterably cruel to one another. In my role as co-facilitator I perpetuated the teaching that Limori had ingrained in us and consequently was rude, callous, dismissive, cutting, manipulative and abusive toward the other members of the group. I wasn't this way at every minute of every day, but I think it is important to note that as co-facilitator I dished out the behaviour I'd seen Limori exhibit. I modelled her. As I've said before, I wanted what she had: certainty about herself and what appeared to be a strong and intimate relationship with God. As co-facilitator, I used all of Limori's techniques to squash any independent thinking or feeling on my own part and in the other members of the group. Of course, I had no idea that that was what I was doing at the time. Looking back, it is embarrassing and mortifying to remember how I behaved. I am so sad about the way that I contributed to the perpetuation of Limori's manipulations. My technique paled in comparison to how Limori herself did it (I never had anyone stand naked in front of me, for starters), but it was still abuse that I was ladling out, in the guise of spiritual training.

Limori had left in her wake what was essentially a pack of dysfunctional wild dogs. As is so often the case with human beings, the abused become the abusers. I, who loathed and feared the way Limori treated me and others, turned around and treated myself and my compatriots the same way. Not to say that I became the master manipulator that Limori was, but when the circle was in session, over and over again, with monotonous repetition, I repeated what I'd been taught.

"You're in your ego."

"Get out of your head."

"Your energy is making me sick."

What anyone felt was never important. And nothing anyone ever did, including myself, was good enough. We met, week after week, the months rolling by into years, and covered the same ground over and over again.

ONE RESULT of co-facilitating the circle with Michael was that our relationship deepened. We had been best friends, but now we were spiritual colleagues as well. Since spirituality was the most important thing in both our lives, this professional partnership meant to me that we were a team.

This strengthening of our relationship and of our emotional and spiritual bond was a bit of a mixed blessing. On the one hand, I loved being partners with Michael in the circle; I loved that we had a shared purpose and that I held an increasingly meaningful place in his life, and he in mine. It meant that we shared focus on Wednesday and Thursday nights, rather than simply being participants and observers in the group, as we had been before. And it created a need for us to spend time together outside the group, occasionally discussing the energy of some of our peers and what needed to be done about them.

But on the other hand, as a result of this I was more tortured about my feelings for Michael than ever. His marriage with Jessica continued, and as one of Limori's disciples I respected its importance in the universal scheme of things. As the months and years passed, my feelings for Michael changed only in that they grew deeper and more intense. I hated myself for feeling that way, but try as I might there was nothing I could do to stop how I felt. Every moment spent with him socially was a joy and an agony. I lived for the times when we went out to a movie or dinner on our own, yet I flagellated myself about enjoying these occasions so much and, after each one, vowed not to need or want them ever again. But like a junkie who swears she will not fix again, I couldn't stay away, despite my logical, best intentions.

No matter how often I saw him, the sizzle of recognition that I felt when our eyes met was there. My body developed a magnetic field around itself whenever he was in the room and it was becoming increasingly difficult to keep my hands to myself. The worst part was, he said he felt the same way— and he was not nearly as reticent about talking about his feelings as I was. Every six months or so, when we could no longer stand the physical and emotional tension between us, we'd sit down to one of our regular coffee or dinner dates and talk about how much we loved one another and how frustrated we were that we couldn't be together. I told him I felt like I had a secret under my hat all the time. When I was among our friends and peers at the meditation circle I felt as though I was hiding something essential about myself because I couldn't share how I felt about Michael with anyone but him.

One night, at a Spanish restaurant on Robson Street, after an hour or more of sharing our feelings about each another and after several glasses of wine, we actually debated out loud about having an affair. Seconds after the question was tabled, though, we rejected it. Ever the good girl, I could not fathom doing something so forbidden and, most especially, could not imagine lying to Jessica and everyone else I knew. Michael said that although he felt more like a parent to Jessica than a husband, he could not bring himself to lie to or betray her.

Besides our own moral qualms about having an affair, our belief system, the one we had learned from Limori, told us that acting on our connection and attraction to one another was not a matter of choice. Michael could not simply choose to leave his marriage. He had not chosen to enter it – that decision had been made for him – but his devotion to his spiritual path and to Limori were such that he would stay married to Jessica as long as God wanted him to. With those barriers always front-of-mind, then, we remained just friends, albeit very close and special friends, and he remained in his marriage, because it was what

God wanted. What we didn't know was that Limori was about to grant our wishes for togetherness in the most diabolical and cruel way possible, a circumstance that would eventually result in my leaving the group and serve to tighten Limori's stranglehold on Michael more than ever.

MUSICAL BEDS

Those who can make you believe absurdities can make you commit
atrocities.
—Voltaire

A guru's followers are everything to her. Without them she is nothing, simply another attention-loving fruitcake with charisma and circular logic. The guru's followers provide material wealth in the form of tithed wages and other monetary gifts (necessary for someone like Limori who was living an increasingly luxurious and extravagant lifestyle). Cult members also provide free labour to the guru, and are willing to perform the most menial, backbreaking tasks in the name of service to the cause. And perhaps most importantly, a guru's disciples provide her with the power and control she so desperately needs. The cult leader controls every move her followers make: where they live, how they live, what they eat, where they work, what they work at, how much (or, more accurately, how little) contact they have with their families of origin and/or children and, more to the point of this chapter, whom they sleep with.

For the guru, so much of her life, status and power rely on the strength of a vertical relationship, from each follower up to her. The stronger the relationship each follower has to her, the more they are willing to do for her and the longer she can expect them to stay devoted to her cause. Therefore, it is essential that the guru constantly strengthen the vertical tie she has to each person. One of the most effective ways to do this is to continually undermine the horizontal relationships between the members; if horizontal ties are weak, then a disciple has nowhere to look but up, for guidance, comfort and love.

Limori weakened the horizontal relationships between group members in a number of ways, including ones I've described, such as shunning certain members at certain times and creating an atmosphere of fear and suspicion among the members of the group. But the very best and most effective way by far to undermine the relationships between group members (the horizontal relationships), and thus strengthen the vertical relationship of each person to the guru, is to ensure there is an absence of personal intimacy between members. If deep intimacy existed between a group member and his or her spouse outside the group, or if it began to exist between two group members, this would threaten the connection between each disciple and Limori. Therefore, she had to continually make sure that our loyalty and any deep feelings of connection were to her alone. If we became too attached to one another, we would weaken the significant role she played in our lives and she would therefore have less control over us. A person can't serve two masters; Limori knew she had to be the ultimate authority in each of our lives and the person we each trusted the most. A guru creates an atmosphere of "us versus them" so that the group is cohesively tied together, while simultaneously ensuring that each member's loyalty is primarily to her and not the others in the group. (How's that for a parlour trick?)

One of the best ways to weaken the horizontal relationships

and inhibit intimacy within a group is to have a group culture that encourages either celibacy or promiscuity. Both states, although they are polar opposites of each other, achieve the same end because they both inhibit intimacy. Our guru chose the promiscuity curriculum and played an ongoing game of Musical Beds with those who were closest to her. She was able to do this by proclaiming that relationships, like everything else in her version of how the world worked, were not matters of choice or feeling, but were instead vehicles to be used for higher learning, getting over ego positions and serving God. Initially there was a small measure of discomfort expressed by my peers about this element of Limori's teaching, although she made sure the discomfort was short lived.

In the early 1990s, Susan (she of the naked workshop) was invited to spend a summer living at Wolf's Den. She and her husband (who did not belong to the group) owned an apple orchard in the interior of BC, but when Limori invited Susan to spend the summer living and working at Wolf's Den, it was an offer too good to be refused. (Susan would have felt honoured by the invitation, just as I had when Limori asked me to move in with her.) I was peripherally aware that this had happened but didn't think anything of it until one day in mid-summer when I received a call from Michael saying that he, Gary, Richard, Jessica and Karen were going over to Limori's apartment in North Vancouver that evening to talk to her about something. He sounded angry and upset, and when he and Jessica picked me up for the drive over I found out why.

Susan was having an affair with Brent, one of the permanent residents of Wolf's Den. Gary, Richard and Michael were particularly upset because, as they put it, "You don't sleep with another man's wife." They all knew Susan's husband and, although he didn't follow Limori, we had met him on occasion. Initially they were mostly angry with Brent for stepping in and violating this part of the male code of ethics.

Limori welcomed six angry disciples into her apartment that evening, but she seemed amused by us rather than concerned about our disapproval. The men outlined why we were there, and Limori waited patiently while they did so. Then she dropped a bomb, explaining that not only did she know about the affair but that she, at God's request, had instigated it. This served to further enrage the men in the room, and she let each man express his moral outrage (Jessica, Karen and I mostly just observed the confrontation) but did not engage with their anger or defend her actions or those of Susan and Brent. When the men had blown off enough steam, Limori pulled out all the stops with her particular brand of rhetoric and, over the next couple of hours, smoothed ruffled feathers, assuring everyone that this was God's will and that, as ever, there was nothing more important than that.

Limori spoke to us for several hours, providing multiple and various reassurances that what Susan and Brent were doing was not only copacetic with God and the participants in this affair (but not Susan's husband – I don't know if he was aware of what was going on at the time), but also that it was important for Susan and Brent's learning. Any impropriety or potential hurt feelings on Susan's husband's part were not as important as the positive energy changes that were happening as a result of Susan and Brent's willingness to follow God's instruction and teaching. We each left the apartment that night a degree or two warmer in our metaphorical pots on the stove than when we had walked in.

I recently learned, while sharing my memories of this event with Gayle, that she was a witness to this relationship from the Wolf's Den side of things because she happened to be there at the time. When this affair happened, Limori was still spending part of her time in the city and part of it at Wolf's Den. A few weeks before our meeting with her, she had been up at the lodge and announced to the group that God said that Susan needed to cure her sexual issues and that the way to do this was to spend a romantic afternoon in bed with Brent in Limori's bedroom. Gayle reports sitting in the dining room of the lodge while this was going on, having the same battle of feelings that I've reported having during circumstances like this – wanting to feel comfortable with God's orders and trying to believe that God was helping Susan, but also struggling with the impropriety and deception of it all. Gayle knew and liked Susan's husband, and her essential self was naturally repelled by Limori's orchestration of sex for "learning purposes." However, she kept her mouth shut, as we all did, and Susan and Brent spent not only that afternoon together, but the rest of the summer. During this time, Limori convinced Susan to stay at Wolf's Den permanently and divorce her husband, although the relationship with Brent ended after a few months.

To date this was the furthest Limori had pushed the group toward the promiscuity end of the cult spectrum, but she lost none of us by turning up the heat in this way. As time moved on and she coupled and uncoupled others in the group, we became so used to the game of Musical Beds that eventually we were immune to it; gradually, orchestrated relationships became the standard for those that took place in the group, such as the marriages between Michael and Jessica and Gary and Karen, which we would witness later. In *The Guru Papers*, Kramer and Alstad describe the phenomenon that I've called Musical Beds like this:

> [A] parental type of authority is at the very core of the guru's power over disciples. The power to name, arrange marriages, and dictate duties and behaviour are ultimates in parental authority... To give someone the power to name or marry you is to profoundly accept their parental role in defining who you are. The ostensible motivation behind this has to do with an

attempt to break the ties of the past so the person can become "new." A deeper reason is that this aids the guru in becoming the center of the person's emotional life, which facilitates surrender."[1]

Each time a relationship began and then ended at Limori's behest, the participants became even more closely tied to their leader, because she was the one emotional constant in their lives.

ON THE EVENING of June 27, 1997, I went with Debbie to a presentation/talk/writing workshop being given by the writing teacher Natalie Goldberg. Debbie and I were both big fans of Ms. Goldberg, and we had a lovely time in the cathedral in downtown Vancouver where the event was held. Afterwards, we crossed the street to the Hotel Vancouver to have a glass of wine in the lounge on the main floor. As we scoped out the lounge for a seat, who should we spot but Michael and Jessica, also having a glass of wine and, quite obviously, having a deep and disturbing conversation about something. As Debbie and I approached their table we could tell that Jessica was upset, but they asked us to join them anyway. I remember first looking at Jessica inquiringly about what was wrong, and then coming right out and asking her, and she was able to answer in one word, which said it all: "Workshop."

Here, the group's loaded language was able to tell me that something very difficult was going on, something that God wanted and Jessica was being resistant to. Little did I know that very shortly, this workshop would intimately involve me. Once Jessica had uttered the magic word, *workshop*, Debbie and I pressed her no further, sensing that the matter was private and deep and that perhaps this was not the appropriate place to ask for details. Jessica collected herself as much as possible and put on a more public face, and the four of us chatted and had a glass of wine.

Three days later, Michael and Jessica and I arranged to go to a local microbrewery that was having an open house. The day before, Michael had called me at work and asked if I would come to their apartment an hour or so earlier than we had originally arranged because he and Jessica had something they wanted to talk to me about. I spent that Saturday morning running errands around town in preparation for a month-long trip to England that I was embarking on two days later. As the morning wore on, I inexplicably became more and more nervous, anxiety filling my stomach and knotting my shoulders. I wondered if the feeling had to do with my trip. The tension and anxiety became so strong at one point that I took a break from my scheduled errands, bought myself a bottle of water and sat on the grass in a park to try and calm down.

"Relax," I said to myself. "Nothing is wrong." I drank the water and focused on my breath, but was able to do very little to calm my jangled nerves. Rather than taking the bus, I walked from where I was to Michael and Jessica's apartment building, trying to burn off the nervous anxiety in my body with exercise. It didn't work.

I could feel the tension in the air the instant I walked through Michael and Jessica's front door that afternoon. Jessica wore the forced smile of someone catering her own funeral. Michael was less obviously tense, but I could still tell that something was up with him. They invited me into the living room.

We sat in a U shape: Michael on a loveseat to my left with his back to the windows that looked out onto False Creek and Jessica on a couch to my right. I was between them on a third couch at the bottom on the U, trying to stifle the anxiety-induced scream that was building in my chest. Michael was sitting very still, with his back straight and his hands clasped in his lap. I recognized the posture as that of someone trying to be centred. Jessica struck an identical pose, although hers was stiff with fear, and her eyes were red from crying. The vibe that came from her was of someone trying desperately to be brave, but I couldn't imagine why she would need to feel that way. All I knew at that moment was that whatever was going on, it was big. In a million years I never could have guessed the reason for this strange and electrically charged meeting.

Michael visibly gathered himself, taking a deep breath and letting it out slowly. And then he began his explanation of why I was there that day and, in doing so, changed my life forever.

He began by saying that two or three months earlier he and Jessica had been out at a concert together. Toward the end of the evening, Jessica made what Michael felt were a couple of ill-timed, unkind remarks to him (the details of which aren't important to our story) and he said that he felt something inside himself snap. He'd had it. Had it with being married to someone he loved but for whom he felt a more parental relationship than a partnership. And he'd had it with constantly feeling controlled by Jessica.

This marriage, as I've noted in earlier chapters, had always been a challenge for him. He didn't want to be married in the first place, and he found Jessica a supremely challenging person to live with and love. He had stayed in the marriage for five years because of his love for serving the God that Limori had him believing in. He had grumbled about it along the way and had had innumerable discussions with Limori, both in person and on the phone, about the relationship and how best to cope with it. As I observed their marriage from the outside looking in, my experience was that it was somewhat fulfilling for Michael because it gave him a concrete project to work on and a purpose to fulfill, but that it was not emotionally supportive or satisfying.

But on the night of the concert, after Jessica's comments, Michael's patience for the project had ended. He was done. He later recounted that the depth of that feeling stunned him a bit. It was over, he felt; something had broken inside him that night and he and the marriage would not recover from it.

I sat quietly and listened to this, not sure where Michael was going with the story. Jessica had said nothing so far. Michael took a deep breath and continued. Limori had called him a day or two after the concert and, he later told me, almost the first thing out of her mouth was, "What's wrong?" They (Limori and Michael) later described it as though she had picked up on his feelings psychically from Arizona, where she was at the time, and called him specifically because she could feel something was wrong. Given what I know now about cult leaders and their uncanny ability to read people, I suspect the call was a coincidence and that as soon as she heard his voice she could tell something was wrong. (We've all had that experience where we can tell a loved one is not doing well simply by the tone of their "Hello" when they pick up the phone.) But, no matter, into our group folklore went the story that she had called because she knew Michael had reached the breaking point in his marriage.

I was not privy to that conversation or the ones that followed and only heard about them afterwards from Michael, but I will attempt to piece together what happened because it is such a perfect example of a) our guru's manipulation of her followers, in this case to ensure that the vertical relationships to her were rock solid and the horizontal relationships between followers were undermined, b) her ability to have her followers (Michael, in this case) be the co-creators of their own manipulation, and c) the astonishingly effective strategy that she used to slowly, slowly turn up the heat so that none of us knew we were boiling to death.

Over the next several days, after the initial call with Limori and probably during several dozen ensuing telephone conversations, Limori and Michael discussed how he was feeling about his marriage now that he'd reached the breaking point. Limori had him tune in to God to see what was to be done (this is where the victim becomes a partner in his own manipulation). Eventually she said that God was saying that, because of the lack of love in Michael's marriage and Jessica's inability to love and support him in a generous way, Michael's connection to God and to the Masters (a specific group of spirit guides that Limori had lately been training Michael to tune into) was blocked. His passion for God was convincing Michael that Jessica was blocking his growth and his connection with God and the Masters. The struggles in their marriage and Jessica's unwillingness or inability to provide loving support to her husband were creating a block between Michael and the one thing he loved most: his work for God.

This was something that Michael could not bear. Everyone has a lever (as Dr. Phil says); Michael's lever is his deep and abiding passion for and devotion to working for God. The need to rectify the situation would trump his innate desire to protect Jessica from any pain. Once the seed of that idea was planted, Limori had only to water it for the next few days or weeks, until the roots of it had taken hold, and then begin to plant the idea that Michael needed love and support into order to connect with God and the Masters, and that if he wasn't getting it from his wife then he should get it from someone else.

Thus, the idea that Michael should take a mistress was born, and before a name for this person was put forth the idea was broken to Jessica. She was told that "her lack of love-flow in the marriage was preventing Michael from reaching energies that he was meant to reach." I can't imagine that that conversation was an easy one for Michael to broach, but he would have been shored up by the belief that he was doing it for God. Jessica was given some time to adjust to the idea and I don't suppose I have to describe how painful that must have been for her —to have her husband come to her and tell her God had said that she wasn't loving enough and that as punishment for this her husband would be having an affair with someone else while remaining married to her. And not just any someone else, but someone she knew. Someone from her closest community of friends.

It slowly began to dawn on me that we had come to the point of my visit and of Michael's story. I sat on the couch in Jessica and Michael's living room and listened to him explain that what was being asked of me was that I become his mistress.

To say I was stunned when Michael reached this punch line is a gross understatement. I could barely process what he was saying. It all felt so absurd that I was sure someone was going to jump out of a hiding place and yell, "Surprise! You're on Candid Camera." I was also deeply, deeply embarrassed that this discussion was being held in front of Jessica, although apparently she had known that this was coming for a couple of months.

Even now, more than a decade later as I recount this story, I can feel the tension and anxiety of that day and that situation re-emerge in my body. My hands, arms and shoulders are filled with a peculiar energized feeling that I experience at times of great stress and my stomach is in knots; feelings that I had all but suppressed on that bizarre and fateful day. My body was telling me, in the only way it could, that this was wrong, wrong, wrong. But my brain had been hijacked and I had stopped listening to my body long ago. I felt the all-too-familiar feeling of my logical brain and authentic self fighting with my cult self, although of course this was a feeling I would not have been able to name at the time. My cult self was by now much more in control of me, naturally, after eight years of indoctrination and exposure to the unusual, unreasonable, damaging and debilitating requests made of us in God's name. But even by the sick and twisted standards that I'd become comfortable with, this seemed a little too ridiculous to believe.

But remember what I said about Limori knowing what everyone's lever was? She knew me just as well as she knew anyone in her sway, so she knew I had two primary levers: Michael and God.

So she took these two great loves of mine and used them to her best advantage.

I remember asking a few questions and reminding them both that the timing of this request was a little questionable, as I was leaving town in two days to spend five weeks hiking in England.

And then I agreed to do what God was asking.

WITH THE BENEFIT OF HINDSIGHT, I can see now that whenever these sorts of bombs were dropped into our lives (for example, that a couple should break up or someone should move to live at Wolf's Den or someone was being used by very dark energy, and so on), Limori made sure to parcel out the information in small pieces. She would not, for example, get on the phone with Michael and abruptly announce, "God says you should take a mistress. It should be Alexandra. Tell Jessica tomorrow and then tell Alexandra." Had she delivered information in that way we would never have been so hooked into her manipulation or nearly as compliant and obedient. She was extraordinarily skilled at easing her disciples into challenging, painful situations very slowly, degree by strategic degree, while always, always maintaining that everything she asked of us was because God had requested it.

Lifton's second criteria for thought reform is mystical manipulation. He describes this by saying, "Totalist leaders claim to be agents chosen by God, history, or some supernatural force, to carry out the mystical imperative. The 'principles' (God-centered or otherwise) can be put forcibly and claimed exclusively, so that the cult and its beliefs become the only true path to salvation (or enlightenment)." Because of this, "the individual develops the psychology of the pawn."[2]

No kidding.

. . .

I LEFT for England on Monday, June 30, and spent a glorious month travelling on my own around the country that I had been dreaming of seeing for years. I even drove on the wrong side of the road, much to the frustration, I am sure, of the other drivers, who had the poor fortune to be sharing the motorways with me. I returned to Canada on a Wednesday evening in late July and on the next night, Thursday, I went to Michael and Jessica's for our closed circle meeting and shared some of my adventures with the group. Michael, Jessica and I hadn't yet told the rest of the group what God had asked of us – that would occur a week later.

And so began the Mistress Period, as Michael and I started to refer to it. Michael and Jessica continued to live in their apartment in False Creek, going about their daily lives in much the same way as ever. We had been instructed that Michael and Jessica would continue to live together and be married and that he and I would be lovers. Michael viewed it as he and I continuing to be good friends who now slept together occasionally, while he continued to be married to Jessica and fulfill the role of husband and primary support person on her spiritual journey. The only concession was that he was to sleep in a separate bedroom.

Despite the twisted context of the relationship, it was a huge relief to finally be able to fulfill my physical longing for Michael. The sexual and emotional tension that had existed between us for so long was released and was replaced by a deep, heartfelt joy at being together. Naturally, the intimacy between us deepened and I was thrilled to discover that we were as well-matched physically as we had been intellectually and temperamentally. My heart still leapt into my throat with excitement and joy every time Michael walked into my sight, but now I felt I had permission to feel the way I felt. I allowed myself to fall even more deeply in love with this man I'd already loved for so long. And I prayed the landing would be soft.

Because we were required to keep this matter secret from

anyone outside the group, no one else in our lives knew about it. Secrets like this served to reinforce the "us versus them" atmosphere in the group. Michael and Jessica continued to visit his parents periodically at their home on Vancouver Island, and went to family weddings and on golf holidays with Michael's friends and to other events, without revealing that there was anything untoward going on in their marriage. I, too, kept the information from my family, co-workers and the two friends I had outside the group, although the hypocrisy in this troubled me. I would wonder to myself, "I thought we were supposed to tell The Truth at all times. Why then are we keeping secrets?" Later, an even more uncomfortable thought crossed my mind: "If this (the Mistress Period) is truly God's will, then why does it have to be secret? Shouldn't we share it with others if it's a good thing?" I was practiced at pushing thoughts like these away.

Michael must have felt like he was slowly being pulled in half. Either Jessica or I, or both of us, was pretty much continuously upset or jealous about something, such as how much of his attention or time the other person was receiving or what our respective importance was to him. It was agony for me when they spent Christmas with his parents and other family members and I went alone to my mother and stepfather's. And it was equally agonizing for Jessica when Michael and I went away on weekends or holidays. Imagine having your husband go away on holiday with another woman and not only knowing about it but feeling you have to agree with the situation because it's God's will. My mind reels at the audacity of it all.

For Limori, the situation served its purpose. I have to assume that it proved to her once again that Michael, Jessica and I would do almost anything that God asked of us. Michael needed time to consider these types of outrageous requests, but his actions had shown that he would eventually come around to her way of thinking, even if it meant hurting someone he loved. The Mistress Period also served Limori by keeping all three of us on seriously unstable ground for a year. I was so focused for that year on stifling, suppressing, working through, working out and mulling over my feelings of jealousy, confusion and inadequacy that I had very little time or energy for anything else. Remember, we were completely convinced that all our feelings and ego positions had to be battled and overthrown for the good of the universe. So putting two women in a situation where jealousy, possessiveness, feelings of inferiority or superiority and myriad other emotions are naturally going to occur was ideal for keeping us under Limori's control. Every time any sort of feeling would come up, which was practically every moment of every day, Jessica and I would point out to ourselves and each other how we were failing God and try harder to not feel these feelings. Which, as any human being knows, is an impossible task.

I can say from personal experience that to give someone an impossible task like that and then make it their fault when they fail is an excellent way to keep people under control. My journal entries from this year reflect this and are a pitiful thing to read. I was filled with the self-loathing of someone who can't stop feeling. It's impossible to not feel, yet I was convinced that the road to salvation lay that way and I continually chastised myself for the love I felt for Michael, the jealousy I felt toward Jessica and the monstrous discomfort and confusion I felt about the situation itself.

It is painfully sad to realize in hindsight how low I was willing stoop for God. Jessica and I were both humiliated in this situation; she, because her marriage was a façade (don't forget, she had been told over and over again that the responsibility and blame for this situation was hers – if she had loved Michael with less selfishness she would have been spared), and I, because my relationship with Michael was a secret. I felt that the underlying message from God was that I wasn't good enough to be an actual girlfriend, just a pseudo one.

And don't think that the man in the middle of all this got off scot-free, either. Michael mentioned at several points along the way how difficult the situation was for him. No matter what he did, he upset or wounded someone he loved. If he went away for the weekend with me, Jessica was deeply hurt, of course. And if he took her to a family event, I was the one pouting. He couldn't win.

But, again and again, like a broken record, the message was repeated that we were "learning" from this experience and "getting over our ego positions" and that this was far more important than petty things like propriety or conventionality. If we were learning, then whatever kind of hell we were going through was justified. Limori could treat people as badly as she wanted because they would learn from it. I put up with a year of agony, as did Michael and Jessica, because I was learning. In several instances in my journal I confess that I wanted to give up, but didn't, because I was learning:

"This is just torture. God is torturing us. I feel like it's too much. I can't do it. I can't be all benevolent and detached. I'm not capable. And yet I can't say no to this because I'd be turning down all these lessons." (October 19, 1997)

AFTER A YEAR of the Mistress Period, all three of us were close to the breaking point. I felt like each and every nerve I had had been individually rubbed raw. I was almost ready to call a stop to the whole thing and break up with Michael (such an absurd phrase when the man was already married). Later, Jessica told me that she had been almost ready to move out of their home. Neither of us made these moves, though, primarily because we were trying to follow God's orders, despite how horrifically painful and humiliating it was. Finally, in the summer of 1998, Limori declared that Michael and Jessica's marriage was officially over and they should move apart and begin divorce proceedings.

8

THE BEGINNING

The significant problems we face cannot be solved at the same level of thinking we were at when we created them.
—Albert Einstein

Our flight to Wolf's Den was delayed, so Michael and I sat playing cards at a small table in the south terminal of the Vancouver airport. It was December 28, 1999, and we were headed up to the fishing resort to spend the final days of the millennium with those members of our "family" who lived there. Even though Limori would not be there, I was nervous about making this trip. It had been Michael's choice to spend the last part of our Christmas holiday this way, and I had gone along with the idea simply because I didn't have the backbone to oppose it. I didn't like being at Wolf's Den; I didn't like the food Limori had Lisa cooked, and I didn't like that we would essentially be trapped in the lodge from morning until night because of the frigid temperatures and the remoteness of the location.

Limori, Susan, Alice and Rosemarie (another member of Limori's travelling entourage) were all in Arizona for Christmas that year. Limori had been renting a home near Tucson for a while; Arizona had replaced Hawaii as her second base-camp. And though she wouldn't be at Wolf's Den physically, I knew from experience that her presence would be felt almost as strongly as if she were.

Sure enough, as soon as we arrived at the lodge and settled in the cabin that would be ours, the phone calls from Arizona began. Limori called to see if we'd arrived safely, then she called back to tell Lisa what she should make us for supper that night, and she called after supper to speak to Michael about the importance of this week, when the world was moving into a new "energetic era" as the calendar brought us into a new millennium. She was so present in the lodge that we should have set a place for her at the table.

That first evening passed unremarkably; it was the next day that things began to go pear-shaped. There were no guests at the lodge while we were there so Michael and I were free to do as we wished. We read in the library and went for a short walk, although the temperature soon drove us back inside. Mid-afternoon the phone rang for the umpteenth time, and, after speaking to Lisa for a while, Limori asked to speak to Michael. He took the phone and began chatting with her and then excused himself and went into Lisa and Matthew's bedroom, which was just off the kitchen. (In the latest game of Musical Beds, Limori's former husband was now paired with Lisa.) He was gone for two hours and when he hung up and came and found me in the library, he was a changed man. His face looked dour and drawn and there was none of the usual spark of life in his eyes. I asked what was wrong and he said he couldn't talk about it, so I left it alone. But I guessed that whatever had transpired during his phone call with Limori had to do with me and that it wasn't good news. I guessed this because of the way he was closed off from me, in a way that he only ever was after he'd talked to his guru. I was certain that she'd delivered the latest message from God that said I was failing Him and also failing Limori and Michael. But I couldn't know for sure because Michael wasn't talking. So I tried not to think about it.

During dinner that night he was obviously more comfortable because we were with Matthew, Lisa and John. Some of his normal lightheartedness began to return. But as we got ready for bed that night, we sat on top of the bedspread for a while, chatting. I tentatively made another query into the topic of his conversation with Limori and, surprisingly, he revealed a tiny bit.

"You're not doing very well," he said.

I knew he meant "energetically." "Why?" I asked. "What's wrong?"

"I can't tell you."

I paused, trying to get my head around what was going on, "So . . . something's wrong but you can't tell me what it is. Is that it?"

"Yes," he said. He was having trouble meeting my eyes and his dour expression was back.

I made an exasperated noise and moved to get up off the bed to brush my teeth.

"You're angry," he said, and somehow I could tell that he was talking not just about the present moment, but about my state of being in general.

"No, I'm not." I defended myself automatically. "Or at least, I wouldn't be if you would tell me what was going on."

"I told you, I can't."

I gave up on the conversation because I could tell it was going nowhere and only making me more nervous than I already was. After we'd cleaned our teeth and added more fuel to the wood-stove in our cabin, we snuggled up against one another under the warm blankets. I felt like crap because of the cold we'd both caught at Christmas, and his nose was red and running, too.

"Do you want to make love?" he asked.

"No," I said. "I don't feel well enough, physically or emotionally." It was true that I didn't feel physically well enough for love-making, but the greater reason that I rebuffed him was that I was saddened and hurt because he was shutting me out of our relationship and I couldn't comprehend opening myself up to him while he was doing that. I was terribly confused about how to deal with this recurring situation, in which he and Limori discussed me behind my back and then wouldn't share what they had been told by God. And I was frustrated because if they wouldn't tell me what was wrong, how could I fix it? I couldn't find a way to be at peace with all of this, although I was frantically applying all the group rules to the situation in my head: "Be in your heart. Limori loves you; you must trust her. . . I shouldn't ever be worried or upset about hearing The Truth. If it's The Truth then it will help me." I fell into a restless sleep, reluctantly curled up against Michael for warmth, and what I couldn't know was that this would be our last night together.

THE LAST TIME I'd had any contact with Limori had been eight months earlier. Her only connection with anyone in Vancouver during this time was with Michael. Perhaps he had always spoken to her so frequently, but during 1999 it became apparent to me that he spoke to her nearly every day, sometimes several times a day. Not that he told me each time he spoke to her, but through references he made regularly to conversations that he'd had with her, I began to understand how close he was to her and how closely he was tied to her.

In March that year, Michael and I spent two weeks on vacation on the Big Island of Hawaii. It was the best vacation I'd ever had. We were finally in a relationship with just two participants and we were deeply in love. This time away from the group and from the drama that had encircled us for the past couple of years lifted our spirits and bonded us even more closely. We snorkelled, which I had never done before, and swam and ate apple bananas from the farmers' market in Kailua-Kona and soaked up the sun like the vitamin D–starved Canadians we were. I had my first drink with an umbrella in it. While wading in a shallow cove, Michael had his toe gently nipped by a tourist-spoiled sea turtle who thought the toe was a potential source of snack food. We avoided hotels and instead stayed in bed and breakfasts in several places on the island and bonded over delicious, exotic breakfasts with our warm and genial hosts. We watched the sunset and drank wine and ate guacamole made from avocados grown where we were staying. After making love I would lie with my head on Michael's chest listening to the song of his heart. With our open balcony door letting tropical air waft over us, we'd hear the ripened grapefruit-sized avocados fall from their trees to the ground with the softest, most earthly and comforting thud. We did not tire of one another even though we were together around the clock. And we were asked every day, usually several times, if we were on our honeymoon. "No," we'd answer, "we're just very happy to be together." It was a moment out of time. No Limori to interfere with us, no fellow group members requiring Michael's spiritual guidance or support. No energy dramas going on. For an all-too-brief moment our relationship existed outside the prison yard it had grown in, and flourished in this glimpse of freedom. I still look back on that vacation as one of the highlights of my life thus far. It was, quite simply, heaven.

A week after we returned to Vancouver from Hawaii, Michael mentioned that Limori was passing through town on her way to Arizona. She and her travelling entourage, Alice, Susan and Rosemarie, would be staying for one night at a hotel in Rich-mond and Limori had invited Michael and me to have lunch with her. During this visit, my eyes would be opened to Michael's rela-tionship with Limori more than ever before. When I look back, if there ever was a moment that was the beginning of the end for me in Limori's cult, this was it.

. . .

We met the four women in the restaurant of the hotel at our appointed time. The six of us sat at a long table and chatted; early on in the conversation Michael mentioned that he and I had just returned from Hawaii but Limori barely acknowledged that he'd spoken. She held court, as ever, and spoke only about the things that mattered to her: energetic changes that were taking place and the challenging work she'd been doing for God lately. This trip she was taking to Arizona was of paramount importance and they were on a tight time schedule to get to Tucson by a certain date because God had said they should. If they didn't arrive by that date there would be disastrous consequences for the universe. After an hour or so of chatting over coffee we had lunch, and it was during this meal that I woke up to a glimpse of Michael that I was not comfortable with.

Limori had a habit of staying at the same hotels over time, and using the same restaurants. Because of her charisma and attention-getting appearance and manner, she usually became well known at these favoured places and was very often treated like royalty. At this particular hotel, she was fond of the Rueben sandwich. When our waiter brought us lunch menus, Limori noticed that the Reuben was not listed, but, being Limori, she ordered it anyway.

"I'm sorry, madam," the waiter said, "we don't serve the Reuben any longer."

"Well," Limori said, her tone and body language conveying the message *Don't you know who I am?*, "that's what I want for lunch. Ask the chef and I'm sure he'll make the sandwich for me." The rest of us at the table sat quietly, well used to this sort of performance. The waiter left our table to go into the kitchen to talk to the chef and was back in a few seconds.

"I'm very sorry, madam, we're just not set up to serve the Reuben since it's been taken off the menu. May I offer you the club sandwich?"

Limori thought about this for a second or two, her hands

clasped over her vast midsection, rings sparkling in the light. Then she set her gaze so directly at the waiter that I was surprised she didn't burn holes through to the back of his skull. "I want a Reuben sandwich," she said. "I've been coming to this hotel for years and I always have a Reuben sandwich when I'm here. You tell the chef that I am the customer, and a regular customer at that, and that I know it's possible for him to make me a Reuben sandwich and that's what I want." She held the waiter's gaze when she'd finished and after a second or two he moved away toward the kitchen again.

Limori got her Reuben sandwich. Are you surprised? I wasn't, but what did surprise me was that when the waiter asked the rest of the table what we wanted for lunch, Michael looked at Limori, and then at the waiter and said, "I'll have the Reuben sandwich as well." This choice was mildly surprising to me because Michael was a health nut and was always fastidious about what he put in his mouth, and a sandwich laden with processed meat would not normally be a choice that he'd make. But more than that, it was the split-second attitude that came across when he placed his order that struck me.

He was sucking up.

He was sucking up to Limori in a way that, if I had witnessed it before, I had been too preoccupied or blind to notice. He wanted her to be pleased with him, I realized, and he wanted to be in with the in crowd. (Alice, Susan and Rosemarie seemed to follow Michael's lead and also ordered the Rueben. I alone had something other than that for lunch.)

Michael had always been a lion to me. He was the one person in our group who stood up to Limori. He'd had many an argument with her, both ones I'd witnessed and ones he'd described after they'd happened. Unlike me, he had never seemed afraid of her. I had always been able to see that he respected her, but this was the first moment I noticed that he wanted her approval, just as I did.

Much to my amazement, his obsequiousness continued for the rest of the afternoon. After lunch, we moved out into an atrium just off the lobby of the hotel. There were several wing-backed chairs and a couch, where the six of us sat for the next couple of hours. Limori sat in one of the chairs and Michael sat to her left, on the seat closest to her. He was soaking her into his every pore. I could tell that he'd have been happy if the afternoon lasted four days. I, on the other hand, could not get out of there fast enough. Limori and Michael talked about the people in the Vancouver group and she commented on everyone's energy and whether it was favourable or not or if they were in their ego or not. Limori referred to Mildred and for the first time ever said that her energy was not very good these days and that Michael should be cautious about being around her. To me, Limori said that negative energies were trying to reach Michael through me and that I should be very cautious, particularly about getting pregnant.

"Whatever birth control you're using," she said, "I'd double it. These energies are trying to plant a negative baby inside you, and they know that this would be one way that they could disrupt Michael." With this one comment, Limori elevated Michael in God's hierarchy by emphasizing that he was so important that the Dark was trying to attack him, while simultaneously keeping me in a state of fear, self-doubt and self-loathing because negative energies were trying to work through me to harm Michael. She paused, listening to her guides, and then said, "For a while, your fear of losing Michael prevented him from reaching the Masters. You'd better get a grip on that fear."

This comment about Michael not being able to reach the Masters was exactly the same as the one Limori had made to Jessica to bring an end to her marriage to Michael. It sent a cold knife of fear and guilt through my heart and, far from helping me to get a grip on my fear, made it worse.

She looked deeply into my eyes. "God says to me now that if

He were to take Michael away from you, you would turn your back on Him."

"That's absurd," I thought. "I love God." But her words foreshadowed the events that would unfold at the end of the year. It was she who would take Michael away from me and I would indeed end up turning my back on her and on the God she had been trying to convince me she spoke for all these years.

As unsettled as I was by these proclamations, I was also deeply concerned about my observations of Michael's behaviour when he was around Limori. I could see that it filled him up to be near Limori, and that he experienced a high just by being able to talk to her in person for a few hours. But I was not comfortable at all with the person he turned into in her presence. This was not the man I loved and admired.

The following day, Michael and I went for a long walk on the beach and discussed what had transpired the day before. For the first (and last) time I questioned Limori's methods directly to Michael's face. I expressed what had bothered me for years: that Limori talked about love but her methodology didn't seem loving. And I was crushed that Limori had said Mildred's energy was bad. I was deeply fond of Mildred and couldn't bear the thought that she, like all the rest of us, was now a screw-up in God's eyes. I had gotten used to the fact that Limori/God thought that the rest of us were all screw-ups, but Mildred had always been exempt from that. She had never been tarred with the same brush that Limori used on the rest of us and thus had always given me hope that it was possible to stay in God's good graces.

"But if it's The Truth," Michael said, "then it's The Truth. Limori was not attacking Mildred; she was simply telling us what she saw. And love does not always have to look soft and mushy. Sometimes tough love is the only thing that will get through to a person. ["Tough love" had lately become a part of our loaded language. Essentially it meant that Limori could treat anyone as badly as she wanted to and was justified by calling it tough love.]

The key question is why does it bother you that Limori speaks The Truth, about Mildred or anyone else?"

His tone was defensive about the fact that I was questioning Limori, and I noticed that and thought about it for a second. Then something radical happened, something that had never happened before and was, I believe, a small, tentative step toward the end of my time in the cult: I actually spoke up about what I really felt. I voiced my actual opinion without couching it in group rhetoric and addressed his defensive tone. "Why is it not OK to ask questions about Limori and her methods? Why do you get defensive any time I do that? She has always invited us to question her, yet when we do we get chastised for it."

I turned my head toward him as we walked and vividly remember the look of controlled confusion on Michael's face. I could practically see the circuits frying in his head. I had addressed, out loud, one of the primary hypocrisies in Limori's teaching and it didn't sit well with either of us. He didn't have an answer for me so we continued our walk in sullen silence.

Years later, I would learn that in this pivotal moment what I had done was challenge the doctrine over person criteria of thought reform. Once again, I'll reference Dr. Robert Lifton to explain criteria number seven:

If one questions the beliefs of the group or the leaders of the group, one is made to feel that there is something inherently wrong with them to even question – it is always "turned around" on them and the questioner/criticizer is questioned rather than the questions answered directly. The underlying assumption is that doctrine/ideology is ultimately more valid, true and real than any aspect of actual human character or human experience and one must subject one's experience to that "truth." The experience of contradiction can be immediately associated with guilt. One is made to feel that doubts are reflections of one's own evil."[1]

. . .

I HAD BEEN bumping into this criteria for membership in the group for years, and would continue to do so for some time, but without realizing it. My perpetual cycle of fear of Limori's methods and guilt about that fear was exactly what is being described above. I had always been afraid of Limori and deep down wanted to challenge her methods and question the supposed benefits of ostracizing, yelling at and abusing group members, but knew that any questions I had would be turned back around to me and my value and commitment to God would be questioned. We had always been told we were free to challenge her but, in practice, we were not. The message always came back that to question her, even by proxy via Michael, meant that the questioner was flawed, evil and unable to see The Truth.

THE REST of that year was easier. We didn't see Limori again and, although I was increasingly conflicted about the group and Limori's teaching methods and philosophies, I kept that to myself. My journals reflect some of that conflict but I didn't dare express a word of it to anyone and am surprised, frankly, that I allowed myself to even think some of the things I was thinking.

For example, in November 1999, I wrote, "This spiritual journey is mine. It's not Limori's or Michael's, it's mine. I've always tended to give my power away. I've been on the path thus far because I felt I needed Limori to approve of me and I needed to be a good girl. Now I feel more in charge of my own life, more responsible for myself, less afraid of Limori."

The part about being less afraid of Limori was mostly bluster, because as we will shortly see, even being in the room when she was on the phone would send me into fits of fearful angst, but it is obvious that I was tentatively exploring the idea that my relationship with God was not Limori's responsibility, nor should she (or anyone) have dominion over that relationship. That was a deeply radical and rebellious thought, which defied everything I'd been taught by Limori up to this point, and I was afraid while I was writing it. I was embattled that fall, my cult self and my essential self duelling it out for supremacy inside me.

In late September or early October 1999, I began asking God to please show me or tell me the truth. "Not Limori's truth," I would say out loud during my prayers at night, "I want to know THE truth. Your truth, God. Is this path with Limori the right one? If it is then I'll accept that, but I want to know for sure, from You. Show me. Get through to me somehow. I want to know Your truth." Every night for weeks I asked this with an urgency that bordered on desperation.

The bright side of that summer and fall was that Michael and I were blissfully happy; after nearly ten years of talking about how much we loved one another we were now able to express it to ourselves and to our friends and family. The relief was enormous and the relationship itself was even better than I'd imagined. The feeling of being soulfully connected to Michael didn't go away, no matter how much time we spent together. My new personal assistant business was growing and it was especially gratifying to have Michael's help and counsel about that. It was another point of connection for us; we both had an entrepreneurial spirit and now I was able to nurture mine, and receive his encouragement, as I learned how to be self-employed.

THE MORNING OF DECEMBER 30, 1999, dawned crisp and clear and freeze-your-nose-hair cold. I pressed myself against Michael's back and wrapped my right arm around him, spooning him for warmth. My state of mind was much the same as it had been when we'd gone to sleep the night before: confused, angry but not admitting it, frightened and dreading the next few days I'd be spending here at Limori's resort, under Limori's thumb, with Limori inserting herself between my beloved Michael and me. But I tried to suppress those thoughts and feelings and focus on being on vacation, although this was a far, far cry from my experience in Hawaii, earlier that year. The outside temperature alone should have given me a clue that I was a million miles away from avocado trees and peace.

The phone call from Limori came shortly after lunch. Michael excused himself to Matthew and Lisa's bedroom. The long phone cord snaked under the closed door and remained there for most of the afternoon. I spent the ensuing hours, while Michael talked to Limori, drifting around the lodge, trying to feel comfortable but losing that battle. I knew instinctively that Michael and Limori were talking about me; it made sense, especially after what had happened the day before. And my body once again knew that something was wrong. I've described having butterflies all the time I lived with Limori; I had them now while I waited for Michael to finish talking. They were fluttering so furiously that I felt nervous all the way up into my throat. (I can feel the feeling now as I write.) I felt so choked with anxiety that I wanted to throw up. I tried to read in the beautiful library that looked out onto the lake, but I couldn't concentrate – it was like there was a marching band standing beside me, belting out tunes that made it impossible to concentrate enough to absorb the words I was reading. I just knew I was doomed. Daisy, one of the lodge cats, came and sat on my lap, and kneaded my chest and purred while I petted her. I was grateful for her kindness and company because I was already feeling abandoned by the humans at the lodge.

Later I moved into the kitchen and worked on a cross-stitch project that I had with me. After four hours of being on the phone, Michael emerged from the bedroom and passed the phone to Lisa, who went into the bedroom and closed the door. I glanced up at him but he wasn't looking at me. Matthew was there at the kitchen counter and I heard Michael ask him if there was any juice. Matthew said no, he thought that we'd finished it all that morning. Michael asked Matthew if he would make some then because he needed something to drink. This was not a good sign; none of us ever asked Matthew to do anything. He was the king of this domain, even if he was no longer married to Limori.

Michael turned and walked toward me, and I'd never seen a look on his face like the one he wore. His eyes were sunken in with dark circles around them, as though he'd aged fifteen years that afternoon. I set my cross-stitching down on the table as Michael asked Matthew, Lisa (who had emerged from the bedroom and hung up the phone) and John to join us. They all sat down and looked at me. Michael began.

"God says that I need to move into the new millennium unencumbered."

PART II

BASTOGNE

I must be gone and live, or stay and die.
—Romeo and Juliet

After the tearful and tense breakfast I described in the prologue, I spent the morning of December 31, 1999, holed up in my cabin, waiting for the time of my flight back home. When it arrived, I dragged my suitcase, wheels grinding through the snow, up the short path to the driveway of the lodge. I left it there and went inside to find out who would be driving me to the airport. Lisa was in the kitchen.

"I'd like to say goodbye to Michael," I said to her, nervously anticipating that this would not be allowed. "Do you know where he is?"

"I think he's in the living room."

"Thanks."

I went through the swing doors that divided the kitchen and living room with my heart in my throat and tears threatening behind my eyes. Michael was seated in one of the dining room chairs in front of the fireplace, reading a book about hockey that his brother had given him for Christmas. He looked up when he saw me approaching, and a rush of thoughts and feelings crowded together inside me, jostling for dominance. I couldn't believe that he could sit so calmly, reading, as though nothing was happening. I felt ashamed about how afraid of him I felt. He had gone from my closest ally to someone I was petrified of in a few short hours. And his face was so calm, like he had not a thought in the world besides what he was reading in his book. I felt frightened of that too; his expression was so eerily calm that it was like he wasn't even there. Our eyes met and I saw that his seemed as hard and vacant as glass. It was as though all that we'd shared and every intimacy we'd experienced together was erased from his memory. Just like that, I was the enemy. Someone he now needed to manage and instruct and, most important of all, keep at a distance.

Rather than provide me with any hope of reconciliation, or a shred of compassion, he took a firm grasp on the knife lodged in my heart and twisted it. "I'm not allowed to hug you," he said, when I reached a distance of two or three feet from his chair.

"Oh," I said. "Okay." I knew from years of indoctrination that this meant my energy was so bad, so dark and devilish, that if I touched Michael, or anyone for that matter, I would contaminate them, the same as if I'd physically been covered in tar. "I'm leaving now, so I guess we'll talk when you get home."

"Yes," he said, and that was it.

Awkward silence.

"Okay, then," I said. I didn't know what to do with my body. I realized I was holding my hands at waist height, intertwining and unwinding my fingers with nervous energy. I took half a step back and turned slightly back toward the kitchen. "See you . . . I guess."

"'Bye," he said.

I walked back toward the kitchen doors, the tears in my eyes threatening to spill over, but I refused to wipe at them until I was out of Michael's sight.

I waited, alone, in the kitchen foyer until Matthew was ready to drive me to the airfield to catch my flight. He talked as we drove and chuckled at me again, as he had earlier in the day. I was conscious that whatever I said would be reported back to the others at the lodge, and to Limori in Arizona, but in any event I had very little to say. Shock and grief had made me almost mute, and I knew that in these circumstances whatever one said would be criticized and corrected. I'd seen others in this position so many times, and had so often been on the other side of this coin doing the criticizing, that I knew any protestations or apologies or heartfelt sharing on my part would be in vain. I mostly kept my own counsel during the fifteen-minute ride, staring anxiously ahead at the snowy road.

Matthew lifted my suitcase out of the truck, said goodbye and good luck and drove off. I went into the Atco trailer and checked in for the flight, which meant telling the woman behind the office desk jammed into a corner of the trailer who I was.

"Flight's a few minutes late," she said, between puffs on a cigarette. "Have a seat." She flapped her hand in the direction of four or five plastic chairs along one wall, so I joined a couple of what I had to assume were other passengers there in the "departure lounge."

Now that I was away from the lodge, I felt that I didn't need to be quite so worried about "hitting" anyone with my energy, and I didn't have to fear that the people surrounding me would mock, chastise or berate me (since they were strangers). My mental defences let down slightly and I began to feel what was going on in my body. I ached as though I'd been pummelled with something heavy for hours. My eyes felt like they'd sunk into my skull a couple of inches, and I felt as though I needed to think about blinking, otherwise it wouldn't happen. The wait for the flight was maybe fifteen or twenty minutes, but for the first time in my life I experienced the phenomenon of the flexibility of time. I felt like every moment, every second, stretched out like the gonging of a bell and the resonant sound that follows it. There were, as the Bard says, days in each minute. I could have read aloud *War and Peace* inside each of those seconds, they were so drawn out.

I was concerned about falling apart, here in the Atco trailer, surrounded by five strangers in parkas and snowmobile boots. I was afraid that if I moved or breathed or turned my head or scratched my nose that I would, literally and instantly, shatter into ten million pieces.

After several years of waiting, we boarded the tiny airplane and eventually lifted off, heading toward home. I remember little of the flight, except for the staggeringly beautiful eagle's-eye view of the Coast Mountains. When we landed in Vancouver, I gratefully moved into task mode: wait for luggage, drag suitcase outside, hail a taxicab, give driver home address, sit through ride, pay driver, drag suitcase into apartment building lobby, proceed up three flights of stairs. It was the most activity I'd had in twenty-four hours.

Just as I stepped into the stairwell of my apartment building, which didn't have an elevator, a woman I didn't recognize came up from the basement and saw me struggling to carry my large, heavy suitcase, purse and carry-on bag up the stairs.

"Do you need any help?" she asked.

"No, I'm fine," I said, almost tipping over backwards with the weight of my bags.

"Yes, you do," she said. "Here, let me." She took hold of my carry-on bag and started up the stairs ahead of me. I was almost undone. Her gentle and spontaneous kindness contrasted so sharply with the cruelty and ostracization I'd just experienced that I was struck dumb. When we reached my floor, which I think was her floor too, I mumbled thanks but was so perilously close to hysterical tears that I was afraid of opening my mouth too far lest I began to wail, so I'm not sure if she heard me. I'm not sure if I ever saw her again. The grief-induced haze I was in prevented me from taking stock of her features or where she went after she dropped me off at my door. To this day, whenever I'm carrying a suitcase up a flight of stairs I think of her and say a prayer of thanks.

AND SO IT BEGAN. I couldn't know it at the time, but every road of my life up to this point had led into this time, and every resulting road would lead out of it. My life was now divided into two halves: before New Year's Eve, 1999, and after. This was my moment, my opportunity to consciously and purposefully choose who I wanted to be and what I believed to be true about the world, about God and about myself.

There is a god in the Hindu religion called Shiva, who represents both destruction and creativity. In my early twenties, in my emotionally immature way, I was never able to grasp this. "How," I would wonder to myself, "can something represent both destruction and creativity? Those two things are, like, total opposites." The early part of the twentieth century would bring home to me, in the most intimate way, the understanding that creativity sometimes sprouts from destruction. Like the new plant growth that can begin only when a forest has been destroyed by fire, sometimes our lives cannot grow in a new direction until we metaphorically burn down our existing life. Martha Beck, sociologist and life coach, describes this situation in her book *Finding Your Own North Star* as a "death you have to live through."[1]

I was dying. Not physically, maybe (although there were days when I begged for that to be true), but emotionally, mentally and spiritually. The way that Limori had had Michael break up with me and the subsequent treatment by those at Wolf's Den and in the Vancouver group (more about this in a moment) made me feel like a splattered bug on the windshield of life. I spent the first few days after my return from that disastrous trip so shocked and stupefied that I could barely string a sentence together and found myself doing things like putting my car keys in the refrigerator and having to consciously remember how to tie my shoelaces. But the result of that messy impact was that I was jolted awake. I loathed and despised and despaired of every second of the subsequent months and years, but what I eventually came to realize was that this was the biggest blessing and greatest gift I'd ever received. It was a course correction, as pilots say, of such jolting and terrifying magnitude that it almost unhinged me, but I now believe it needed to be that big, that shocking, that devastating, in order to get my attention. Anything less and I would have skirted around it with cult rhetoric.

I KNEW NONE OF THIS, of course, when I entered my apartment in the darkness of early evening on the last day of 1999. I drifted around, thinking I should unpack or eat something, but was unable to be still anywhere long enough for any activity to be completed. After an hour or so of this, I called Debbie, the person from the group whom I was closest to. I knew that she was having a few of the women from the meditation circle over for a New Year's Eve party. As briefly as I could, I explained what had happened and she invited me over to join the group, who would be arriving shortly.

Because my presence was unexpected (everyone knew that Michael and I were supposed to be up at Wolf's Den until the third of January) and because it was blatantly obvious to everyone that I was completely wrecked, moments after I walked through Debbie's front door I explained everything that had happened. Tellingly, no one expressed a great deal of surprise; we'd all become familiar with the game of Musical Beds. Jessica especially could empathize with every gory detail of what I was feeling at that moment. They expressed mild condolences, but group etiquette required that they remember to distance themselves emotionally from me and not express too much sympathy, lest they risk being drawn into my dark energy.

Over the next few months my relationships with each of the women in the room, Debbie, Amber, Karen and Jessica, would gradually disintegrate, but at the time, they were all I had to hang on to. I emotionally clung to each of them like I was drowning.

The evening passed and we toasted the New Year and the new millennium at midnight. I was a nervous wreck and excused myself as soon as I could. When I got home I caught myself wondering what Michael and the gang at Wolf's Den were doing to bring in the millennium. I imagined it would be highly cere-monial and that the spiritual events, whatever they were, would go on for hours. As I crawled into bed I could smell Michael on the pillow he had slept on the last time he'd stayed overnight.

Until that moment I'd thought "crying oneself to sleep" was just an expression.

ONE OF THE cruellest aspects of Limori's strategy of jettisoning me from Wolf's Den and from Michael's life was that I was not given an explanation for why it was happening. Other than Michael's initial statement that he had to "move into the new millennium unencumbered" and that the karma between us had been cleaned up, I had not been given a single reason for what was happening. When Michael eventually returned to the city, I requested a meeting with him to find out more about the cause of all this disruption and heartbreak. He sat, with sunken eyes and a hardened expression, on my couch and I faced him from a chair. He looked as bad as I felt, which was saying something. Part of what I experienced in him was that he was so angry with me he could barely contain himself. He adopted the spiritual posture of straight spine and waggled his head every few minutes, tuning in, but his body language could not hide the fact that he was furious with me, and deeply disappointed in me, for causing this blow that had clearly devastated both of us.

Once we'd dispensed with small talk and got settled, our conversation bordered on ridiculous.

"Is there anything you can tell me about what's happening?" I asked.

Head-waggle to tune in. "No, just to search for The Truth and search for God in your heart," he said.

I was afraid (as ever) to press him for more, but also afraid that not asking for more information was the wrong thing to do. "Is there anything I can do to . . . I don't know . . . fix this?"

Another head-waggle and a centring breath. "Just find The Truth in your heart and let go of your ego."

The conversation went on like this for a few more minutes. He revealed nothing specifically of what I had done wrong or was doing wrong. I was left to guess and flounder, which I speculate was one of the desired outcomes of Limori's strategy, and Michael was clearly operating under her strict instructions. And, in fact, he said as much a couple of times: "I'm not allowed to tell you any more."

Michael is a naturally compassionate and kind person, helpful to the extreme. A more loyal friend you could not ask for. I had watched him spend the five years he was married to Jessica bending over backwards, spending endless hours counselling her and offering emotional, spiritual and intellectual support. If he could have physically hauled her up to where he felt she needed to be in the spiritual hierarchy he would have done it. He primarily loved two things in his life: God and his friends (okay, three – golf should be on this list, too). He wanted those he loved to love God as much as he did. He couldn't bear the thought of anyone he loved being left behind (i.e., being cast into the outer darkness with the rest of Them). I could clearly see as he sat on my couch that raw January day that it was ripping him to shreds, not just being split from me, but the thought that I was slipping away into the darkness. Whatever Limori had said to him, whatever spiritual levers she had used to convince him to dump me, they were working. He was a man on the edge of collapse and, as much as my heart ached for my own loss, it redoubled when I was face to face with him and could see how broken up he was about having to toe the hard spiritual line with me. Yet such was his commitment to Limori and to her brand of The Truth that, despite the pain and sorrow he was experiencing, he would not defy her authority. He would not and could not make the choice to continue our relationship. Our guru had convinced him that God wanted us to be apart and, come hell or high water, those were the orders that he was going to follow. It didn't matter that we loved one another. It didn't matter that this was not what either one of us would have chosen at that moment. It didn't matter that we were both devastated and heartbroken. It didn't matter that a third party had decided our fate. He believed he was following God's orders and that was enough for him.

I felt the grim reality set in for both of us that day. He was thousands of miles away, sitting there across from me in my living room, and there was nothing I could do to bring him closer. Begging wouldn't work, I knew. Saying, "This is ridiculous. We love each other," wouldn't work, because logic didn't matter then, to either of us. Throwing myself on his mercy wouldn't work, because he believed that this wasn't his choice; he was desperately trying to follow the instructions of a higher power that he believed in absolutely and, even while his own heart was breaking, he would not defy that ultimate authority.

To add insult to injury, Limori used the fact that Michael loved me as one of her levers to get him to commit to this break-up. "If I try to help you," he said, "you will never learn the things you need to learn." So, in other words, he believed he would be hurting my chances in the spiritual realm if we stayed together or he helped me or told me any more of what Limori had told him were the reasons for the break-up and my resulting ostracization. "You need to figure this out for yourself. I cannot help you. But if you do figure it out, then you'll be saved. You need to win this battle." There was an edge of desperation in his voice.

What battle, for Christ's sake? I thought. I don't have a clue what's going on.

Limori had engineered the perfect diabolical situation that served her purposes. Michael was led to believe that he couldn't advance spiritually unless he broke his ties to me. With one fell swoop Limori had gotten him to prove his loyalty to her without a shadow of a doubt and had, at the same time, made me the bad guy who Michael now had to avoid like the plague. She could praise him for his exemplary service to God and at the same time keep him emotionally and physically as far away from me as possible, simply by telling him that if he helped me he would be damning me further. A few months later Michael and I bumped into each other on the street near his office and he confessed that the only thought that was helping him through the terrible time he was having over the loss of our relationship was that what he was doing was helping me spiritually.

I have to assume that this was a make-or-break situation for me in Limori's eyes. Her primary objective was to cement Michael to herself in that essential vertical relationship the guru must have with each disciple, that much is very clear, but if as a result I had also strengthened my loyalty to her, I'm sure that would have been a welcome by-product of this event. A guru can always use another blind servant. Sucks for her that it didn't turn out that way.

EVERY TIME MICHAEL and I saw each other at the meditation circle in January and February of that year, and at the one or two private meetings we had, his face had an increasingly familiar expression of grim resolve mixed with grave disappointment in me. I am at a loss to explain how painful it was to look into the face of someone I loved so much and see disgust and disappointment when he met my gaze. I stared at the floor a lot during this time and met his eyes only when I couldn't avoid it.

In the autumn of 1999 Michael and I had purchased tickets to a music concert that was to take place in the early part of 2000. As the time for the concert approached, I hesitantly called Michael to discuss what we should or would do with the tickets, but didn't leave a message because I was afraid to press him about anything at that point and I thought the concert was still a few weeks away. The next time I saw him was at a Wednesday night group meeting.

As I helped Jessica and Amber set up the chairs in a circle, Michael approached me with thunder in his eyes. "Karen and I went to the Buena Vista Social Club concert last weekend," he said. "I asked her to go with me since I knew you and I couldn't go together."

"Oh," I said. I was sad and hurt that he'd taken it upon himself to use the tickets without asking for my input about what to do with them, since we'd bought them together. Such was our connection with one another that he saw this thought cross my face and responded to it before I could say anything.

"I saw on my call display that you had called and figured that was what it was about, but I couldn't face calling you back to talk about it. So I just went ahead and invited Karen." He was excusing himself but I didn't find his explanation comforting. He continued, "You were VERY angry that you weren't there with me."

"What?"

"You were VERY angry that I went to the concert without you. I felt your energy hitting me the entire night. Karen saw it. I was in agony the whole time. My head hurt for two days after. You were furious."

"But . . . I didn't even know when the concert was," I said. "I thought it was next weekend or the one after."

"Doesn't matter." He was clipped and impatient, as though speaking to a disobedient dog. "Your energy hit me all night long, to the point where Karen and I left the concert early because I couldn't take it any more."

I was paralyzed; the depth of his contempt for me was so unfamiliar and so unlike what our relationship had been before that I was having trouble catching up to reality. Plus, even in my mind-controlled state, his logic did not seem sound to me.

"I . . . I . . . Michael, I don't know what to say. I thought the concert was still to come. I had forgotten the date and didn't have it written down but I thought it was next weekend at the earliest." He continued to glower at me. "How could I have hit you if I didn't even know the concert was happening?"

"I don't know," he said, clearly exasperated with me. "I don't know how these things work. All I know is that I was in agony that night and that Karen witnessed it and that it must have been you hitting me because the tickets were originally ours."

I stared at him, still paralyzed and goggle-eyed; his circular logic was spinning me and I did not have the mental wherewithal to joust with him. I flapped my hands slightly, exasperated, and then walked away, giving up. Even as a trained cult member, I found what he was saying completely illogical. It was a classic double bind; he didn't know "how these things worked" but at the same time he was certain that whatever he was experiencing was my fault.

I HAD HAD A VERY small taste of what being shunned felt like in 1994 when I was asked to move out of Limori's house. That experience was small potatoes compared to what I went through in early 2000. Bereft of my romantic relationship, I naturally turned to my friends in the group for solace and comfort, but much to my dismay, found myself rebuffed.

Karen was the most effective at ensuring that I felt like a black sheep. She was sympathetic with me, although cautious in her sympathy, when I first spoke to her after returning from Wolf's Den. On January fifth, she had coffee with Michael and after that my relationship with her was over, although I wasn't able to acknowledge this for quite some time. Whatever Michael told her, whatever spiritual reasons he gave for needing to break up with me, they scared Karen enough that she could barely look at me from then on.

Amber and Debbie were slightly less obvious with their shunning behaviour. They continued to be able to spend time with me, although I was relegated to hanging around the edges like an invisible person in the room. I had become someone not to be too attached to or to let down their guard with, because who knew what negative energy I would then attach to them.

I could feel all this happening at the time but I refused to face it; it was too much to cope with all at once. I acted as though I couldn't tell that my friends were afraid of my energy and I pretended that I was unaware that they would rather not be around me.

THE BITTERSWEET AGONY of seeing Michael at Wednesday and Thursday nights didn't last long. In mid-February, a message was relayed from Michael to the group via Karen that he was in seclusion and would not be coming to the meetings for the foreseeable future. Until this occasion, seclusion was something that only Limori herself had participated in. Every once in a while, when she was still living in the city and leading both Wednesday and Thursday nights, she would stop coming for a few weeks and we would be told she was in seclusion. This meant that God had requested that she spend her days meditating and doing spiritual work and not receive guests or take phone calls. However, during these times she would always have Alice at her side and one or two other minions serving her.

In Michael's case, though, seclusion would be taken to an extreme. He lived alone and worked almost alone. His friends now consisted of those in the meditation group, except for me, plus his business partners. I realized that he would be, in effect, alone almost all the time, day and night, weekday and weekend. My heart and body ached in sympathy for him. I was suffering acutely from the abrupt loss of his companionship and of our relationship, but I still (temporarily) had the solace of spending time (albeit strained) with Debbie and Amber. I also had two loyal and loving friends unconnected to Limori's group, whom I was leaning on for comfort and companionship. Michael would have none of this. It was yet another test of his loyalty to Limori and once again he seemed to be willing to do anything that she asked of him.

I don't know how he survived this time. To this day when I think of the amount of pain we were both in, and on top of that his almost solitary confinement, I wonder how he did not go completely crazy.

As early as January 4, 2000, my authentic self was rearing its head and trying to get my attention. I was so desperate to fix whatever was wrong with me that I spent the night of January 3 lying awake for most of the night, wondering if I should sell all my belongings and my car, close my business and move to Wolf's Den "to learn and become clear." But by morning I had rejected this idea and wrote in my journal, "There is more than one way to serve God." This thought was unprecedented, and I would not voice it out loud to anyone in the group for months. But, like crocuses in the spring, it was a sign of change and the blossoming to come. A few paragraphs later I wrote, "I still believe in Limori and all that she stands for. I believe she and those with her serve God," so I still had quite a way to go before I began to think for myself. But the seeds were there, struggling through the fertilizer toward the sun.

Each day crawled by, more agonizing than that last. My thought-reformed brain swirled away like a dog chasing its tail, trying to find the elusive Truth but only getting more tangled up and confused. This was my first experience with grief and so not only was it uncomfortable and unrelenting, I had no skills or even the slightest awareness of how to comfort or be patient with myself. And, of course, since Limori had taught us that emotions are pure ego, I heaped guilt upon myself for feeling anything about what was going on. I honestly believed that I should happily and with a willing heart just accept what God had instructed Michael and me to do and not moan about the love I had lost or being rejected by my peers and friends. I expected myself to feel nothing and yet I was feeling more than I ever thought possible. I felt like I was walking around without skin; the slightest unexpected noise or loud voice would slam into me and cause me physical pain. (For close to three years I couldn't listen to music. Even a quiet symphonic piece would tear at me like razor blades.) Days went by when all I could manage to eat was a banana. In less than two weeks I lost twelve pounds. I woke up every day between 4:00 and 5:00 a.m. Each day, I'd spend that half-second between sleeping and waking in blissful ignorance about my life, but then everything that was happening would come rushing back. It was like reliving the whole thing over again each morning in the winter darkness. I would try to get back to sleep each day, but would just lie on my back, desperately sad, incredibly lonely and utterly lost.

I had spoken to my mum a couple of times since returning from Wolf's Den and explained what was going on. She was furious with Limori and Michael, which made me feel even more loyal to them, but more than that she was worried about me. I must have sounded worse as the days went by, because by the third week in January she said, "Sweetie, you need help. I think you should go and talk to a counsellor."

It was a testament to my desperation that I immediately agreed. Under normal circumstances, therapy would have been looked upon by those of us in Limori's group as something akin to quackery. Why would any one of us seek therapy from a mere mortal when we had access to The Truth from God via Limori? But I was on an emotional precipice that was frightening me. My emotional state was so fragile that on top of everything else I was terrified of how unglued I felt. The feeling that I'd noticed in the airport while leaving Wolf's Den, of being a hair's breadth away from shattering into ten million pieces, stayed with me, lived with me at almost every moment. It was like a demon breathing on the back of my neck all the time. I woke up with it and carried it around with me all day and the short hours of sleep that I could snatch were the only respite from it. So when

Mum suggested professional help I leapt at the idea. I hung up the phone after talking with her and immediately dialled a career counsellor I knew, to ask if she could recommend a therapist.

She was actually at her desk when the phone rang. "Certainly," she said. "What kind of help are you looking for?"

I wasn't sure what she meant, so I launched into a brief explanation of what was going on but immediately dissolved into tears that threatened to escalate into uncontrolled sobbing if I continued.

She kindly interrupted me, "So, someone for personal work?"

Sob, sniff, shuddering breath. "Uh, yes, I guess so," I spluttered.

She gave me the names of two people she knew of and I thanked her. I hung up and immediately dialled the first number and left a message asking for an appointment. Not too much later the therapist called back and we booked one. When we'd chosen a time and date I asked her where her office was located. She gave me the address and suite number and explained that the building was close to Oak Street and Broadway. "That address seems familiar to me," I thought. As soon as I hung up I realized why; her office was in the same building as Michael's. God does have a great sense of humour.

HER NAME WAS Mary and without hyperbole I can say that she helped saved my life.

I didn't know what to expect from therapy, having never been shrunk before. Mary herself was an impressive figure. As she came across the waiting room floor to greet me, my immediate impression was one of elegance. She was not dressed in an overly fancy or formal way, but her bearing and movements were refined, patient and calm. Exactly what I needed. She was tall and slender and had a pretty face topped with a mop of medium-length grey hair, and I guessed that she was in her early to mid-sixties.

When we sat down in her office she asked me to explain why I was there and I embarrassed myself by immediately bursting into tears, and as I told my story my weeping only got worse. It is incredibly difficult to sound coherent when you're sobbing so I was fighting a losing battle to regain control of myself while giving her the gist of what was going on.

"Breathe," she reminded me gently a couple of times during my narrative.

I think that for most of that session she made enquiries about my past and what was going on now with Michael and the group, but I can't say for sure because I was so emotionally overwrought that mostly I just remember sobbing. At the end of the session we booked another appointment for a couple of weeks out and I left feeling that I had an ally, even if she was a virtual stranger, and that I had a safe place and a safe person to hold onto. I had been buffetted with so many emotions and contradictory thoughts for the couple of weeks since the break-up that I felt like I was drowning most of the time. The calmness and support I felt from Mary were a welcome respite from the tornado in my head and body.

We met a couple more times in the following few weeks and then, at the end of one session, she gently suggested that I might want to come in to see her every week (instead of every other week) because of the intensity of what I was going through. I agreed even although I was in a precarious place financially; my personal assistant business was less than a year old and I was deeply in debt and seemed to be sliding further that way with each passing month. I had a few steady clients and was gaining more all the time, but building the business had been financially challenging even before my life went to hell and was now proving to be even more so. For the next year or so I would use a line of credit to finance my visits to Mary, which drove the financially responsible part of my brain completely berserk, but in hindsight it was the best money I ever spent.

Interestingly, not once, not ever, did Mary use the word *cult* in my presence. I don't know how soon she realized that I was in a thought-reform situation, but at some point it must have become obvious to a professional familiar with the darker sides of human nature. Yet she never, ever, attempted to influence my decision-making process with her opinion of what was going on. She simply listened and mirrored to me some of what I was feeling and asked gentle but important questions that required me to reflect on what I was really feeling, rather than on what I felt I was supposed to be feeling. It is a testament to her skill as a therapist and her nature as a human being that I gradually felt safe enough to begin to think and voice things that would have been considered heresy in the group's eyes. I remember that my feelings gradually progressed from fear of even thinking about the things that were coming up for me, to tentative acceptance that yes, I was actually thinking something that Limori would disapprove of, to a tremulous willingness to share those thoughts with Mary, to eventual feelings of rebellion.

Eventually, after voicing something like "I do feel sad that Limori made Michael break up with me. It doesn't seem right somehow," I started to think "HA! I thought that thought and even said it out loud and the world didn't explode." And then I'd wonder, "What does that mean? How can that be, when Limori, whom I trust, told me that the consequence of thoughts like that would be deadly?" Over time, as I acquired more and more references to instances in which I was able to feel my feelings and think my thoughts and there were no biblical repercussions (no plagues descended, no earthquakes swallowed the city whole, I didn't feel in the grip of a devilish possession), my curiosity naturally grew.

Mary's kind and gentle questions only reinforced this growing sense of safety in my own thoughts and feelings. "How does that feel to you?" she would ask, or, "What do you think is true?" For the first few months I would answer her with group rhetoric but then gradually I began to see her point, and I would travel inside, briefly and tentatively at first, and check with myself: "How do I feel?" Initially I had not the first clue about how I felt about anything, but with practice my confidence in naming my feelings began to grow.

The only time we ever strayed close to using the word *cult* was many months into my work with her, when she loaned me a copy of a book called *The Guru Papers: Masks of Authoritarian Power*. I was more than slightly confused about why she was loaning me this particular book, but I trusted her and took it home with me that night and began to read it. I was absolutely staggered by the time I got to the end of the first chapter; it was as though the authors of this book had been flies on the wall at all of Limori's workshops and all of our Wednesday and Thursday night meditation circles. Some of the phrases that the authors used, as examples of ones that manipulative, coercive gurus use, were almost, word for word, things that Limori would say to us. I would be reading the book on my couch and have to put it down in my lap, simply to marvel at the information I was absorbing; it was all hitting so close to home. I returned the book to Mary at our next appointment, sharing with her how much I related to the material, and very soon went out and bought my own copy. Then I read it through again, this time using a pink highlighter to mark everything that rang true for me. After that I sat at my computer and typed up a document of everything I'd highlighted so that I could take it in to Mary and show her all the parallels between the what the authors were saying and what I'd experienced.

But here's one of the utterly fascinating features of thought reform and the journey of recovery from it: even after having read the book twice and recording the parts of it that were telling my story exactly, I still did not use the words *guru* or *cult* in reference to Limori or my experience, and I would have been horrified and defensive if anyone else had. A disciple's fierce loyalty to her guru outlives her participation in the group. Although I would soon permanently say goodbye to Limori's meditation group, I wouldn't be able to bring myself to use the "c word" in reference to it for several more years to come.

THE DAYLIGHT HOURS began to lengthen as winter turned to spring and then summer. The brightest spot in each week was my appointment with Mary; the rest of the time was an ongoing exercise in the humility of grief and loss and personal Armageddon. One of my personal low points came about midway through the year. I was working at a downtown management-consulting firm. I went into their office once or twice a week to provide backup administrative support, doing things like database entry or covering the switchboard at lunch. I was sitting in a back office one afternoon at a computer and while I worked I kept silently saying to myself, "Okay, you got through that moment; now you can get through the next one." I'd take a cleansing breath in through my nose and let it out through my mouth and then say to myself again, "Okay, you got through that moment; now you can get through the next one." I was in so much pain that it took this kind of conscious effort simply to navigate the territory from one moment to the next.

I was losing everything that had meant anything to me. I had lost Michael, someone I had loved for my whole adult life to that point. I had lost any sense of right and wrong – what I was going through felt incredibly wrong, but I was being told by the people I still believed in that it was the best thing for me. I had lost my spiritual community and spiritual home because everyone in the group was treating me as though I didn't exist. My faith in and understanding of God, which meant so much to me, was breaking down. I had no sense of self to rely on and no solid personal foundation upon which I could rest. I was sleep deprived and probably nutritionally deficient because I could hardly eat. And I was very, very lonely. My closest friends from the group were acting as though I was an unwelcome and personal-hygiene-challenged guest whenever they saw me and although I had successfully avoided acknowledging this to myself earlier in the year, now it was so obvious and awkward that I was beginning to have to face it.

Breathe in. Breathe out. Okay, now do that again.

MY RELATIONSHIP with my mother had remained intact after she left Limori's group back in 1992, although it was somewhat strained at times given some of the beliefs I had about "us versus them." These beliefs tainted my estimation of my mother's value; she had, I thought at the time, turned her back on God. Also, I had been required to keep many secrets from her, including the one about the Mistress Period, which did nothing to nurture the intimacy between us. From her side of the relationship, she says that it was difficult to observe me being so tied into the group and she worried, knowing that if I did leave I would lose nearly everyone I knew and loved.

When I did leave she became an integral part of the support that I needed. I called her nearly every day for a couple of years and cried into the phone. To her credit, she did exactly what I needed at the time, which was simply to listen. She was also able to provide a unique perspective on the situation because she knew Limori's practices and teachings intimately. She reassured me that I was not the evil and negative person I was accused of being by the group, but it would take me quite a while to believe her.

I felt blessed and infinitely grateful to have my mother to turn to at this most difficult time in my life. I was so alone, but my mother was always as close as the nearest telephone.

. . .

THE WORST THING that had ever happened to me was being inflicted upon me by the people I trusted most in the world. This was a paradox I could not reconcile within myself. I kept trying to understand how we could use words like *love* and *truth* and yet not act in a loving way or tell the truth.

I was gradually, with Mary's help, learning to separate what I had been taught by Limori from what I tentatively believed to be true in the depths of myself. It was, as I've said, an unfamiliar process to me to think something or feel something and then test inside myself whether or not I believed it to be true. My compass had been firmly outside myself until now and bringing it inside was like learning any new skill; it took time and patience and I failed quite a bit at the beginning, but eventually began to get the hang of it.

By the fall of 2000, nine months after Limori ended my relationship with Michael, I had learned enough about myself and about giving myself permission to feel that I realized how uncomfortable I was at the Wednesday and Thursday night meditation meetings. I was being treated like an outsider, and I felt like one as well. I also felt that I was being insincere and hypocritical by continuing to go to the group meetings because I was beginning to recognize that my feelings were out of alignment with the group beliefs. I was starting to disagree with the group ideology as a whole. This was incredibly dangerous territory for me and I didn't discuss it with anyone in the group. I felt frightened by my thoughts of disagreement with Limori's teaching, but I also felt that continuing to believe them was intolerable. It had stopped making sense to me that we talked about love and truth and yet contradicted those values over and over again. And it was beginning to infuriate me that we used God's name to do it. For several weeks (which really isn't that long at all, but at the time it felt like forever) I waffled in this No Man's Land, not sure of anything. The most dominant part of myself believed that I would be betraying God by questioning Limori and her group philosophy. What if all that she said was really true? What if it WAS what God wanted? What if Limori's behaviour, which I experienced as controlling and abusive, was actually the way to learn? I turned these questions and others over and over in my head until I was dizzy. As I said earlier, I was not yet examining whether or not the group was a cult; it had not yet occurred to me to use that word or apply it to our situation. I was simply wrestling with whether or not I believed any longer in what Limori had told us was The Truth. And with the question of whether or not leaving the group meant leaving God.

What I couldn't know at the time was that I was bumping into the internal conflict caused by the final criteria in Dr. Robert Lifton's eight for thought reform: the dispensing of existence. "Since the group has an absolute or totalist vision of truth, those who are not in the group are bound up in evil, are not enlightened, are not saved and do not have the right to exist. If one leaves the group, one leaves God."[2] This is what I was desperately afraid of.

By one Saturday in mid-October, 2000, I had grown tired of these questions and their endless loop in my head. I sat down in my mediation chair after lunch and told myself that I had to decide one way or the other. I was extremely uncomfortable with the uncertainty that I'd been living with for these past months and wanted to step over to one side of the fence or the other.

I closed my eyes and took a few centring breaths and tried as best I could to feel calm. I was shaking with fear from the inside out; my hands and arms trembled. I was questioning the one sacred premise that Limori had taught us in so many ways never to question. "Is Limori doing God's work or not?" I asked myself. "What do I believe?" I sat there, quiet and afraid, and after a few minutes realized that for me, the bottom line was this: What I believe in, at the deepest parts of myself, are love and compassion. It seems to me that Limori is teaching us to act without those two values, though she talks about them. If she IS representing God on Earth, then that means that God does not value love and compassion. I am beginning to recognize that I value these things enough that I cannot operate without them. Limori's values and my values are not lining up, and I don't think I can be a hypocrite and continue to follow her while that is going on.

I took another deep breath and faced the most terrifying aspect of this conundrum: That means that I am willing to choose love and compassion over Limori's god. If she turns out to be right, and I am turning my back on actual God, then so be it. I can't live without love and compassion any longer.

I'm paraphrasing, of course, as I recount this moment. It was as much felt as thought. I honestly believed at the time that I was turning my back on God, but the pressure from within myself to resolve the contradictions I was beginning to perceive in Limori's teaching was strong enough to make me willing to try and resolve my conflict. When this moment was over and I knew I had come to what was for me the centre of the matter, I opened my eyes and took another huge breath— and actually felt lighter. A few tears of relief trickled down my face and slowly my hands stopped trembling and my body began to relax slightly in the chair. I was still afraid, because now I was living without the doctrine I had held so dear for so long, but it was a different kind of fear. It was the fear of the unknown, rather than the fear that had been created because another human being was in control of my life.

For the first time in a very long time I was free.

PART III

IT AIN'T PRETTY BUT IT'S REAL

Although the world is full of suffering, it is also full of the overcoming of it.
—Helen Keller

The long road of recovery

After having made my decision to leave Limori's cult, I shared my decision with the group at our next meeting and was met with the indifference that I'd suspected I would receive. I was, after all, an outcast at that point; the fact that I dared to speak out loud to the group was the most energy-charged moment of that evening. Michael was not there, because Limori still had him in seclusion, and we had not seen Limori herself at a Wednesday night for years, so it was just to nine or ten of my peers that I made a short speech about needing some time to figure things out and not coming to the meetings for the foreseeable future. I think we all knew I would never be back. With the exception of Debbie and Amber, I never heard from anyone in the group again, including Karen, with whom I had been very close. I tried to stay friends with Debbie and Amber but I was flogging a dead horse. They were afraid to be near me for fear of catchng my negative energy and although I put on a happy face I found that it was difficult to be with them as well, now that our beliefs about what was right and true were diverging.

One night a couple of months later, I exited my neighbourhood movie theatre after seeing a seven o'clock show, and as I walked past the line-up of people waiting for the nine o'clock show, I spotted Debbie, Amber and Karen, waiting together to be let into the theatre. I stopped briefly to say hello and they asked how the movie was. Floating around all of us like a bad smell was the unspoken recognition that this chance meeting signalled that my relationships with them were over. In the past I would have been part of their group, waiting to see the movie. Now I was there alone and they were together. That was the moment I knew I had finally lost virtually everything and everyone who had ever mattered to me.

I had never imagined that one body could contain such grief and loneliness. I had lost so much that made me who I was: beliefs, the security that comes with belief, and people, including myself. I had no idea who I was or what mattered to me. Without the structure of the cult dogma, I had no tools with which to navigate life. What was the truth about life? What did I believe to be true about God or myself or peanut butter sandwiches? I had no idea. To have my values and understanding about how life worked stripped away, on top of losing my entire community of friends, was like living without skin.

I worked each day for the clients in my personal assistant business and on evenings and weekends I went through the motions of buying groceries and doing laundry while I tried to keep a firm grip on the very few threads of sanity and normalcy I had left. But there was no me at the centre of me. I was building that person up from scratch and it was damn hard work. Luckily I had the support of my therapist, Mary, and, as I've said before, my session with her was the highlight of each week. I continued seeing her for years and when she closed her practice I moved on to working with another therapist she recommended.

I grieved the loss of my dear Michael, shocked that the sun had the audacity to rise each morning when my life felt like it was finished. Because his office was in the same building as Mary's, Michael and I would occasionally bump into each other as I was going into the building for an appointment and he was coming out to go home. The unexplainable, mystical connection between us continued; I would wake up some mornings and my first conscious thought would be that this was a day I would see

Michael. Even if it wasn't one of my therapy days, my body was always able to predict with unerring accuracy when I would see or hear from him and, sure enough, in a few hours, I'd bump into him at Granville Island or I'd drive by him standing on a street corner or I'd receive a voice mail message from him wishing me a happy Christmas. It was both eerie and gratifying to know that the connection between us still existed even though we'd been forced apart. It also added to my heartbreak and made my frustration about what was happening almost unbearable. I railed mightily against circumstances that seemed so unfair and unjust. Love is so precious and difficult to find, and it seemed such a profound waste for Limori to insist that Michael toss this love away as though it meant nothing.

TIME ALONE HEALS NOTHING. Let's be clear about that right up front. Walking away from any sort of traumatic experience, including being in a cult, and pretending that it didn't happen will leave your wounds festering and weeping forever. I'm being purposefully as graphic and as blunt as possible to emphasize that healing is work and we have to work at it, and that if we don't, no matter how many years pass, it will be as if the trauma happened yesterday.

If you have been in a cult, I am not too proud to get on my knees and beg you to get professional help and to work at your healing so that the rest of your life can be lived as freely as your spirit intended. Preferably, you will find help with someone who is familiar with how cults work, but failing that, almost any skilled and compassionate professional counsellor will be able to assist you. I bumped into someone once whom I knew from Limori's cult, who had left the group but done no healing work. I could almost see the damage to this person's soul and heart, it was so close to the surface. I could tell that just seeing me triggered this person and brought memories and pain rushing back to the surface, like a cork in a bathtub. Dr. Phil (love him or hate him, he uses great imagery to get his points across) talks about unhealed wounds being like a beach ball that you are desperately trying to keep under water. As you sit on that beach ball in the ocean of your life, keeping it pushed down below the surface takes tremendous energy. And if you tip even slightly off balance that ball will bob to the surface with no effort on its part at all.

If you were in a cult, don't waste another ounce of energy trying to keep that beach ball submerged. By getting professional help with your wounds, you will be taking back your life from the guru who stole it. By not getting help, you are simply gifting your abuser with even more months and years of your precious life. Your abuser does not deserve such a precious gift.

As I've mentioned earlier, I didn't begin to use the word *cult* in reference to Limori's group until several years of my recovery had gone by. In late 2003, I felt psychologically strong enough for the first time to consider that the group wasn't simply dysfunctional but fell into the category of coercive mind control. I pulled my copy of *The Guru Papers* off my bookshelf and read it for the third time. During this reading the pieces began to fall into place for me, and I began to be able to apply words like *cult* and *thought reform* to my situation. Until then it had been unimaginable and far too painful to consider that this was the truth. I then began what I would later recognize as part of my personal method of healing: gathering information about how cults work and why I had been vulnerable to one. Finding understanding was one of the primary ways I found solace and healing. I began reading as many books about the phenomenon as I could get my hands on and, more often than not, when I found a particularly informative book I would read it two or three times while my brain slowly wrapped itself around what I was learning.

It was more than a little unsettling to recognize myself and my experience in the pages of books written about cults, and I found that my ability to process what I was learning would come in waves. For a few weeks or a couple of months, I'd be gripped with curiosity and read books borrowed from the library or bought locally and surf the internet for additional information and articles. Then I would need a break and stop reading for months at a time, allowing what I'd learned to integrate, until I felt curiosity and the need for greater understanding overtake me again. With each new wave of exploratory energy, I found that my understanding deepened and my comfort about addressing what had happened to me increased. And, of course, as all this was going on I moved through layers of feelings about what had happened to me and to those I loved: anger, frustration, sorrow, rage, loss, grief, relief and guilt about being free.

Unlike a snake that sheds its old skin all in one go, recovering from being in a cult was, for me, a piecemeal experience. I had so much to learn and so much to heal from that I could only face the task one small step at a time, although I made absolutely sure that I left no feeling unexamined. I knew, instinctively, that the only way to heal from this experience was to bring it out into the light and look at it as clearly as possible. If I buried it, if I sealed it up in a box and pretended it wasn't there in my heart every day, I would only be awarding Limori even more years of my life, and she had already stolen too much. I wasn't prepared to give her one more second.

I needed primarily to learn to trust myself again. I had lost every bit of faith or trust I had in myself; after all, I'd believed to the very tips of my toes that Limori spoke for God and that everything she said was true. Yet I was waking up to the fact that I'd been completely wrong about that; this awareness was incredibly painful. How could I ever trust anyone or anything again? How could I ever know what was true about life and what was not, if I'd been so profoundly wrong about this? The feeling that I'd lost my ability to trust myself filled me with such sorrow that I almost couldn't stand the weight of it inside my chest every day. I had been used to turning outside myself for answers. Now I needed to turn inward, but there was nothing there. I was utterly and completely lost. I had a body and a brain but no self. It was terrifying and, no matter how much ice cream I ate, I couldn't make the feeling go away. I have never, before or since, known a feeling of such helplessness, fear and loss. It was almost intolerable.

And yet, as these things so often are, it was also my salvation. That yawning gulf where my self should have been was an empty plot of land patiently waiting for me to build a new foundation. And so, brick by brick, over the years that followed, I slowly, slowly built myself a new me. I began tentatively, exploring my beliefs about easy topics like my hairstyle or movies I liked to watch. I noticed the rigidity I felt about the ways I believed other people should live their lives and questioned myself about this. I thought about gardening and Brussels sprouts and wearing dresses and wondered if I liked them because I liked them or because Limori had said I should. With each day, there were new experiences available to me to try out my new internal compass on. I was awkward, like a new foal learning to walk, wobbly and unsure of myself. But I got my legs underneath me eventually and after several years was even able to laugh again.

As I said in part 2, I tried to approach the experience of leaving the cult as though it was an opportunity. I refused to allow ten years in a cult to ruin the rest of my life and deliberately made the choice to concentrate on how I could use the experience of loss and personal ruin to my best advantage to achieve the things I wanted to achieve—becoming more peaceful, more authentic, more confident. I committed myself in every way to my recovery. I tried very hard to make lemonade out of the lemons I'd been handed and I am happy to report that the person I am now is the person I'd often hoped I could be. I would not have achieved this had I not had the experience of leaving the cult. As the Buddhists say, the lotus flower grows in the mud.

CENTRAL TO ALL THIS DRAMA, of course, was my relationship with God. Suffice it to say that rebuilding that relationship was challenging then and continues to be now. I felt deeply betrayed by God immediately after leaving the cult, and it took me a long time to work through those feelings. At the time, it felt like there was nowhere in the universe that I could turn for help. In the early days of my recovery I was not available to me and I could not trust that God was there for me either. I was utterly alone. But, once again, my determination to feel at peace guided me to keep working at healing myself and my relationship with the divine. Leaving the cult was a faith-rebuilding exercise of the greatest magnitude and, as ever, in hindsight, I am grateful that it happened and that I had the opportunity to find out what really mattered to me spiritually.

Eventually, I also had to learn to feel safe to reawaken my need to have a spiritual community in my life. I thought for a few years that having my own personal relationship with God would be enough, but as I healed, the need for spiritual community grew in me and I felt a deep void in my soul without it. This topic of spiritual community, almost more than any other, is fraught with danger, given what I experienced at Limori's hands. One of the first feelings that came up for me when I considered finding a new spiritual community was fear about what I would do if I ever lost the community – if I ever decided I had to leave or if the community fell apart or took a direction I was not comfortable with. This fear, of course, comes from the memory of the tremendous loss I experienced when I left Limori's community. So I cautiously and carefully make my way through this emotional minefield one step, one feeling, one experience at a time. I have learned to be gentle with myself during these sorts of explorations and not to expect myself to find solutions or healing or answers overnight. I trust myself and my process now and know that everything will unfold as it should. I allow myself to feel my feelings and to trust that what I'm feeling is true and acceptable, even if it's uncomfortable. I have tried on several spiritual communities for size and fit and was disappointed to find that they were not right for me. But I continue the quest, because the need feels so great, and because I know that I am healing more of the wounded places within me by doing so.

Despite all the healing work I did after leaving the group, or perhaps because of it, I find myself more than a little empathetic whenever I meet someone who is grieving or bump into grief myself again. For the three years after I left the group, I lived every day, every moment, in such a cavern of despair and loss and grief and loneliness that it's as though that experience has imbedded itself in each cell of my body. If someone I know is grieving I feel myself return to that place and it's as though my heart is being pulled out of my chest, right through my sternum. Even if it's someone on the *Oprah* show, who is talking honestly and with heartfelt sincerity about what grief feels like, a part of my self wakes up and remembers. Remembers the way there were more colours in the spectrum and too much light. The way music and loud voices and car alarms that were blocks away physically hurt me. The way time slowed. The way I could sit on my couch and stare out a window, seeing nothing, for hours. The way that I was eventually softened and made aware of the true meanings of compassion and love.

I don't know if this response to my own and others' grief will ever go away. I'm not sure I want it to. It reminds me that I am human and therefore vulnerable and that life can be hard, messy and painful and that the search for perfection is vastly overrated and that what matters far more is the constant need to connect. With myself, with others and with life.

The reason I use the phrase "the long road *of* recovery" rather than "the long road *to* recovery" in this section of my book and as its subtitle is that I have finally figured out that recovery is indeed, as the cliché says, a journey and not a destination. The experience of being in Limori's cult will always be with me, in large ways and small. It changed me and, as I move away from the experience, it continues to change me. I work diligently on my healing because I refuse to let one more second of my life be hijacked by someone with less than pure motives.

Reflections about my guru

The name of Limori's cult is not one you would recognize. That's the question I get asked most often: "What was the name of the group you were involved with?" I suppose people expect that a group needs to be large and well known, like the Moonies or Heaven's Gate, in order to qualify as a cult. But ours was simply a small group of people who wanted to learn to meditate and who each, in their own way, had the mix of personal characteristics that was necessary to make them vulnerable to someone who was willing and able to seduce, manipulate and coerce them.

One of the questions I had during my recovery was, "How did Limori know how to use and apply the exact mix of criteria that turned us into mind-controlled zombies?" I'm assuming she didn't ever go to guru school. The short answer came back from those cult professionals that I consulted: people do what works. Cult leaders are often masterful at reading other people. What looked like psychic ability in Limori was, I suspect, a potent mix of some small bit of intuition mixed with a powerful talent for reading and understanding her followers' body language, facial expressions, words and deeds to know what our fears, desires, motivations and levers were.

Looking back, it's so easy to see how she moved us all around like pawns on a chessboard. At the time, it all seemed so mystical and magical and special, but now, with the benefit of ten years of hindsight, I can see that so much of what she did was motivated by her need to control us and tie us ever closer to her.

Limori was the centre of my world for so long, but at the same time she was also something of an enigma. To describe it as giving my life away to someone I barely knew seems absurd now, but that's exactly what happened. By the time I met Limori she wasn't as much a person as a persona (not that I could have made this distinction at the time). When she was in the room the only topics available for discussion were God and the spiritual workings of the universe. We were discouraged from making small talk in her presence, because it was considered inane and unimportant in the context of saving the universe from the forces of darkness. To interject into that atmosphere a question about Limori's family history or friends, so that I could get to know her better, would have felt ridiculous, and it wasn't until I began writing this book that I realized how very little I actually knew about our illustrious leader. I never asked Limori how she came to be a psychic working in Vancouver or who her friends were before she became our leader. She didn't reveal much about herself or her past, unless a story could be offered in the context of her path to becoming God's right hand. Upon reflection, I can see that chatting about who she was and what her past looked like and what her dreams might have been before we met her would have brought her down to our level, and that was something she would have wanted to avoid. What she needed us to believe about her was that she was omniscient; sharing details of her childhood or non-spiritual experiences from her adult life would have dulled the lustre of the image she was constructing for us.

There's nothing more dangerous than a little bit of the truth

Some of what Limori said was admirable and true. I think this was the most dangerous thing about her (and possibly about other gurus – I am grateful that my experience extends to only one). "Learn to meditate – it's good for you." "Be in your heart – try not to judge people." These things are true and noble and right no matter who says them. The fact that my heart and mind and body resonated with the truth of some of what Limori said made it difficult for someone as young and confused as I was to separate the wheat from the chaff. I don't know if that's everyone's experience of their involvement with a cult, but it was mine. Unfortunately, in order to follow someone like Limori one is not allowed to choose which pieces of the dogma to believe and which parts to dismiss; it's an all-or-nothing deal. You're either with us or against us. The parts of her doctrine and teaching that were true made me want the rest of what she said to be true as well.

As I said in Chapter 1, it was my spiritual yearning and a desperation to find meaning in my life that led me to Limori. I now believe that spiritual yearning is so common in human beings that it is one of the primary reasons cults exist. We are all part of the divine; we were all created by the great creator, be that an old man on a throne of clouds with a flowing white beard or the universal force that quantum physics is getting close to being able to explain. Whatever it is, we are part of something, of that I am convinced, but our humanness, our bodies, which make us feel individual, and our thoughts, which separate us from each other, deceive us into believing that we are separate and different from the divine, the universe, God, the Force, call it what you will. But somewhere inside each of us our instinct knows this is not true. We are not separate. And so, most often without consciously realizing it, we look for ways to close that gap, to experience connectedness. I believe that this is one of the reasons that people can become vulnerable to cults.

The little bits of actual truth that Limori spoke convinced me that the rest of what she had to say was the truth. My desire to belong and my need to feel connected to God made me selectively ignore the parts of Limori's message that did not ring purely with the truth. When Limori told me she could hear God talking to her, I grabbed onto that idea like it was a winning lottery ticket and I hung on, even though she dragged me through hell.

Money

The guru–follower relationship is a symbiotic one. I needed Limori to provide me with a sense of self and a sense of purpose. She gave meaning to my life. And she needed those who followed her to provide her with the twin possessions of power and money. I've spent the first section of this book talking about the power she had over us, but very little time talking about money. I think it's important to touch on that now. Limori's group of disciples was eventually able to provide her with a lavish and luxurious lifestyle. As I've said, when I first met her she was earning a small living providing psychic readings out of her home. But gradually, as the years went by, she was able to wring a significantly more extravagant living out of those of us who provided for her.

Her first major acquisition was the property of Wolf's Den. A few years after she and Matthew were legally married, the group was sitting in a Thursday night meditation circle talking. As ever, Limori was sitting at the top of the circle, and Matthew was there on her right-hand side. While she talked to us she had her right hand on Matthew's left knee, in the fairly common gesture of partnership and affection that she'd adopted. Out of nowhere, Limori looked at Matthew and said, "God says the title for Wolf's Den should come to me."

Other than candy, the greatest love in Matthew's life was Wolf's Den. He was an unflappable, quiet, jolly sort of man; like Santa Claus without the beard. He never spoke ill of anyone and never raised his voice to anyone. I never saw him angry; only content, amused and pleasant. (Although he did have an annoying habit of laughing at people who were in pain.) He tended to sit and observe on Wednesday and Thursday nights, and the rest of the time let everything simply slide over him. He questioned nothing that Limori did, which I suppose was some of his appeal to her. For several years, including the ill-fated months that I lived with Matthew and Limori, he worked for a local cable company in the Vancouver area. But his one dream, the only thing he wanted out of life, was to leave the city and move up to his beloved property at Wolf's Den, which he had inherited from his father. He complained weekly to Limori when I lived at the house that he wanted to do this. She would assure him that the time would come and eventually it did. After that, every time I saw him at Wolf's Den he was like a kid in a candy store. Limori was master and commander at Wolf's Den, but Matthew exuded the vibe of a grizzly bear protecting his territory. He didn't have to say anything or do anything to prove this; he was king of that particular piece of forest. In his quiet way, the pleasure and joy that he felt about every moment he spent living in the small piece of wilderness he and his father had carved out was readily apparent.

As sometimes happened, large, ultimately shocking and/or hurtful, pronouncements were often introduced apropos of nothing, like the one Limori made about Matthew transferring the title of Wolf's Den over to her. She would interject them into unrelated conversation and then not refer to the subject again for days or weeks. This type of technique did give me the impression that it was God speaking through her. She would just pop out minor, or sometimes major, changes that people needed to make in their lives and then let the topic go, while the person affected stewed about what was said. I have to assume that this was to allow the recipient of the news to adjust to what he/she was being told. In the Wolf's Den instance, Matthew said nothing, and in his calm and confident way seemed to take it all in stride. I never heard anything about the matter again myself and it wasn't until I began writing this book that I remembered this event and wondered what had ever happened about the title to Wolf's Den.

Limori is now the sole owner of Wolf's Den. Matthew's name is nowhere on the title. When I asked a friend experienced in this sort of thing to do a title search, I was not surprised at all when he discovered this. Matthew's beloved Wolf's Den is no longer legally his. I can see, in hindsight, that it was not much of a stretch for Limori to realize that if she wanted to build an empire she would need a place to put her throne. Wolf's Den must've fit the bill perfectly: remote enough that the practices there wouldn't cause too much fuss, yet a business location, offering lodging for fishermen and hikers and operating as a restaurant for the lodgers and the local community, which could and does bring in an income. Better yet, payroll doesn't cut into the revenue because the disciples at Wolf's Den work for free.

In order to appear extraordinary and deeply in God's favour, Limori cultivated an image of wealth and status. Her clothes have long been custom made by Susan. She wears jewelry that may not be the most expensive around, but is dramatic and eye catching, especially when paired with her wardrobe and charisma. The suite she had added for herself at Wolf's Den was eye-poppingly lavish the one time I saw it: elegant, dark wood furniture upholstered in white, white area rugs, porcelain vases decorating the mantels, floor-to-ceiling picture windows that looked out on the lake, Gayle's beautiful and arresting art hanging on the walls. When I walked through the door into the suite for the first and last time, it was as though I had been transported in a time machine to how I imagine an elegant hotel in 1920s Paris would look and feel. All this, in the middle of the Canadian wilderness.

And, as I've previously mentioned, Wolf's Den was not Limori's home year-round. She took to travelling extensively in the mid-1990s and then to staying for months at a time in Hawaii and Arizona. Each home she rented and occupied would be furnished and outfitted to the standard she was used to, i.e., to that befitting a queen. She travelled first class when she flew, partly because of her self-appointed status and partly because of her girth; she would be hard pressed to fit into a coach seat on an airplane.

So where did the money for all this lavish and expensive fluffery come from? Well, for starters she often used her charm to finagle fantastic deals on what she purchased from a storeowner or, even better, to get the storeowner to gift her the purchase outright. Limori always attributed these types of gifts to the fact that people recognized her as the right hand of God.

Second, she always carried quite a bit of debt in order to live her lifestyle. She complained frequently about the debt but always followed up with, "God will make sure that the bills get paid. I'm just doing what he tells me to do. I don't want to do all this travelling to Monte Carlo and Hawaii, but He insists, so I go."

And, as with most gurus, Limori's disciples played a large part in keeping her in the style to which she wanted to become accustomed. I was never flush with money during the time I knew Limori, so I was never subjected to much mandatory donating to her cause, except for chipping in for things like the Wolf's Den mortgage and the fees for workshops. But I have heard stories from others. For example, Gayle was coerced into giving Limori fifty thousand dollars, some of which was the widow's benefits she received when her husband died.

It is important to note that Limori always kept these types of financial transactions and gifts secret from those not directly involved. Money was one example of our social structure where the rules that applied to the group about always telling the truth did not apply to Limori herself. This always bothered me when I became aware through rumour or innuendo that someone had made a large donation to Limori's cause, although I was loath to acknowledge it at the time.

One of the hardest truths I have had to face in my recovery was that, financially, Limori lives off the backs of those who follow her. She lives a lifestyle of comfort while her disciples work tirelessly and for free. Acknowledging this added greatly to my feelings of betrayal.

Disciples

The images that we most often see of cults are of almost overwhelmingly large groups, and those that we see of gurus are of people who are successful at recruiting new members to add to the flock, which increases the guru's power and income.

I've often reflected on how ineffective Limori was at recruiting new members to her cult. For whatever reason, she was not the type of guru who was able to attract new members while simultaneously keeping a tight reign on those of us already indoctrinated. The Wednesday night group reached its peak numbers in the very early 1990s. When Sheila split off from the group, some of the faithful followed her. After that, the numbers in the group dwindled. The attendance at Thursday night was at its peak possibly fifteen people, but gradually Limori pushed a few of these faithful away or alienated them in some way, including Gary, Richard, Norman and his wife, Nelly, and others who haven't been a part of my narrative. So, thankfully, she is left now with only a handful of true believers, including Michael, as opposed to some gurus, who command the attention and pocketbooks of thousands of people.

I'm not enough of an expert on cults and gurus to know why this is the case with this particular group leader. I would need to understand thought reform in more depth to know what part of Limori's technique failed to attract new followers. But I can make an educated guess based on my experience. I think that once she reached a certain level of power with those of us who were involved, and had successfully indoctrinated us and held us to her, she became a little drunk with her own power, and this was repellent to any newcomers. She believed her own spin a little too much for the tastes of those who had not met her before. At a certain point, she seemed unable to be patient with the seduction phase of drawing someone new into her orbit; she would immediately go into fast forward with almost total strangers. She often had new people on her fishing line but she would lose them because she would try to pull them into the boat too quickly.

If her aim was to have hundreds or thousands of followers, like other gurus, another significant tactical error on her part was that she stopped coming to Wednesday nights and moved away from Vancouver. She was the reason we had all joined the group, so with her gone, there was no charismatic leader left to reel in new recruits. Wolf's Den is so remote that it would be hopeless to try and recruit new members in that area. I often wonder why she left the city and stayed on the move or at Wolf's Den. It seems a counterproductive strategy, for someone who wants to control people, to diminish her own influence by leaving the faithful, and the heavily populated city where she'd started her recruiting, behind. Was she beginning to be wary of confrontation as more members left her fold? Was she afraid of exposure as a fraud as a result of having all those ex-members out walking around freely and alive? I don't have an answer for this.

As of this writing, as far as I know, there may be only seven or eight people living at Wolf's Den, the last of the faithful few. I have no idea what has happened to the nine or ten women who were still going to the Vancouver group when I left it. I don't even know if the group still meets. I do know that Jessica cottoned on to the fact that she was being manipulated and left the cult a year or so after I did.

Gender bias

It is only with the benefit of hindsight that I was able to recognize that Limori often treated her male followers better than she treated those who were female. Limori treated the men more like peers than subjects. It was a very subtle difference in approach; the men were still subjected to the same seduction and thought-reform techniques that the women were. But I rarely witnessed her subjecting a man to the heights of soul-crushing abuse that she levelled at the women. I've puzzled over this for years but have finally concluded that the reasons for this difference in approach may be, ultimately, very simple to explain.

First, there were far fewer men in the group than women. In the Vancouver group, during the heyday of the early to mid-1990s, the ratio of women to men was probably ten to one. But in order to play her game of Musical Beds with us, Limori needed men to be in her sway. My observation was that she treated them therefore with slightly less abuse than she treated the women so that there would be less risk of losing them. Her rate of failure in converting the men to true believers had to be lower than with the women, simply because there were fewer men to lose.

She also needed men to do the heavy work of building and renovating at Wolf's Den. Construction has been going on there continuously for almost twenty years, with constant improvements and upgrades, not to mention new cabins being built. It is challenging, backbreaking work and although it might be possible to do it without men, it is much easier with them.

Third, men in general seemed less willing to put up with poor treatment from Limori. In the very few instances where she seemed to apply the same level of abuse to a man as she did to a woman, the men didn't stand for it and ended up leaving the tribe. Limori may have learned from these experiences that she needed to tread more softly with the male gender, whereas group members like Lisa, Rosemarie, and Susan have been put through hell again and again, and yet they stay with Limori, as loyal as ever.

Zombies

When I first met the woman I've called Alice in these pages, I immediately wanted her job. Physically she was a mix of contradictions: she was probably approaching fifty years old but she had a short, spiky haircut, like some sort of youthful rock star. Her oversized glasses were slightly outdated and her clothes seemed to be a simplified version of Limori's. She always wore skirts paired with a blouse, usually belted in the middle. And always heels, never, ever running shoes or flats. I've referred to her as Limori's handmaid and have never seen a closer embodiment of that word on display in the real world. She sat beside Limori everywhere they went and fetched everything Limori needed: her coat, her reading glasses, her glass of water, whatever. Sixty percent of Limori's sentences began with, "Alice, get me my . . .".

Alice herself rarely spoke unless spoken to. If Limori asked her to, either inside the circle or outside of it, she would tune in and volunteer the information Spirit had given her, which always agreed with whatever Limori had said. She worked like a dog at all times doing whatever Limori asked of her. When they were living in the Vancouver area it was Alice who did the cooking and cleaning. When groups of us would go to Wolf's Den for workshops, Alice was the head cook, and believe me, it was no small task cooking three meals daily for twenty people in a kitchen not yet equipped for such large output. Alice shopped with Limori, she drove for Limori, she constantly cleaned and tidied Limori's environment. She helped Limori dress in the morning and undress in the evening. When Limori beckoned her to come and sit and meditate, she did that. When Limori instructed her to make lunch for a group that had dropped by the house, she did that. If Limori said, "Tonight is a night we watch movies," Alice sat and watched. If Limori said, "This morning we pack a bag and fly to Tucson," Alice packed her back and went. She knew

Limori's every preference for food, wine, water, clothing fabric, hair dye and toenail polish. She was the ultimate definition of a personal assistant except that she never got paid and it was a 24/7, 365-day-a-year job.

As I became more involved in Limori's group in the early 1990s, all I ever really found out about Alice's background was that she had grown children and an ex-husband. Limori used to tell a story of Alice arriving at Limori's door one day saying she had left her husband and wanted to stay with Limori and serve God from then on. They had met for the first time at some point before this, but I never learned how or when or where.

As far as personality goes, I never really saw one in Alice. It wasn't that she was shy or retiring; she looked everyone directly in the eye and was not ever reluctant about sharing the painful 'truths' that 'Spirit' was channelling to her. She laughed uproariously when the situation called for it and apparently had quite a temper. Or so Limori used to tell us; I never saw it for myself. But what I noticed most about Alice was that she wasn't there. I wanted to know more about her, at first because, as I said, I wanted her job. I was so taken with Limori and with the life of someone like Alice who served God twenty-four hours a day that I wanted to *be* her. I wanted the life of fulfillment and service that she had. But even when I lived with Limori for those few tumultuous months, I never got any greater sense of who Alice was. She existed only to serve. Her own personal opinions about anything were never put forward. And I realize now, it was not just her opinions that were absent; her thoughts and feelings were missing as well.

I assumed during all the years I knew Alice that she had always been this way: vacant, quiet, absent, subservient. But it was only when I began to observe these exact personality traits emerge in my friend Lisa that I realized that this zombie-like countenance was a direct result of the way Limori moulded and trained people in her sway. Much, much later, while writing this book, I would come to realize that achieving this thought-less state of being was a necessity for those who served Limori in such an intimate and unrelenting way. Those who became especially close to her, those who served her every day and lived with her permanently, had to develop this way of being absent while they were present as a means of surviving what they were being put through. Alice, and later Lisa, were life-sized examples of the process that Robert Lifton calls thought stopping.

The first stage of my understanding of thought stopping came by surprise and was completely unconscious. At Wolf's Den in 1999, a day or so before Michael and Limori terminated our relationship, all of us present at the lodge were sitting down in the kitchen for lunch: Matthew, John, Lisa, Michael and me. The topic of what a magical place Wolf's Den was came up and, in his characteristically enthusiastic way, Michael was extolling the virtues of the lodge, its inhabitants and its energy. He was always so attractive when he was fired up about something, and my heart swelled with affection as he talked about how much he loved being there and how great it was to work for God and to have such a special place in the world to come to and to be with others who did God's work. Although I was happily soaking up the joy radiating off Michael, I was quiet while he said his piece because I didn't feel the same way. My fears about being around Limori, even when she wasn't physically around, were as present as ever and though it tortured me, I felt myself reluctant to join in for three choruses of "Wolf's Den and Its Leader Are So Great," so I kept quiet. But eventually Michael noticed.

"Don't you agree, Alexandra?" he asked. "Isn't it wonderful up here?"

As ever, I was torn in half about how to answer this question. The absolute truth of my heart was that, no, I didn't think it was so wonderful at Wolf's Den, with Limori controlling everyone's every move, even from two thousand miles away, and I thought the Germanic-style food she had Lisa serve was heavy and bland,

and I was bored and cold all the time and just wished I could go home. However, somewhere in my subconscious, I had finally figured out that speaking my truth was only considered The Truth when it fit in with Limori's vision of how things were. So, voicing this actual truth of my heart, which was not in line with what the group wanted to hear, would be unacceptable. Consequently, I simply mumbled something insincere about what a good time I was having and hoped Michael would move on. No such luck.

"Are you kidding me?" he said, offended by my lack of rhapsodic response. "It's amazing up here." At that moment, Lisa was standing beside him clearing a couple of lunch plates off the kitchen table. "Look at Lisa!" Michael said. He gestured toward her, his hands open-palmed like a game show hostess revealing the Grand Prize. "Since she moved up here, she's undertaken such an amazing transformation."

SHE'S A ZOMBIE!! I wanted to yell at him in response.

I came so close to letting these words explode past my throat and out of my mouth that almost ten years later I can still feel the pressure I had to use to bite them back. And yet, at the time, I didn't understand why I felt Lisa was a zombie; I simply had the almost uncontrollable urge to shout it out. Coupled with my confusion about why I would think something so treacherous was my shock at how close I had come to betraying the group code of conduct by stating my thought out loud. I was so shocked that I just sat, stunned and frightened, and said nothing to Michael, blinking at him with what was, I'm sure, a stupefied look on my face. There was a battle going on in my mouth and in my heart but he couldn't know that, and at the time I couldn't have explained what was happening. He held my eyes for a few more seconds, waiting for my response, and then gave up and helped Lisa clear the table, chatting with her about Wolf's Den and how much they both loved it. I immediately got to work inside myself, pushing away the feeling of wanting to point out to

Michael that Lisa had become a zombie. It was too uncomfortable for me to consider, although the power of what I felt and the energy it took to repress saying it was monumental.

Lisa had turned into a zombie, just like Alice. I had known her fairly well when we both lived in Vancouver and attended Wednesday and Thursday night meditations. She had started out as normal and unique as any of the rest of us; she had an excellent sense of humour, a delightfully cheeky mischievousness, a kind and caring heart and, not least of all, three beautiful children. And now she was like a clone of Alice: silent, obedient, working around the clock, absent even when she was present.

WHILE I WAS HAVING my own experiences with Limori and being pulled ever more deeply into the group she helmed, I watched Lisa become what cult experts call a true believer. I could probably write an individual chapter on my observations of all of my friends in the group, but it was Lisa whose transformation was the most dramatic.

When I met Lisa through the group, in 1989 or 1990, she was married and the mother of one toddler, living in a distant suburb of Vancouver and travelling into town twice each week for our evening meetings. She was also spending time with Limori at her home. When I compare and contrast Lisa's journey with my own and with those of others in the group, I find the perfect example of the Frog in Boiling Water analogy. Lisa and I joined the group at almost the same time, and yet, while watching her journey from spiritual seeker to true believer, it became clear to me that she was not only prepared but eager to endure faster-rising temperatures than anyone else at that time. The flame burned brightly under her. Limori knew who among us could be brought along at this fast-track pace, and Lisa was the most rapidly accelerated disciple I would ever witness.

I recognized in Lisa the same devotion that I felt for Limori. I could see in her face the love she felt for Limori and the space in her soul that Limori was filling up. I could see it because I felt the same way, and yet at times I was jealous of Lisa because she seemed less conflicted than I felt. For a couple of years Limori groomed Lisa by making her the treasurer of our meditation circle, by spending one-on-one time with her and (again, I can only see this in hindsight) by testing her devotion. There was the typical period of seduction and flattery, which involved, among other things, Limori declaring that Lisa was the incarnation of the Angel Gabriel. She presented Lisa with a ring that signified her spiritual purity and significance, and I never again saw Lisa's right hand without the ring present.

While Lisa's devotion to Limori grew, she was also building a family, and gave birth to two more children, the last being born in the late spring of 1993. Lisa left her husband shortly thereafter, which, as I have explained, was an essential move in order for Limori to have more control over this follower of hers who was proving to be the ideal disciple. A few months later, Limori arranged a short-lived relationship between Lisa and group member Victor. Lisa was obviously willing to do whatever Limori asked of her and this relationship was an ideal test of that loyalty; at the time, even in my mind-controlled state, I could see that Lisa had no feelings whatsoever for the man she had been matched with. He was at least twenty-five years her senior and it was so obvious that no romantic feelings existed on Lisa's part and she was only doing this because God asked her to, that to see them together in the circle was cringingly uncomfortable. Yet Lisa gave herself to the situation fully, proving to Limori that she was ready for the next temperature increase.

Consequently, that relationship was over almost as soon as it began. In the meditation circle one night in mid-1994, Limori announced that Lisa's name was being changed to Numi and she was moving to Wolf's Den to work for God full time. While Lisa prepared for her departure, Limori encouraged her to tune in at every opportunity, took her shopping and generally spent as much time with Lisa as Lisa could spare away from her children. Lisa glowed in Limori's presence and began dressing similarly to those women like Alice who lived with Limori full time; they wore dresses, never pants, and all sported an uber-short haircut that the group had begun referring to, jokingly, as the "cult cut."

In short, Lisa could do no wrong, and at the time I was jealous of her special relationship with Limori and felt threatened by it. Limori praised her often for being such a good spiritual student, and there developed a joking familiarity between them, similar to that of people who are falling in love. They shared jokes and private references in front of the group, giggling intimately.

So, in the summer of 1994, Lisa packed up her life and her three children and moved up to Wolf's Den. Coincidentally, in September of that same year I fell and broke some ribs and had to take some time off work to heal. I called Limori at Wolf's Den to talk to her about what had happened and see if she could give me the spiritual answer as to why this had happened to me. She invited me up to Wolf's Den for a few days to convalesce. I flew up to the lodge, moving agonizingly slowly and carefully, and Matthew picked me up at the tiny airport. It was immediately and painfully apparent to me that Lisa's honeymoon phase with Limori was over. Lisa's children had already been banished back to the city to be raised by their father and grandparents. Limori was not calling her by her new name, Numi, but was referring to her as "Scum" and, on my first day there, the others who lived at the lodge were instructed to do the same. And she was clearly, even to my mind-controlled eyes, being ostracized, while still moving among her peers. I had seen this happen a number of times before at workshops, but the ferocity with which Lisa was being treated was stunning even to me, even though I had become slightly immune to these type of techniques that Limori called spiritual.

As we sat outside at two picnic benches for lunch on the first day, Limori was at one bench with Alice and Matthew and the rest of us were at another. Limori would call over from her bench and ridicule and berate Lisa, all without speaking to her in the first person.

"Look at her eat! She eats like a pig. Here, piggy, piggy." This was followed by oinking noises. "Would you like some more food, piggy?" Limori proceeded to pelt Lisa with whatever food items were handy at her table. Lisa ducked slightly to avoid receiving a pickle to the side of her head and Limori mocked her for that: "Don't you want it, piggy, piggy?"

There was a small pause as Limori turned away and continued to eat her lunch, but it didn't last long. She hurled a cherry tomato at Lisa and then said, "Here! Scum, pick that food up off the ground. You're going to attract mice and raccoons. You're such a pig. Look at the mess you've made. Disgusting! Pick that up."

Lisa got up from her seat, picked up the bits of vegetable and fruit that Limori had lobbed at her and put them in a napkin in her fist. When she sat back down again, Limori launched into her: "What are you doing? Go to the kitchen and throw that stuff out. We don't leave rotting food lying around. Get going, Scum!"

Lisa rose again off the bench and set off down the slight hill to the lodge and into the kitchen, always keeping her eyes downcast.

As always happened in these cases, Limori began to mutter to the rest of us about how dark Lisa's energy was and how wicked she had become. The rest of us were silent, except perhaps for the occasional murmur of assent from Alice. When Lisa returned to the table, the verbal jabs from Limori continued, as they would for the rest of the few days I was visiting.

The following day, after continuing to watch the unrelenting workshop that Lisa was going through, the likes of which I had not witnessed before, I sidled up to Lisa in the kitchen in a rare moment when we were alone and asked her if she was okay. I was concerned because of the elevated ferocity of what I was witnessing, but also because Lisa was the only person who had moved to Wolf's Den after I had come to know her. All the others who lived there at that time, with the exception of Matthew, were people I had never known in Vancouver; they had moved to Wolf's Den almost immediately after I joined the meditation circle. I had a closer tie to Lisa; she was real to me. I had babysat her children and had been to her house when she and her husband held social events for some members of the group. I had driven up to Wolf's Den with her for workshops on more than one occasion and, before she moved up there, considered her to be a friend, even though at times I was jealous of her relationship with Limori.

She answered my enquiry by saying, "I just want to get through this. I know it will make me spiritually stronger."

It was not until I was writing this book and putting all the pieces together for myself, trying to explain them in a coherent way, that I realized that Alice's and Lisa's zombie-like countenances were exactly what Robert Lifton was referring to when he coined the term *thought stopping*. Lisa and Alice, and the others closest to Limori, have learned to stop thinking for themselves and are suppressing their thoughts and feelings to such a degree that it's as if they're not in their bodies any longer.

What I had assumed was Alice's original personality was, in fact, the result of years of being in Limori's presence. Her truest self is so buried, so suppressed, that it's as if she's not there, even when you speak to her directly. And this is what I noticed happening to Lisa when I wanted to shout out to Michael that she had become a zombie.

As of this writing Lisa is still living at Wolf's Den. Her name has been changed at least one more time that I am aware of since the days of being called Numi or Scum. Her three beautiful girls were banished from Wolf's Den a few months after they arrived with her. (The task of raising the children eventually fell entirely to their grandparents, when their father passed away in January,

1997.) Lisa's loyalty had to be to Limori and no one else. Gurus cannot tolerate children, especially small and needy children, dividing a parent's loyalty, so Lisa's daughters were dispatched. Of course, Limori would assure Lisa that this had to happen for energetic reasons; nothing is ever demanded of anyone unless God is asking that it happen.

Lisa was someone who was on the true-believer fast track and to this day whenever I think of her I shudder with a "There but for the grace of God go I" glance heavenward. Each of us who got involved with Limori, for a long or short term, had our own reasons for being there, our own motivations for accepting the bill of goods that she was trying to sell us, our own voids to fill. For me, seeing what happened to Lisa was like looking in a mirror. She was keen, as I was. We were almost the same age. She was pleasant and compliant and earnest in her desire to serve God: all qualities that I saw in myself at that time.

For someone like Lisa, the temperature that Limori had her cooking at just kept steadily rising until Lisa found herself living at Wolf's Den, without her husband or her children or the name she had been born with. Reports from old friends who know Lisa and keep in touch with her say that she has blithely referred to spending time living in the root cellar under the lodge as penance for periods of having bad energy. Her hands shake with a Parkinson's quiver now, but she says that she has not been diagnosed with a specific disease.

Thought reform trumps love. It overrules the primordial, instinctual, life-giving love of a mother for her children and, very often, even the personal instinct for self-preservation.

An ever-fixèd mark

In December 2004, Michael and I got together for dinner at a local tapas restaurant. We hadn't seen each other in person for a couple of years, but when we met it was like we'd seen each other yesterday. As I removed my coat at the entrance, I looked across the restaurant and could see him sitting at the table he'd been given. I was delighted to discover, as I joined him, that the indelible connection between us was there, as strong as ever. I was at once excited and nervous to see him. Excited because I longed to hear and see how he was and catch up on all the things I didn't know about his life. Nervous because I knew that our interactions were always tainted with the shadow of his guru's mind control. And because I knew what his beliefs told him about me and my negative energy.

Our visit had been prompted by a Christmas card. Earlier in the month I had sent him a card, which was not something I had done since we'd broken up. Though we had been apart for five years, I had acknowledged to myself that I loved him as much as ever and wanted to say hello, even if it was via a greeting card. He called me a few days after he'd received the card and requested that we get together for this meal. I confess that I jumped at the opportunity to see him. Yes, I had logged thousands of hours of therapeutic and recovery work at this point and knew without question that it was a cult he was involved in; my head was so shrunk I was often surprised it was still visible on top of my shoulders. But the truth was that I loved him still, despite everything, and needed no convincing at all to spend an evening with him.

Five years had passed, almost to the day, since our relationship had been severed. We chatted for hours, although it seemed like minutes, about his business and mine, our lives and our friends and family and ourselves. Our waitress finally came and requested that we pay our bill because she wanted to finish her shift. We looked up from the deeply pleasurable well of reconnection, stunned to find that it was almost midnight and that we were the last customers in the restaurant.

His face was so familiar to me, and so beloved, and yet as we talked I realized that he was now a stranger. He was quite obviously more deeply attached to Limori and her other followers than ever. For the first time, he was referring to her as Lady Limori, saying that she had claimed a royal title that was rightfully hers. I could barely stop myself from snorting and rolling my eyes. The good news was that I had done enough of my own healing and recovery work that I could listen to the cultic pronouncements that snuck into his conversation with a measure of detachment and compassion. I was also able, for the first time, to clearly see him switch back and forth from his authentic self, when he talked about his business or his niece and nephew, for example, to his cult self, when he talked about energetic things that had happened to him or recited a new bit of cult rhetoric that I hadn't yet heard, and I was able to feel empathy for his cult self and deep, abiding, almost overpowering love for his authentic self. It was blissful to be so physically close to him and excruciatingly painful to feel that he was six million miles away.

After we settled up with the waitress, she assured us that we could sit and talk for as long as we wanted. Michael then came to the reason for his request to see me.

"The past five years," he said, "have been an intense learning process for me and I believe that was the intention for both of us when our relationship was broken up. But through it all I maintained the hope that somehow, someday the stars would align to bring us together again." He paused. "I never really let you go."

I was stunned and listened as quietly and with as much presence as I could. I had wondered for the past five years if he felt this way because it was how I felt. We had been forced apart without our consent but, for me, that hadn't meant that my feelings for him had changed or disappeared. It was extraordinary to hear him say out loud what I had felt all along. He paused again to sip some wine and then gathered himself to carry on. It was clear that what he was saying was difficult for him, but I could also see his spiritual resolve shoring him up.

"I've learned a lot, thanks to Lady Limori." He smiled with

affection and devotion when he said her name. I wanted to gag. "It hasn't been easy but I keep going because I've known for twenty years that whatever my fate is, I have much to learn in order to be ready for it, and I feel strongly that she can teach me."

I understood, by him saying it hadn't been easy, that he was emphasizing to me his belief that I had given up on God when the going got tough and he had stuck it out because of his greater love for God. His cultic beliefs required him to place the responsibility for our break-up at my feet. I knew that he couldn't allow himself to consider that Limori might not have ALL the answers in the universe, and that it was possible to be a good person and serve God outside her realm, because if he began thinking thoughts like that his entire belief system and his sense of self would be brought into question, and that is dangerous territory.

He continued. "I understand that you now consider everything that comes from me tainted by my choice of teachers. But whether or not you were able to cope with the manner of teaching is, unfortunately, not the main issue between us. At this point you have chosen a road that I simply cannot go down, and you seem determined to maintain it. So be it. I am very, very sad that it has to be this way, but at this point there is no choice but to let you go."

If I had thought about Michael's reason for meeting me, I suppose I might have thought that it was just for old times' sake. So I was stunned, and devastated, by this announcement. On the one hand, I was surprised at his vulnerability in sharing the fact that he had held onto me and the hope that I would return to the group for so long. At the same time, all at once, my feelings about the love between us were confirmed. In his own twisted, mind-controlled way, his authentic self was telling me that he loved me as much as ever and as much as I loved him. And that he had been waiting, with hope, all this time, just as I had.

But, with the very same words, his cult self was telling me that it had won this battle. He was no longer going to listen to his feelings for me because they didn't matter. What mattered was serving his guru, Lady Limori, and his God. He had believed for five years that the only reason we were apart was because I refused to serve God and face all my ego positions. He believed that if I hadn't been weak, and unwilling to face The Truth, I would have continued to follow Limori myself and we'd be together.

I listened, knowing that his mind and thoughts were controlled and that there was no way I could reason with him. Thought reform is kryptonite where logic is concerned. Trying to reason with him would have been like trying to get through to someone who is high on heroin. You're not talking to the person; you're talking to the drugs or, in this case, the cult doctrine. I sat there in the quiet, empty restaurant, powerless and defeated. It was so painful and bittersweet to hear what he was saying, especially to hear his words and understand them from both sides of my awareness, that I began to feel that peculiar sensation that comes with shock, where I feel like my head is inside a bell and time slows down and the world shrinks to a two-foot radius around me.

His cult self was angry and deeply disappointed with me. For five years, with the very little contact we'd had, he'd been trying to get through to me with the doctrine he believed to be true, and I had dismissed it while I tried to find the actual truth for myself. I could see frustration, coupled with pain, all over his face. I'm sure it mirrored the look on mine. We were sitting two feet apart but we could not have been farther apart if we'd been sitting on two different planets. Both of us were desperate to bring the other person over to our way of thinking, and both of us were failing miserably.

We sat there at our corner table, replete with wine and those delicious Spanish potatoes that tapas restaurants make. I looked at him and his beautiful face that I love so much and knew that there was nothing, nothing, I could say or do that would help him to see that his brain was tied in knots. The powerlessness of that moment made me ache until I thought I would burst wide open, right there at the table.

And the agony wasn't over yet. He was so disappointed in me that he wrote me a letter a week after our dinner to reiterate what he had said at the table. He outlined to me in print, in case I had missed his point while we were talking, that I was arrogant and served only my own ego and had no grasp of the spiritual heights he had advanced to by not giving up on following Limori, as I had. As I read the letter I once again was swamped with the strangest feeling of being pulled in half, because I knew exactly what his thoughts were telling him and I completely understood why he thought that I was to blame. Yet I was now living with a free mind and knew how the guru he believed in was lying to him. It was like stepping back and forth through a funhouse mirror. On one side of the mirror Limori ruled the world, and I understood exactly why Michael believed in her so strongly and why he was so angry with me for turning my back on her and on her god. On the other side of the mirror, I was free to think and feel what was most authentically me and knew that no one could grant or remove my relationship with God or with myself. Despite the fact that I could see both these realms, I was not able to reach through the glass and pull Michael over to my side. I allowed his letter to drift down to the coffee table in front of me and, not for the first or last time, wept with sorrow and frustration.

Every single day I think of Michael and send him love. Every day I wish there was a way for me to reach him through that looking glass. Even after our dinner conversation that night I continued to hold onto the hope that he would encounter a situation that would spur him to leave Limori's clutches. But leaving a cult, as I had discovered for myself, means turning away from everything you believe in, including your own self. It is a terrifying, mind-bendingly awful experience, one that our minds convince us to avoid at all costs. If there is no compelling reason to leave, most people stay.

To be unable to rescue Michael from this has been almost unbearable. I live with that sorrow and longing every day, like an extra shadow cast by my heart. My journey of recovery enabled me to save myself. I have not been able to save my darling Michael.

I have not seen Michael or had contact with him since that painfully precious dinner we shared in December 2004. A little more than two years later, in early 2007, he left his business in Vancouver, sold his car and moved north to live at Wolf's Den full time.

Love stories

The title of this book is a deliberate attempt to emphasize the principle behind the quote included at the beginning of Chapter 1: Nobody joins a cult. In 1989 what I joined was a group of like-minded people who all wanted to learn to meditate and improve their lives and contribute to the world in a positive way. Eventually I would come to love many of them, including our illustrious leader.

There is love that exists in cults; it's just not the most obvious element that we think of when we see images on the news. In a way, it is a tragedy that this love does exist, for without it many of us probably would have left Limori's sway much, much sooner. I loved the other people in Limori's cult, especially those I shared Thursday night meditations with for years. I was incredibly close to Debbie, Amber and Karen. In our own twisted, confused way we tried to help one another cope with the stresses and strains of following what we didn't know was a cult doctrine. Despite the inherent dysfunctionality in the group, these were some of the closest girlfriends I've ever had.

I loved Limori. I trusted her and yearned for her approval. I cared about what happened to her and wanted her to be safe and free to pursue the things that mattered to her. Was it a healthy love? No, it was more like hero worship, but there was true affection there for the woman I followed.

Did she love me, and the others? I doubt it. I don't know that anyone who is capable of such abuse could also be capable of love. She needed us; without her subjects, a queen is nothing. But I don't think she loved us.

And, of course, I loved Michael. For whatever reason, I was able to feel a deep and abiding love under the umbrella of contradictions and manipulations that I became so used to. I will be forever grateful to him for seeing me when no one else seemed to, and for listening to me with his entire body when I spoke. He tried to teach me that I was valuable, but that was a lesson I wouldn't absorb until long after we'd parted.

At the root of everything, there was each person's love for God. That was the greatest love story of all. If we hadn't loved God, we wouldn't have been there in the first place. Each person had such tremendous love for the divine, for the goodness in the universe, that they were willing to allow their own lives and spirits to be ripped to shreds in order to try to fulfill the promise of that love. The irony and tragedy of this lives with me every day and I shake my head and my fist at this paradox that allows people like Limori to use and abuse those who are pure of heart. That is the saddest part of this love story.

Writing this book is also a gesture of love. By telling my story I am loving myself by giving myself back the voice that was silenced for so long. I am contradicting so much of what Limori taught me: that I didn't matter, that she was the only person who had any significance or anything significant to say, that my feelings and thoughts meant nothing, and that I only mattered to God when I was pleasing Limori. All these things were lies, and by addressing them as such, I am trying to offer love to myself and to anyone else who has had the experience of being controlled and abused in this way. I received so much comfort, solace and, indeed, love from the books about cults that I read when I was ready to explore what had happened to me, that I wanted to find a way to pay that love forward, and say to anyone else who has had a similar experience, "It's going to be alright, I promise you." And, "I understand," which were the two most comforting words in the world to me when I realized I'd been in a cult. Being able to name the experience and find that I was not alone in it was, all by itself, immeasurably healing.

EPILOGUE

W hy did it take me ten years to leave Limori's cult? And why do some people continue to stay, in that group and in other, even more abusive groups?

I found the most succinct and poignant explanation for this in, of all places, the animated film *Kung Fu Panda*. Panda's teacher asks him why he doesn't quit trying to be a Kung Fu master, when they both know he is ill-suited to the role, both physically and temperamentally. Panda replies that he stays with his master because the rigorous training he endures is less painful than being just himself, in his regular life, working at his father's noodle shop. He stays because he hopes his master can make him "not me."

I fell in love with Limori and with all she promised because I felt she was the one who could make me not me. Among the other contributing factors for my involvement was a gross lack of self-acceptance, which drove me into Limori's arms and kept me there as she continued to promise she could change me. Even when she hurt me, over and over again, I believed that she was trying to help me leave behind the me that I believed wasn't acceptable and attain the me that was. But this was all a lie.

Thankfully, just like Panda, I eventually learned that I was good enough just being me.

So many of us have voids where self-acceptance should exist, voids that we are unconsciously or consciously trying to fill. We use alcohol, drugs, sex, work, plastic surgery, video games, self-importance and food, among other things, to try to drown the voice inside us that says, "I am not good enough. If only I were different, then I would be acceptable." This becomes a cycle that has no end. No matter what we achieve, there are always more changes to make. The search for spiritual enlightenment can be just one more way we do this.

Although I don't have any scientific data to back up the following statement, my experience tells me that staying in any abusive situation, including a cult, has nothing to do with how intelligent the victim is and everything to do with what he or she believes and feels to be true about themselves. If we believe we are not good enough, we will stay and endure in order that we might one day fulfill the promise of being acceptable.

Cults won't exist any longer when we, the only species that has the ability to reflect on our own existence, learn to accept every part of ourselves as beautiful and miraculous. That is a pretty tall order, one that I don't expect to see fulfilled in my lifetime.

Until then, if you or someone you know has been in a cult, treat that person gently. Give them as much love as possible. And tell them, every day, "You are so much more than good enough. You are perfect, exactly as you are."

UPDATE: NOVEMBER 2014

In late January 2013 Limori died. She had apparently been fighting a battle with cancer for some time until she finally succumbed.

Relief was the emotion I felt most keenly on the day I was told. Relief that she couldn't hurt anyone any longer. Relief that she would not be able to pull anyone new into her trap. And hope. Hope that perhaps those who still believed in her would, with time, be able to let the knots untangle in their brains and live their lives free of her destructive influence.

The influence of a cult leader outlasts death, however. Those who were living with Limori at Wolf's Den are still there as of this writing, still mostly cut off from their families and hanging onto the beliefs their guru implanted.

I HAVE SPOKEN to Michael once, very briefly, since our dinner in 2004. Sadly, his father passed away in December 2009. I had remained close to Michael's parents and visited them regularly at their Vancouver Island home after my relationship with Michael ended. When his mother told me of his father's passing, I felt the need to call Michael and express my condolences, even though I knew he would probably not enjoy hearing from me. As a result of my call he would, I suspected, have to spend days clearing the bad energy that he would feel had arrived at the resort. It was therefore selfish of me to do so, but I called Wolf's Den anyway. Limori was still alive at this point and it was terrifying to put myself within her orbit, even just by telephone. But I did it, motivated by the sense of loss I felt and by the still-present love I felt for Michael.

It was he who answered the phone. "Good afternoon. Wolf's Den Resort."

Hearing his voice was like a balm to my soul. In the nanosecond after he spoke my whole body filled with delight and love at hearing him speak. Similar to the feeling you get when the sun comes out and bathes you in warmth on a cold, cloudy day, except this warmth came from my core and radiated out. I can still feel it now, as I write this, five years later. He was speaking in that moment in an unguarded way, because he didn't know it was me (a.k.a., the Devil) on the other end of the phone.

I told him who it was calling and could hear the shock in his voice. He said, "Oh!" I said that I was calling to express my condolences. He said thank you, but his walls had instantly gone up. As soon as I'd announced myself his tone had changed. He became clipped and brusque. His cult self was immediately in charge.

I asked him how he was doing. He said he was okay, given the circumstances. He began to say goodbye. It had been, at most, half a minute since we'd started talking. It was stilted and deeply uncomfortable.

And then, a hail Mary pass. His authentic self reached out past the walls of his cult self, just as I was about to hang up. "How are you?" he said, in a tone more reminiscent of the one I knew from our years of friendship. The question was genuine and warm. Suddenly it was a different conversation. It was as though a light had been turned on in a darkened room. I could feel his honest desire to connect. As it had been at our dinner in 2004, the looking-glass feeling of him shifting back and forth between his two selves was there again.

I can't remember exactly what I said, though I know it was brief. I probably just said I was doing well.

And then the light was gone, as quickly as it had been lit. "Well, thank you for calling," he said, his cult self in charge again. "Goodbye." And then, sanctimoniously, "God bless."

I hung up, almost wishing his authentic self hadn't broken through for that moment. My heart ached. The connection, and then the loss of it again so quickly, was deeply painful. But, I told myself, it was reassuring to be reminded that no matter what, the light at the centre of each of us can never be extinguished.

AS OF THIS WRITING, there are seven people left living at Wolf's Den, and a handful in the outside world, who still believe in Limori. I don't know if they will ever give up their mind-controlled ways of thinking, even though she is not there any longer to reinforce the beliefs. All of them gave up so much in order to follow Limori. If they begin to let doubt and critical thinking creep in now, all these years later, and allow their thinking to become freer, they will then have to face the feelings that arise when they realize they were lied to and manipulated. Feelings of betrayal when they realize that the person they loved and trusted most in the world, who they thought embodied God, was actually just a cunning, totally self-absorbed abuser who used them for her own gratification. I remember feeling so ashamed and embarrassed that I had given ten years of my life to someone who was lying to me and using me. I felt like such a fool and I felt those ten years were completely wasted. (They weren't, but that's how it felt in the early stages of my recovery.) I can only imagine how that feeling would multiply exponentially for those, like Lisa and Susan, who gave up their children. Or Michael, who gave Limori twenty-five years of his life and who so deeply needs to feel he is fulfilling a purpose. Therefore, I suspect the potential price for those who remain loyal to Limori to free their thinking is greater than the one they pay by sticking to what they know and continuing to hold onto the beliefs Limori taught them.

I hope they prove me wrong.

It is a long road out, and it requires a tremendous amount of courage to begin that journey. It is worth it, in my experience. I have not had an experience as gratifying as the one of rebuilding myself from the ground up after leaving the cult. But it is not without its daunting hurdles. Sometimes, for a cult member, the cost of clearing those hurdles is too great.

Despite this best guess, based on my own experience and my research and understanding about cults, I continue to pray that eventually everyone who was touched by Limori is free. Free to think and feel and live in a way that expresses the beauty of their essential selves. Free to develop their own relationships with the world, with their families and friends, and with the divine.

UPDATE: JANUARY 2017

And then there were four.

The number of Limori's former disciples living at Wolf's Den now numbers four: Michael, Matthew (who originally owned the resort), Lisa, and Mildred, who is now in her late 90s.

The other three disciples who had been living at the resort – Susan, Debbie, and a young woman from Austria who I will call Hilde – moved away in December 2015. Susan and Hilde moved to Pemberton, and Debbie moved back to Vancouver.

Limori had recruited Hilde after I left the group. She was the daughter of Limori's best friend in Austria. Hilde contacted me in the summer of 2016. We had never met and she had heard nothing but terrible things about me, of course, but she had enough courage and curiosity to reach out. She had read this book and was just beginning to recognize what had happened to her. We met and chatted for a few hours over lunch that summer. Her heart was broken by the betrayal she felt, and I recognized the look of pain and sadness in her eyes. She had given Limori ten years of her life, as I had, and the shock of understanding how deeply and completely she'd been manipulated was just beginning to sink in with her.

She shared some of the horror stories that she had lived through, especially when Limori was dying, and some of the stories of insanity and paranoia that went on at the resort. Including that before her death, Limori had taken to telling people that I was colluding with a resort across the lake from Wolf's Den. According to Limori, this resort had installed a high-powered telescope in one of its windows and trained it at Wolf's Den so that the resort owner could spy on the goings-on at Wolf's Den and report back to me. I'm sure I don't have to explain that this was not true. Limori's inflated sense of her own importance was matched only by her need to demonize those who disagreed with her and dared to embrace independent thought.

Hilde has now moved back to Austria to be closer to her sister and other family members. She was out of contact with her family almost the entire time she lived at Wolf's Den because of Limori's practices of separating loved ones and making sure her followers' loyalty was directed at her alone.

After Limori died, her only child, a son, inherited Wolf's Den. Very quickly he sold it to a businessman who owns another resort on the BC–Alberta border.

IN LATE 2016, I was interviewed by a woman who had read this book and who was writing a book of her own about using the creative process to express and release grief. During the course of the interview she asked me if I knew the term *disenfranchised grief*. I did not, so she explained to me that the term is used to describe grief that is not acknowledged or recognized by those around the person grieving. She said that based on reading my book she expected that this was the type of grief I had experienced after leaving the cult.

I think she is right.

As I've explained earlier in the book, I did not feel entitled to feel or express any of the terribly turbulent and unhappy emotions that I was experiencing early in 2000 and in the years that followed. We had been taught that our greatest purpose in life was to serve God, and therefore I believed that anything that transpired was God's will and thus should be something that I was joyful about participating in.

But what that ingrained belief did was force me to simply ignore how sad, traumatized, lonely and betrayed I felt. I was facing the greatest loss of my life to that point – all in one moment I had lost my boyfriend, all my friends, my spiritual home, and my understanding about my relationship with God. But the indoctrination that I had experienced told me that I shouldn't feel grief or loss about any of that. That I should carry on happily and joyfully, knowing I was doing God's work.

So there is still grief inside of me all these years later that comes to the surface occasionally, such as during the conversation with the woman who interviewed me for her book. While we talked, I felt myself getting choked up, and had it been appropriate I might have let myself weep while I was speaking to her. This is something I'll want to work on healing in the coming years months and years, now that it has come to my attention that there is still some unprocessed grief within me.

On the subject of grief

My brother, who was a kidney transplant patient, died in early January 2016. Brynley and I were very close, and lived just a few blocks apart in Vancouver. We had always been close as siblings, and were our biological parents' only two children. In May 2012, he was diagnosed with kidney disease and this caused us to become even closer. I was his only family member in the Vancouver area, and the person who was able to provide him with the support he needed during the next few years.

For three and a half years, we worked together to manage the disease and the complications it added to his life; I went with him to many of his doctors' appointments and all of the medical procedures that he had to endure during that time. I dropped by to see him at dialysis once a week to keep him company. He was so incredibly brave about everything he had to endure, and then this period came to a very happy close in August 2015 when he received a new, functioning kidney from a deceased donor.

Sadly, there were complications with the anti-rejection medication that all organ donors take, and when I hadn't heard from Brynley for a couple of days in early January 2016 I went to his apartment and found that he had passed away. Thankfully, he died peacefully in his sleep, having a nap on his couch.

Thus began a very difficult time, as anyone who has lost someone close to them unexpectedly will understand. But here's the reason I'm telling this story. As I sat in the lobby of Brynley's apartment building the night I'd found him, with a dear friend who had come the instant I called, answering questions from the police officers who attended the scene and waiting for the coroner, I noticed that my body began to have a visceral and frightening reaction to the shock and grief that I was experiencing. For the next twenty-four hours I shook with adrenalin. It was the same feeling you get when you're outside in cold weather and your body has become chilled. Perhaps you don't have a warm enough jacket on, or you've been outside for too long. I began to experience a similar kind of internal tremor that filled my entire body. This shaking lasted for a little more than a day.

I now realize what was going on: after my previous experience of loss and grief, the entire Limori community had turned their backs on me, and I was unconsciously expecting this same sort of response from my community to the current shock, as illogical as that sounds. I didn't even realize that that's what I was bracing myself for, until a day or two later.

In the ensuing few days after Brynley's death, the people in my life who care about me naturally turned *toward* me, not away. Friends showed up at my apartment in a continuous stream of support and connection, making sure that I was not alone until such time as I wanted to be. Flowers arrived from friends, family and ex-co-workers. I received calls from the kidney unit at St. Paul's Hospital, checking in to see if I was coping. My close girl-friends brought food and wine and sat with me, letting me cry or tell stories about my brother that made me laugh. They came with homeopathic remedies and books about grief. They offered to help with cleaning out his apartment, and arrived with pickup trucks, hatchback cars, strong backs and cleaning supplies to help me with that unimaginably painful chore. They called every single day for weeks to see how I was doing, and in the months after that continued to regularly check in to see how I was coping with my grief. They did research online to find resources that I might need or be interested in, including a grief group at the Vancouver Hospice that I joined later that year and found immeasurably helpful.

This was an entirely unexpected experience for me, and not the one I had been bracing myself for. It was the polar opposite of what I had experienced with the cult. And when I finally realized what was happening and, explained my experience to a friend a few days after Brynley's death, it made me sob with relief.

"People aren't shunning me," I said, shocked. "Everyone is turning toward me."

(Logically, I shouldn't have been surprised. My friends are wonderful, amazing, loving people. But trauma can reside at length in our very cells without us even realizing it.)

My body and my cellular memory of grief and loss had assumed that I would experience the same thing over again that I had in 2000 and the years that followed. Some part of me assumed that I was in for another seven or eight years of hellish trauma, because that was the only experience of grief I'd had thus far. But what I realize now is that experience of grief – the one I had with the cult – was not the norm. It was trauma. It was disenfranchised grief. It was emotional and psychological abuse masquerading as spirituality.

Throughout 2016, I was able to process my grief about the loss of my darling brother in a much healthier way than I had ever done after the loss of the cult.

As I write this update, in January 2017, it is the 17-year anniversary of the terrible time in my life when Michael dumped me in such a cruel and unceremonious way, and I experienced, for the first time in my life, a broken heart.

The irony I am now able see is that what Limori, Michael and I could not have known on that cold and overcast afternoon of December 30, 1999, was that they were giving me what would end up being one of the greatest gifts of my life.

Limori, and by extension Michael, set me free.

I will always and forever be grateful to them that, ironically, they saved me. They gave me my life back. I, unlike others in the group, including Michael, was able to rebuild my life in a way that involved my own personal choices. I was not, from then on, influenced by the manipulation and control of other ill-intentioned people.

It is my fervent prayer and wish that anyone who has ever been involved in a cult one day gets to experience this freedom.

UPDATE: JULY 2019

DUELING MEMOIRS

You're probably aware, having read to this point, that I wrote *Cult, A Love Story* for a number of reasons. First, I wanted to help those who had had a cult experience to understand what had happened to them. Second, I wanted to help family members of those in a cult understand why their loved one would do something that, from the outside, looks so destructive and painful.

And the third reason, which I don't talk about much, is that I wanted to save the man I loved, "Michael," who was still in the cult. This book is dedicated to him, and it was my fervent hope that he would read it and reconnect with his authentic, loving self.

In May 2019 Michael released his own book about his experiences with the woman I call Limori. Of course, I bought it the minute it was available and read it immediately.

Since then, I've been thinking about my response to his book. I thought of leaving a review on Amazon but realized I had more to say than would be appropriate in a review. Then I realized I could leave my thoughts here in one of my updates.

So here goes.

. . .

MICHAEL'S BOOK is called *Into God's Light* (by Timothy Noble) and is a retelling of his life since the late 1990s, when he began following the woman I call Limori. It details some of the spiritual and mystical experiences he had, which he attributes mostly to her. The book takes us from before Michael knew Limori through their first connections and into their deepening guru–follower relationship, on through her death and into the present day. He goes into detail about many of the extraordinary spiritual experiences that he's had and some of the lessons he's learned; he also explains his devotion to Limori and all the things he believes she stood for.

The gist of the book is that, in Michael's opinion, Limori was a mighty spiritual being who blessed everyone around her with her amazing divine energy, spiritual mastery, and magnificence. He describes Limori as having an "awe-inspiring connection to the Beings of Light and to God himself."

He does mention that Limori was a "tough" teacher, but qualifies this a few times by saying that in order to get through to her followers' egos, she needed to be that way.

The book is a competently written short read, and the reader definitely comes to understand that the author is and was utterly devoted to Limori and thinks she was a great spiritual teacher and master. Aside from that, however, I'm not sure what the book's purpose is, other than an exercise in stroking the author's ego and that of his deceased guru. It doesn't teach or inform the reader in any way.

What I see

Here's my main problem with Michael's retelling of life with Limori: he leaves out 80 percent of the experience of being near her. I recognized many of the events he describes because I was there too, but he omits any part of the story that is not flattering and complementary to Limori. It's like he's describing a rattlesnake to someone who's never seen one: "It's long and thin and has scales." He neglects to mention the sharp fangs or the venomous, life-threatening bite.

His only concession to that side of his guru is, as I've said, to mention once or twice that she's a "tough teacher." The swath of destruction Limori left in her wake is never discussed. There is zero mention of the families and relationships that were ripped apart, or of the psychological and emotional abuse those around her had to endure. He doesn't discuss the manipulation we withstood for Limori's own benefit. Or the way she, as every cult leader does, was able to teach those following her to blame ourselves for everything bad that occurred, and give her credit for anything positive.

He talks about her global lifestyle and the elegance with which she presented herself in order to point out how special she was, but fails to mention that she lived that lifestyle off the backs of her followers, who gave her many hundreds of thousands of dollars over the years, and also very often worked for her for free.

He mentions that, early on, dozens of people came to her meditation circles, pointing out that people were magically drawn to her presence, but fails to share that this period was short-lived and that at her death there were almost no followers left.

Michael neglects to mention the way Limori controlled our lives and demanded that her every wish and whim be satisfied, despite the fact that Lisa, the woman he's currently in a relationship with, had her three very young children ripped from her and sent away to be raised by their grandparents, a familial rupture so devastating that those children are still living with the effects, more than 25 years later.

Here's a perfect example that shows how Michael shares the portions of events that are complimentary to Limori and then

255

leaves out the more unsavoury facts, sharing only 20 percent of the picture instead of the full story. He spends part of the chapter called The Resort explaining how Matthew found and purchased the piece of land that I call Wolf's Den on a lake in the Chilcotin Plateau. He describes how Matthew "fell in love" with the parcel, and how it "felt like home" to him.

However, what he doesn't mention is that while I was following Limori, she got Matthew, who was then her husband, to sign the deed for Wolf's Den over to her. This part of the story is simply left out, as is the fact that when Limori died, she willed the resort not back to Matthew, but to her son (a man not related to Matthew). So Matthew, who struggled to raise the money to buy the land, and finally did, and nearly lost it to the banks several times, but persevered, ultimately lost the slice of paradise he worked so hard to hold onto. He gave it over to a woman he loved and believed in and was left with nothing.

But as I said, Michael shares only the parts of this story that are flattering to his guru. He takes us into his spiritual home but only shows us the parlour, which has been cleaned and polished, and ignores the other rooms where the paint is peeling, the floors are rotten, and piles of garbage are creating a horrible stench. It's almost like he's gaslighting *himself*, which, while I was reading the book, felt both strange and eerily familiar.

ONE OF THE biggest flaws in any devoted cult follower's logic is that the end justifies the means. Michael's book is firmly planted in the defence of that position. In fact, it seems to be the book's raison d'être. He doesn't detail how abusive Limori was, but by referring to her as simply a "tough teacher" he justifies her every despicable and disgusting behavior. How she treated people is beside the point, he is saying. What matters is that she was "serving God."

My thesis, as you will likely have understood if you've read this far, is the opposite of that. How we treat each other matters. If we don't treat each other with love, compassion, and kindness, it doesn't matter which deity we say we're working for. As you have read, my finally being able to see that disconnect was the reason I was able to leave Limori's cult.

Michael's position is the same as Limori's was: that breaking down a spiritual disciple's ego is more important than kindness or compassion, than trusting that each person is as valuable as the next. I believe that "breaking" people, in any way and no matter what deity you say you serve, is an approach that is indefensible.

Lynda

Yours truly features in a chapter of Michael's book called Those Who Fell Short, a title that leaves readers with no doubts about how he feels about me and anyone else who stopped following Limori. Franky, I'm amazed he mentions me personally at all.

Michael shares his views about why he broke up with me and why, in his opinion, I left the group. I made the decision to "turn away from the Light," he says, and I was being engulfed in negative energies. He refers to me as a "princess of darkness," and therefore had no choice but to break up with me, given his status as a Light Being.

Of course, I disagree with his assessments of both my character and the reason Limori had him break up with me, but you've just read an entire book about that, so I don't need to reiterate.

Here's one puzzling thing, though. In that chapter, he calls me "Lynda," and this is the only pseudonym he uses in the book. I'm assuming he uses that name because I was called Lynda until I was 19. My parents named me Lynda Alexandra when I was born, but at 19 I decided I liked Alexandra better and began using it. (I'm astonished that he remembered that; the name change happened a few years before I met him.) What I can't figure out is why he changed my name and no one else's. Is it because he doesn't want to drive traffic to this book? That's my best guess.

I'm not sure he's read this book, but he does mention it (not by name) and says that in his opinion I wrote it in order to destroy Limori and Wolf's Den. This is categorically untrue, and one of the reasons I changed everyone's name was specifically to protect the privacy of those I discuss, including his and Limori's. I've been asked at author readings and other events to give Limori's real name and have always refused.

We all have blind spots

Reading Michael's book helped me to see that I was entirely blind to how devoted he was to Limori and to the fact that his spiritual journey was the primary focus of his life.

In his book, he mentions that he had an insightful, spiritual, world-dissolving moment of blinding light before he met Limori, which he describes in part by saying "...the world was going to change in huge and dramatic ways, and ... I had a part to play in it."

He had shared this story with me a number of times when we were friends, and I heard him but clearly didn't really understand how that experience informed his character and defined him, in a deep and lasting way. He was and is still willing to do anything to fulfill the promise of that experience.

In hindsight, I was also utterly blind to how much that pivotal spiritual experience mattered to him and how deeply he felt the drive to fulfill the destiny that he felt was calling him. Even when I wrote this book, I hadn't connected those dots. It is only now, in 2019, having read his story from his point of view, that I finally get it.

He describes in his book how, after that moment of blinding light, he searched for years for a teacher before finding Limori. I do remember him telling me that he searched for so long that he thought he'd missed the thing he was supposed to find. I remember him saying that when he found Limori, he was hugely relieved. He decided that she was The One.

Why now?

When I tell people that Michael has written his book, often the first question out of their mouths is "Why?" Of course, I can't know for sure, but here are my thoughts on that.

Limori died in January 2013, as I detailed in a previous update. As of this writing, six years have passed since her death. Having been one of Limori's disciples myself, having learned about how cults work to control our minds, and having experienced firsthand what happens when we leave a cult and those knots in our heads begin to unwind and our authentic self begins to rise up again, I can only wonder if Michael is experiencing something similar. Limori is not with him any longer to reinforce her spiritual dogma. So, I expect that writing his book is Michael's way of digging in his heels and reinforcing his commitment to her. However, no one else is insisting that he continue to believe in her: it is as though he is trying to convince himself. It is with our own selves that we wrestle most, isn't it?

Michael does have the advantage of being at Wolf's Den with the other two of Limori's most loyal disciples, Matthew and Lisa, who are also deeply invested in maintaining their devotion to her. (Mildred moved away from Wolf's Den to a retirement residence at some point.)

You see, it would be incredibly painful for those three if they began to see how Limori had manipulated, controlled, and abused them. They would each have to look back and realize they'd been living a lie for the past 25 or 30 years. For Lisa especially, I imagine this would be excruciatingly painful, as she would have to face the fact that she'd given her children away simply because Limori wanted them out of the way. The three small girls were merely pawns in a game of control and manipulation, not living, breathing children who needed their mother's love and care. I can only imagine that it would be nearly impossible for Lisa to turn and face that truth. I'm not a parent, but even I can see that facing that kind of truth has the potential to drive a person mad with grief and regret.

It is heartbreaking to think of this, and I am heartbroken, too, for Michael and the other two lovely, loving people still living at Wolf's Den and hanging on, tooth and nail, to their belief in Limori. The work she did during her lifetime has ensured that her legacy is living on past her death, something I'm sure her gigantic ego would be thrilled about.

READING Michael's book felt like a full-circle moment for me. Although it was difficult to read, especially the repeated emphasis on his love for and blind devotion to Limori, who did not deserve it, I appreciated finally hearing his side of the story. Naturally (and, I confess, narcissistically), I was especially interested to read how our breakup unfolded from his viewpoint. He is succinct and focuses mostly on the "energies" involved (i.e., mine are The Worst, and his and Limori's are Divine), leaving emotion entirely out of the equation. "I hung up the phone and broke up with Lynda," is his summation of that event.

I am mostly left feeling sad, once again, that a manipulative, charismatic, and controlling narcissist was able to ensnare so many people and destroy so many lives. The ripples from Limori's actions continue to flow outward even though she has left this earth. I feel deeply sad for Michael, Lisa, and Matthew, all still living and working at Wolf's Den, now owned by a stranger. But perhaps they are happy in their Limori-created bubble.

Recently a new acquaintance and I were talking about the

cult experience, and I remarked that I've noticed that it seems to be a very human desire to put people on a pedestal and to follow those who call themselves leaders, even when they are undeserving of our attention. We do it all the time: in politics, in business, in families, and in spiritual matters. I'm not sure why that drive is within us, but I see it everywhere.

So, as you can see, reading Michael's book left me with many mixed thoughts and feelings. As a cult survivor myself, and one of Limori's ex-disciples, I'm able to fully understand Michael's beliefs and explanations. At the same time, with nearly 20 years of recovery behind me, I can also see the circular logic, denial, and mind control at work.

And then, ultimately, underlying all those mixed thoughts and emotions, I am once again feeling deeply grateful to Michael for jolting me awake and unintentionally setting in motion the events that gave me my life back.

> *Out beyond ideas of wrongdoing and rightdoing,*
> *there is a field. I'll meet you there.*
> Rumi

NOTES

Chapter 1

1. Margaret Thaler Singer, Ph.D., Thought Reform Exists: Organized, Programmatic Influence (*The Cult Observer*, Vol. ii, No. 6 (1994): 3–4)

2. Janja Lalich and Madeline Tobias, *Take Back Your Life: Recovering from Cults and Abusive Relationships* (Berkeley, California: Bay Tree Publishing, 2006), 72.

Chapter 2

1. Tara Brach, Ph.D., *Radical Acceptance: Embracing Your Life with the Heart of a Buddha* (New York, New York: Bantam Dell Publishing, 2003), 10.

2. Joel Kramer and Diana Alstad, *The Guru Papers: Masks of Authoritarian Power* (Berkeley, California: Frog Ltd., 1993), 47.

Chapter 3

1. Joel Kramer and Diana Alstad, *The Guru Papers: Masks of Authoritarian Power* (Berkeley, California: Frog Ltd., 1993), 9.

2. Joel Kramer and Diana Alstad, *The Guru Papers: Masks of Authoritarian Power* (Berkeley, California: Frog Ltd., 1993), 52–53.

3. Steven Hassan, from his website.

4. Janja Lalich and Madeline Tobias, *Take Back Your Life: Recovering from Cults and Abusive Relationships* (Berkeley, California: Bay Tree Publishing, 2006), 10–11.

5. Robert J. Lifton, *Thought Reform and the Psychology of Totalism* (New York, New York: W.W. Norton and Co., 1961), 419.

6. Robert J. Lifton, *Thought Reform and the Psychology of Totalism* (New York, New York: W.W. Norton and Co., 1961), 429–430.

7. Robert J. Lifton, *Thought Reform and the Psychology of Totalism* (New York, New York: W.W. Norton and Co., 1961), 425–427.

8. Robert J. Lifton, *Thought Reform and the Psychology of Totalism* (New York, New York: W.W. Norton and Co., 1961), 423–425.

9. Robert J. Lifton, *Thought Reform and the Psychology of Totalism* (New York, New York: W.W. Norton and Co., 1961), 420–422.

10. 2. Joel Kramer and Diana Alstad, *The Guru Papers: Masks of Authoritarian Power* (Berkeley, California: Frog Ltd., 1993), 86–87.

Chapter 5

1. Robert J. Lifton, *Thought Reform and the Psychology of Totalism* (New York, New York: W.W. Norton and Co., 1961), 427–429.

2. Steven Hassan, *Combatting Cult Mind Control* (Rochester, Vermont: Park Street Press, 1988, 1990), 72–73.

Chapter 7

1. Joel Kramer and Diana Alstad, *The Guru Papers: Masks of Authoritarian Power* (Berkeley, California: Frog Ltd., 1993), 105.

2. Robert J. Lifton, *Thought Reform and the Psychology of Totalism* (New York, New York: W.W. Norton and Co, 1961), 422–423.

Chapter 8

1. Robert J. Lifton, *Thought Reform and the Psychology of Totalism* (New York, New York: W.W. Norton and Co, 1961), 430–432

Part 2

1. Martha Beck, *Finding Your Own North Star: Claiming the Life You Were Meant to Live* (New York, New York: Three Rivers Press, 2001), 265.

2. Robert J. Lifton, *Thought Reform and the Psychology of Totalism* (New York, New York: W.W. Norton and Co, 1961), 433–437.

GLOSSARY OF MOST FREQUENTLY USED LOADED LANGUAGE

Clarity: Not having any ego positions or an ego at all. Limori was the clearest of all, but others of us could briefly achieve clarity when in Limori's good graces. For everyone but Limori, however, the situation was always short-lived.

Ego position: Any thought, behaviour, action or belief that contradicted what Limori said was The Truth.

Energy: A force that was in everything: people, animals, plants, but most especially thoughts. Our thoughts alone could move energy that hit Limori and caused physical events, such as the plate breaking in Chapter 5.

God: An omniscient being who rules the universe with an iron fist. Limori is the only person on the planet who has access to this god's thoughts and instructions about how the world should be run. We were constantly asked to strive for God's approval, yet rarely received it. In the context of the group, God was constantly punishing and berating us for failing him, and offered praise or approval sparingly.

The negative: Forces in the universe working in opposition to God. Almost anything could be controlled or influenced by the negative: thoughts, actions, beliefs. Being in one's ego or not being in one's heart was purported to attract the negative into one's thoughts and body so that it could use one for its evil purposes.

Spirit: Initially Limori claimed to be guided by Spirit, which was a generic term used to describe the positive guiding forces in the universe.

The Truth: As described in the text, a concept that only Limori had access to, this sole access being the ultimate example of her clarity and access to God's instructions and direction. Any feeling, thought or belief that did not agree with what Limori wanted could be dissolved by being labelled as not The Truth.

Workshop: A group retreat, taking place over several days, and/or the treatment received and the struggles faced when Limori was trying to convince someone of an ego position. Being berated by Limori, either privately or in a group setting, could be referred to as having a workshop or "being workshopped." The word and phrase could also refer to the struggle that ensued when one of us resisted the life instructions that had come from Limori (this is the context in which Jessica uses the word in Chapter 7). Any resistance to Limori's teaching or instruction could be referred to as a workshop.

Be in your heart: A state that one has to be in to solve any problem or resolve any workshop. In other words, one has to stop resisting Limori's instruction/teaching and surrender to doing what she wants one to do. The complementary phrase is get out of your head/ego.

Trust your heart: As described in the text, what one has always to do, except when it contradicts what Limori says/does/wants.

RECOMMENDED RESOURCES

Books about cults

Combatting Cult Mind Control and *Releasing the Bonds* by Steven Hassan

Cult Encounter: An International Story of Exit Counselling by Helen and Rick Larsen

The Guru Papers: Masks of Authoritarian Power by Joel Kramer and Diana Alstad

Take Back Your Life: Recovering from Cults and Abusive Relationships by Janja Lalich and Madeleine Tobias

I Can't Hear God Anymore: Life in a Dallas Cult by Wendy J. Duncan

Support organizations and individuals

International Cultic Studies Association (ICSA) A global network of people concerned about psychological manipulation and abuse in cultic groups, alternative movements, and other environments. ICSA's mission is to apply research and professional perspectives to the problems encountered by family members and former group members adversely affected by a cultic involvement and to forewarn those who might become involved in potentially harmful group situations. **ICSAHome.com**

Rosanne Henry. A professional counsellor based in Colorado who helps people evaluate harm in cultic groups. Rosanne is a member of the board of the ICSA. **CultRecover.com**

Joe Szimhart. A cult information specialist who provides consultation, education, research and non-coercive intervention that addresses controversial, high-demand groups, cults, psychotherapies or relationships that use undue influence and thought-reform techniques. **JSzimhart.com**

Steven Hassan. The author of what is probably the best-known book about cults, *Combatting Cult Mind Control*, as well as *Releasing the Bonds: Empowering People to Think for Themselves*. Steven's website is a great resource for information about cults and recovery. **FreedomOfMind.com**

FactNet.org A website and resource portal focused on discussion, resources and support for recovery from the abusive practices of religions and cults. **FactNet.org**

Other resources that might be helpful and useful for recovery

Anything and everything by Martha Beck, but especially *Finding Your Own North Star: Claiming the Life You Were Meant to Live* and *Leaving the Saints: How I Lost the Mormons and Found My Faith* **MarthaBeck.com**

Radical Acceptance: Embracing Your Life with the Heart of a Buddha by Tara Brach, Ph.D. **TaraBrach.com**

APPENDIX

Robert J. Lifton's eight criteria for thought reform

Summary from *Thought Reform and the Psychology of Totalism: A Study of Brainwashing in China* (New York, New York: W.W. Norton & Company Inc.)

Any ideology – that is, any set of emotionally charged convictions about man and his relationship to the natural or supernatural world – may be carried by its adherents in a totalistic direction. But this is most likely to occur with those ideologies which are most sweeping in their content and most ambitious or messianic in their claim, whether a religious or political organization. And where totalist exists, a religion, or a political movement, becomes little more than an exclusive cult.

Here you will find a set of criteria; eight psychological themes against which any environment may be judged. In combination, they create an atmosphere which may temporarily energize or exhilarate, but which at the same time pose the gravest of human threats.

1. Milieu control

The most basic feature is the control of human communication within an environment.

If the control is extremely intense, it becomes internalized control – an attempt to manage an individual's inner communication.

Control over all a person sees, hears, reads, writes (information control) creates conflicts in respect to individual autonomy.

Groups express this in several ways: Group process, isolation from other people, psychological pressure, geographical distance or unavailable transportation, sometimes physical pressure.

Often a sequence of events, such as seminars, lectures, group encounters, which become increasingly intense and increasingly isolated, making it extremely difficult – both physically and psychologically – for one to leave.

Sets up a sense of antagonism with the outside world; it's "us against them."

Closely connected to the process of individual change (of personality).

2. Mystical manipulation (planned spontaneity)

Extensive personal manipulation.

Seeks to promote specific patterns of behavior and emotion in such a way that it appears to have arisen spontaneously from within the environment, while it actually has been orchestrated.

Totalist leaders claim to be agents chosen by God, history, or some supernatural force, to carry out the mystical imperative.

The "principles" (God-centered or otherwise) can be forcibly and exclusively claimed, so that the cult and its beliefs become the only true path to salvation (or enlightenment).

The individual then develops the psychology of the pawn, and participates actively in the manipulation of others.

The leader who becomes the center of the mystical manipulation (or the person in whose name it is done) can be sometimes more real than an abstract god and therefore attractive to cult members.

Legitimizes the deception used to recruit new members and/or raise funds, and the deception used on the "outside world."

3. The demand for purity

The world becomes sharply divided into the pure and the impure, the absolutely good (the group/ideology) and the absolutely evil (everything outside the group).

One must continually change or conform to the group "norm."

Tendencies towards guilt and shame are used as emotional levers for the groups controlling and manipulative influences.

Once a person has experienced the totalist polarization of good/evil (black/white thinking) he has great difficulty in regaining a more balanced inner sensitivity to the complexities of human morality.

The radical separation of pure/impure is both within the environment (the group) and the individual.

Ties in with the process of confession – one must confess when one is not conforming.

4. Confession

Cultic confession is carried beyond its ordinary religious, legal and therapeutic expressions to the point of becoming a cult in itself.

Sessions in which one confesses to one's sin are accompanied by patterns of criticism and self-criticism, generally transpiring within small groups with an active and dynamic thrust toward personal change.

Is an act of symbolic self-surrender.

Makes it virtually impossible to attain a reasonable balance between worth and humility.

A person confessing to various sins of pre-cultic existence can both believe in those sins and be covering over other ideas and feelings that s/he is either unaware of or reluctant to discuss.

Often a person will confess to lesser sins while holding on to other secrets (often criticisms/questions/doubts about the group/leaders that may cause them not to advance to a leadership position).

"The more I accuse myself, the more I have a right to judge you."

5. Sacred science

The totalist milieu maintains an aura of sacredness around its basic doctrine or ideology, holding it as an ultimate moral vision for the ordering of human existence.

Questioning or criticizing those basic assumptions is prohibited.

A reverence is demanded for the ideology/doctrine, the originators of the ideology/doctrine, the present bearers of the ideology/doctrine.

Offers considerable security to young people because it greatly simplifies the world and answers a contemporary need to combine a sacred set of dogmatic principles with a claim to a science embodying the truth about human behavior and human psychology.

6. Loading the language

The language of the totalist environment is characterized by the thought-terminating cliché (thought-stoppers).

Repetitiously centered on all-encompassing jargon.

"The language of non-thought."

Words are given new meanings – the outside world does not use the words or phrases in the same way – it becomes a "group" word or phrase.

7. Doctrine over person

Every issue in one's life can be reduced to a single set of principles that have an inner coherence to the point that one can claim the experience of truth and feel it.

The pattern of doctrine over person occurs when there is a conflict between what one feels oneself experiencing and what the doctrine or ideology says one should experience.

If one questions the beliefs of the group or the leaders of the group, one is made to feel that there is something inherently wrong with them to even question – it is always "turned around" on them and the questioner/criticizer is questioned rather than the questions answered directly.

The underlying assumption is that doctrine/ideology is ultimately more valid, true and real than any aspect of actual human character or human experience and one must subject one's experience to that "truth."

The experience of contradiction can be immediately associated with guilt.

One is made to feel that doubts are reflections of one's own evil.

When doubt arises, conflicts become intense.

8. Dispensing of Existence

Since the group has an absolute or totalist vision or truth, those who are not in the group are bound up in evil, are not enlightened, are not saved, and do not have the right to exist.

"Being verses nothingness."

Impediments to legitimate being must be pushed away or destroyed.

One outside the group may always receive their right of existence by joining the group.

Fear manipulation – if one leaves this group, one leaves God or loses their transformation, for something bad will happen to them.

The group is the "elite," outsiders are "of the world," "evil," "unenlightened," etc.

GRATITUDE

A few years ago, a dear friend of mine was undergoing a house reconstruction after a fire had claimed her family's home. When the framing of the house had been completed, and with the drywall not yet installed, she asked several of her close friends to come over to the house one Saturday afternoon. She presented us with buckets full of children's paints, markers, glitter pens and crayons and asked us to draw on the walls. For the next hour or so we individually moved around to each room of the house, at random, writing and drawing on the plywood walls and floors of her home messages of hope, safety, peace and love. The intention of this exercise was that as a community we would leave marks of love and support that, once the home was finished would be unseen, but would always be felt there beneath the drywall, paint and hardwood. My friend and her precious family would be surrounded at every moment by affection and support while they built a new life and a new home within those walls.

I would like to thank the following people who have figuratively written on the walls of my life with their own messages of love, support, caring and comfort. Without you my recovery would not have been possible.

Enormous, eternal gratitude and love to Kelly Novak and Steven Freeland, the only two friends I had left when my life fell apart. You may not have known it at the time, but your friendship, each in unique ways, kept me going and gave me many reasons to believe in love, when I thought I shouldn't any longer.

To the counsellor I call Mary; words cannot express how grateful I am to have found you at what was the nadir of my life thus far. For years, your office was one of very few places on Earth that I felt safe. Your gentle, compassionate, loving way of working had a profoundly positive effect on me and you will stay in my heart forever. The gift you gave me when we completed our work together sits on my desk now as I write this, a daily reminder of your beauty, grace and loving support.

Linda Hamilton, you have taught me to give myself permission to feel, and that is a gift I will carry with me for the rest of my life. I may never be able to find the words to express how much that means to me so I will keep it simple and say, "Gracias, Amiga!" Many thanks as well to your wonderful husband, Dean Hamilton, for his research assistance. And a big shout-out to Caitlyn and Kasandra, who, just by being themselves, bring so much joy and love into my life.

My friend "Gayle" experienced things at Limori's hands that are far, far worse than anything I have described in these pages. She had the unfortunate experience of living with Limori at Wolf's Den for several years, and being trapped in the web of lies, deceit and abuse 24/7. Gayle, even I cannot fathom the courage it took for you to leave in your frozen little car and the subsequent tenacity you had to have to build a new life. I am humbled by your strength and by the grace that seems to guide your every movement. You are an amazing woman and I am so proud to call you my friend.

To the man I call Luke in these pages; thank you for your generous willingness to share your recollections with me. I do not take lightly the gift of your vulnerability and sharing and I appreciate it so much.

My gratitude to Captain Frank Noble for his genealogical expertise and his gracious research assistance, especially when I called him out of the blue.

To Arthur Buchman for being willing to speak to a stranger about a difficult topic. Arthur, your courage and resilience inspires and humbles me.

To Martha Beck: you don't know me, but you have had an incalculably positive impact on me in these, my healing years. Thank you for sharing the unique gifts and talents you possess. May you long continue to thrive and bring your brand of love and light to the world. I am profoundly blessed to have found you and irrevocably changed for the better.

My love and thanks to the five extraordinary women in The Authors Circle who gave me the opportunity to learn to feel safe in a group again and who offered one hundred percent of their hearts, minds and entrepreneurial acumen month after month for five incredible years: Claudette Bouchard, Natalie Forstbauer, Linda Hamilton, Teresia LaRocque and our dear Debrah Rafel Osborn. (Debrah, I do so miss your large emotional landscape.)

Heaps of love and appreciation to my dear friend Lorraine Carol, who was also my companion through this lonely writing wilderness. My life would be a much less happy place without the laughter and caring and constant connection of your friendship.

My thanks to my father and stepmother, Colonel Paul Hughes and Bev Hughes, for their support. And thanks also to my dad for the appreciation of the natural world that he instilled in me.

All the love in my heart and soul to my mother, stepfather and brother, Beverley McCormack, John Thrasher and Brynley Hughes. Thank you each for not giving up on me and for welcoming me back into your lives and hearts after I'd been away for so long. Your ongoing support ever since has been a balm to my soul and has given me strength and courage I never knew I could possess.

ABOUT THE AUTHOR

Alexandra Amor is the author several novels for children, a series of historical mystery novels, and of the award-winning memoir *Cult: A Love Story*. She belonged to a quasi-Eastern New Age cult in Vancouver, Canada from 1989 to 2000.

She says, "The road of recovery from cult mind control is a long and arduous one and a discovery I made early on was that it is often a very lonely journey. For that reason, I wrote this book – to say to other cult survivors, 'You are not alone. There are others who understand how you feel.'

"I also wrote the book for the families and friends of all those who are involved in a cult. It is so difficult to imagine why anyone would put themselves in a situation as abusive and soul-destroying as a cult. If you have a loved one who is involved with a cult, I'm sure you've asked yourself a thousand times how it is possible that the intelligent, sensible person you know cannot see that they are being manipulated. In the book I chronicle my personal descent as a model of how one gradually becomes coerced into believing that a guru is telling the truth, even when it causes personal pain and loss and the erosion of one's spirit.

"I've chosen the title of my book very deliberately to highlight the tragic, abominable paradox of cults: often love is the lever that gurus use to seduce their victims and then to keep them in line and in their sway."

Cult: A Love Story was the winner of a 2010 Independently Published Book Award in the category of Autobiography / Memoir.